THE CONQUEST OF WAR

Sponsored by
THE ALTERNATIVE DEFENSE PROJECT

THE CONQUEST OF WAR

Alternative Strategies for Global Security

Harry B. Hollins, Averill L. Powers, and Mark Sommer

with contributions by
Kenneth Boulding and Roger Fisher

WESTVIEW PRESS
Boulder, San Francisco, & London

Published in 1989 in the United States of America by Westview Press, Inc., 5500 Central Avenue, Boulder, Colorado 80301, and in the United Kingdom by Westview Press, Inc., 13 Brunswick Centre, London WC1N 1AF, England

Library of Congress Cataloging-in-Publication Data
Hollins, Harry B.
The conquest of war : alternative strategies for global security /
Harry B. Hollins, Averill L. Powers, and Mark Sommer
p. cm.
Bibliography: p.
Includes index.
ISBN 0-8133-0786-4 (hc)
ISBN 0-8133-0787-2 (pbk.)
1. Security, International. 2. Deterrence (Strategy). 3. Nuclear disarmament. I. Powers, Averill L. II. Sommer, Mark.
III. Title.
JX1952.H69 1989
327.1'7—dc19

88-28216
CIP

Printed and bound in the United States of America

(∞) The paper used in this publication meets the requirements of the American National Standard for Permanence of Paper for Printed Library Materials Z39.48-1984.

10 9 8 7 6 5 4 3 2 1

Contents

Acknowledgments xi
Introduction, *Kenneth Boulding* xiii

1 Conquering War: The Next Step in Human Evolution **1**

The Shared Interests of All Nations, 2
Barriers to Agreement, 4
The Urgent Need to Change the System, 5
Linking Principles and Pragmatism, 6
Precedents for a System Change: The Case of Slavery, 7
Planning for Peace, 8
Notes, 8

PART ONE
THE UNITED NATIONS AND SIX ALTERNATIVE APPROACHES TO GLOBAL SECURITY

2 Introduction to Part One: Beyond the Balance of Power **13**

Early Efforts to Create a Global Security System, 13
The Era of Arms Control, 1962–1987, 14
Alternative Security: A Renaissance of Global Thinking, 15
Defining a Security System, 15
The Format of Part One, 17
Stepping Stones, 18
Notes, 19

3 The United Nations: A Tool Neglected **20**

Origins of the United Nations: The League and Its Legacy, 20
The Formal Structure of the UN Charter, 21
Collective Security in Theory and Practice, 24
Weaknesses of the UN Security System, 26
The Emergence of Peacekeeping, 27
Three Kinds of Peacekeeping, 28
Sources of Success, 30
The Recent Fate of Peacekeeping, 31
The Lebanon Debacle: Hazards of Bypassing the UN, 32
The Unknown UN: Its Specialized Agencies, 33
Conclusion: The Future of the UN Security System, 33
Redesigning the Tool, Remodeling the Structure, 35
Notes, 36

4 A World Peacekeeping Federation: The Clark-Sohn Plan **38**

Grenville Clark and Louis B. Sohn, 38
"A Federation of Free Peoples," 40
Stimson: "Go Home and Figure Out a Way," 40
Dublin One, 41
From *A Plan for Peace* to *World Peace Through World Law,* 43
Elimination of "Excess" National Forces, 45
Control of Remaining Forces 46
Institutions for Conflict Resolution, 47
Disarmament Proposals of the Early 1960s, 47
The Decline of Disarmament and the Rise of Arms Control, 50
Conclusion: The Near-Miss at Reykjavik, 52
Notes, 53

5 Minimum Deterrence: How Little Is Enough? **54**

The Origins of Minimum Deterrence, 55
Recommendations from the Academic and Scientific Community, 56
Recommendations from Policymakers, 57
Attaining Maximum Stability, 58
Transition Problems, 60

Strengthening Nonnuclear Forces: A Conventional Buildup, 61
Future Prospects, 62
Notes, 62

6 **Qualitative Disarmament: Eliminating the War-making Capability of Nations** 64

The Conversion of a Military Strategist, 64
The Hoover Plan, 66
The Recent Revival of Interest: Randall Forsberg, "Confining the Military to Defense," 68
Common Security Through Qualitative Disarmament, 71
The INF Agreement and Strategic Arms Cuts: First Steps Toward Qualitative Disarmament? 73
Remaining Military Forces, 74
Control of Remaining Forces, 75
Conflict Resolution Mechanisms, 75
Conclusion: A Minimalist Approach to Global Security, 76
Notes, 76

7 **Nonprovocative Defense: Protection Without Threat** 78

Nonprovocative Defense and Qualitative Disarmament, 79
Defense in Depth, 79
The Swiss Model of General Defense, 80
Sweden's Total Defense, 81
Yugoslavia's General People's Defense, 82
Characteristics of Nonprovocative Defense, 82
Restructuring the Alliances Toward Defense, 83
Questions About the Strategy, 85
Notes, 87

8 **Civilian-based Defense: The Strength of Bare Hands and Stubbornness** 89

Sources of Nonviolent Power, 90
The Importance of Preparation, 90
Defense at Every Village Crossroads, 91
Deterrence by Resistance, 92
Facing Down Nuclear Blackmail, 92
The Phased Transition to CBD, 93

Forces Remaining and Who Controls Them, 94
Institutions of Conflict Resolution, 95
Eliminating the War-making Capability of Nations, 95
Evaluating CBD as a Global System, 95
The Philippine Revolution: The People Protect the Army, 97
Conclusion, 98
Notes, 99

9 Strategic Defense: Armor or Apocalypse? 101

Background, 101
The Strategic Defense Initiative, 103
The Soviet Strategic Defense Program, 104
Diverse Definitions of SDI, 105
Problems Facing SDI, 112
SDI's Effect on the War-making Capability of Nations, 118
Soviet Opposition, 120
Notes, 121

PART TWO
KEEPING THE PEACE:
ISSUES COMMON TO ALL APPROACHES

10 Verification: Substituting Information for Weapons 129

National Technical Means, 129
National Nontechnical Means: Human Intelligence, 132
Existing Cooperative Measures, 132
Proposed International Means of Verification, 133
The Future of Verification Technologies, 136
Verification Under Comprehensive Disarmament, 136
A Political More than a Technical Challenge, 139
Notes, 140

11 Bringing Law to Bear on Governments, *Roger Fisher* 141

Notes, 148

12 **Economic Conversion: Making Peace More Profitable than War** 150

Precedents for Conversion, 151
The Structure of the Military Economy, 152
The Supply Side: Resources Released by Disarmament, 154
The Conversion Process, 158
The Demand Side: Identifying Specific Conversion Possibilities, 160
Financing Conversion, 168
Obstacles to Conversion, 169
Conclusion: The Long-Term Benefits of Conversion, 171
Notes, 171

PART THREE
PROSPECTS FOR TRANSFORMATION

13 **Toward a Common Security System: A Proposal** 177

Strengths and Weaknesses of Each Approach, 177
Integrating Approaches: A Proposal for a Common Security System, 182
Notes, 191

14 **The Peril and the Promise** 192

A Broader Definition of Self-Interest, 192
Toward a Movement to Dismantle the War System, 193
Voices for the Abolition, 194
Our Choice, 195
Notes, 196

Appendix: Current Proposals for Arms Reduction 197

Arms Control vs. Arms Reduction, 197
Nuclear Systems, 198
Other Weapons Prohibitions, 199

Conventional Force Reductions, 200
Nonmilitary Measures to Enhance Common Security, 201
Notes, 202

Selected Bibliography 203
Index 213

Acknowledgments

This book is the product of a collaboration between three generations. Harry Hollins, the elder among us, has been instrumental in projects to study and promote thinking about global security alternatives for more than forty years, first in his work with the World Federalists, later in founding the World Law Fund (now the World Policy Institute). Mark Sommer, representing the middle generation, has spent the past decade surveying and stimulating the development in North America and Europe of new approaches to global security and national defense. Averill Powers, the youngest among us, worked at the World Policy Institute and as an independent consultant before cofounding the Alternative Defense Project (ADP) with Harry in late 1985. Averill was the first director of ADP and is now at the New York University School of Law.

Collaboration is a difficult proposition in the best of cases, and with each additional contributor the complications multiply. So it is with great satisfaction that we complete our collective enterprise still better friends than when we began.

We gratefully acknowledge the scholarly assistance of Michael Closson, Lloyd Jeffry Dumas, Dietrich Fischer, Roger Fisher, Richard Garwin, Frank von Hippel, Robert Irwin, Saul H. Mendlovitz, Betty Reardon, and Louis B. Sohn, whose comments and suggestions greatly strengthened the manuscript. We also wish to acknowledge the valued secretarial services of Carol Main and Catherine Seiling Moore, whose patience was often tested by frequent retypings of chapters, and of Terri Clemens and Michael Coar.

We would like to thank all those who have given financial support to this undertaking and especially the John Merck Fund, the Miriam and Ira D. Wallach Foundation, and Joan Warburg. It is thanks only to the faith and trust of those few who recognize the value of such ideas as are contained in this book that they are given expression and a life in the world.

Finally, we wish to extend our personal thanks to Elizabeth Hollins and Sandi Sommer, wives of two of the coauthors. Elizabeth's close reading of the manuscript and insightful suggestions for improvement greatly enhanced its readability. And Sandi graciously accepted more than her share of the tasks on a many-dimensional farm in order to free the time for her partner to work on the book.

To all these valued colleagues and friends, we offer our sincerest thanks.

Harry B. Hollins
Averill L. Powers
Mark Sommer

Introduction

This is a book of many valuable uses. It draws together succinctly and in very clear language the ideas, the problems, the issues, and the organizations that participate in a worldwide movement at many different levels to diminish the probability of war and ultimately to abolish it. The book is well named *The Conquest of War,* for all the great variety of movements, institutions, and processes that it describes have one thing in common—they see war as an enemy of the human race, which, if not conquered, will destroy us. Up to now, war has been a recurrent, but manageable disease, which has created great misery and distress, death and suffering, but which has not stopped (although it may have hindered) the evolution of the human race toward the realization of its extraordinary genetic potential for knowledge and for the good life. With the advent of the nuclear weapon, however, and the long-range missile, and the very real possibility in the future of what Herman Kahn called the "doomsday machine," war has become a deep threat not only to the continued evolution and development of the human race, but to the whole evolution of life on this planet. The human race has had an extraordinary capacity for increasing its powers of production, but along with this has gone an increase in its powers of destruction. The great question for the future is whether the powers of destruction are going to overcome the powers of production and lead perhaps eventually to a lifeless and desolated planet. The conquest of war, therefore, has become the highest priority of the human race.

This book is a remarkable survey of what might be called the "battleground," the conscious processes by which the conquest of war may be achieved. It covers such subjects as national security policy, which the book shows convincingly cannot really give us security in the modern world; proposals such as the Clark and Sohn proposal for a world political organization; analysis of deterrence; problems of disarmament, especially qualitative disarmament; nonprovocative defense; civilian-based defense; verification; international law; economic conversion; a common security system; and so on. The book will be useful as a reference book to those who are working in the field and as a general introduction to the field for the general reader, for it is very well written and explains many technical details in language that the concerned but unspecialized reader can understand. It will also be extremely useful as a textbook in courses in the burgeoning field of peace and conflict studies.

What the book does not do—and is not intended to do—is set these conscious processes ("conquest") in the larger setting of the overall evolutionary process, especially of the human race and the societies that it creates, toward what might be called the learning of peace. These processes are largely unconscious, involving the development of skills in peaceful living, which often develop almost as unconsciously as we learn our native language as a child. Consciousness, of course, can play a role in assisting these learning processes, as when we learn to drive a car. Once we have learned to drive, however, the skill becomes almost unconscious. Similarly, we learn to drive the subtle and immensely complex vehicle of our bodies and minds in our relationships with other people and the world around us in ways that prevent our running into people, running over cliffs, and galloping into wars.

We see these unconscious processes at work even in the international system, which is the prime source of war. Over the last 150 years or so, for instance, we have developed an increasing area of stable peace in the world, which probably did not exist before. This process began perhaps in Scandinavia after the Napoleonic Wars, when the Swedes and the Danes stopped fighting each other. It spread to North America after the U.S. Civil War, in developing peaceful relations between Canada and the United States, and between the United States and Mexico, which is even more surprising, as the United States "stole" Texas and the Southwest from Mexico in the Mexican War of 1846.

We now have a great triangle of stable peace from Australia and Japan, across North America, to Western Europe, with perhaps eighteen countries who have no plans whatever to go to war with each other. They are not even all allied. Alliances against a common enemy are very fragile, as the historical record shows very well. Stable peace has happened without anybody planning it very much, just by a kind of evolutionary change in national images. The conditions for stable peace are fairly simple: Change in national boundaries has to be taken off everybody's agendas, except by mutual consent. There has to be a certain minimum degree of intervention in other nations' affairs, though it is not easy to say just what that minimum is. And there has to be a certain abandonment of grandiose expansionary visions, a shift from the image of the state as a conqueror to the image of the state as a convenience, somewhat arbitrarily defined. The present area of stable peace has been achieved with remarkably little organization.

There is a parallel to stable peace in personal behavior, in the development of courtesy, the disappearance of dueling, the change in personal images that lay stress on "winning friends and influencing people," rather than dominating and beating people down. These changes are all part of the substitution of what I call "integrative power" (generally accepted legitimacy, community, and so on) for threat power, which, incidentally, turns out to be not very powerful unless it is legitimated. The growth of law and respect for law is also part of this almost unconscious evolutionary process, as Roger Fisher brings out so well in this book. This movement is both an evolutionary and a learning process. The selective processes select out the threatening and the armed in favor of the nonthreatening and the productive. We see this even in biological evolution—*Tyrannosaurus rex* and the saber-toothed tiger are extinct and the mouse and the cockroach survive. The evolutionary race is to the adaptable and the productive, not to the threatening or the destructive.

A very interesting question is how the conscious processes described in this volume can fit into the underlying unconscious processes and perhaps accelerate them as we become more conscious of the unconscious processes. There are certainly conscious institutional structures, like the United Nations itself, the development of disarmament treaties, and of world political institutions (which might not actually resemble any known government), that would facilitate the spread of stable peace. It needs to spread, first of all, around the whole temperate zone, between the United States and the Soviet Union and their respective allies, then to the areas of more intense conflict, like the Middle East, Central America, Sri Lanka, and so on. This book provides excellent illustrations for the steps along the way that may be taken toward a world in stable peace. To see a "city on a hill" that has no road to it is merely frustrating. The fact that stable peace exists, however, shows that it must be possible, and the fact that it has grown shows that it can grow further. This book is an important guidebook to the road ahead. The more people read it, the more likely we are to take that road that leads to genuine security and a better world.

Kenneth E. Boulding
Institute of Behavioral Science
University of Colorado at Boulder

CHAPTER ONE

Conquering War: The Next Step in Human Evolution

When we get to the point, as one day we will, that both sides know that in any outbreak of hostilities, regardless of the element of surprise, destruction will be both reciprocal and complete, possibly we will have enough sense to meet at the conference table with the understanding that the era of armaments has ended and that the human race must conform its action to this truth or die.

—President Dwight D. Eisenhower

We live in an in-between time. For the greater part of a century, a broad consensus has been building across national and social boundaries heretofore thought insurmountable that war as an institution has outlived its usefulness (if ever it had any) and that some less costly means must be found to resolve conflicts between nations. A perennial plague of human history, war in our era has become so lethal and damaging, and preparations for it so exceedingly expensive, that as a species and a planet we can simply no longer afford it. But most of us do not yet believe peace is possible. Those institutions we have established for resolving conflicts between nations languish for lack of use and support and there remains powerful resistance to giving them the means to do the job.

Nor have nuclear weapons abolished war. They may have made superpower conflict less likely, but only at the cost of making it far more catastrophic if or when it does occur. Meanwhile beneath their umbrella, lower-intensity conflicts of immense cumulative destructiveness have continued to proliferate. "Nuclear peace" is not a stable and enduring condition but a fragile truce, a cease-fire without a settlement. It is a strange and anomalous state of affairs, not quite war and not yet peace.

Which way the balance tips will depend in large measure on our collective ability to answer the fundamental question posed by President John F. Kennedy a generation ago: *How can the world be made safe for our differences?* Religions, ideologies, languages, values, and political and economic institutions all vary widely between nations and within them, supplying abundant fuel for conflicts. These differences are too fundamental to be ignored. But they need not be seen as innately destructive, for many of them add immeasurably to the vitality and wonder of life on this small planet. The conflicts resulting from these differences cannot magically be made to disappear, but they can be managed in such ways that resorting to force to settle them finally becomes an unnecessary and unacceptable option. This book explores alternative systems and strategies for security by which these conflicts can be carried on, and ultimately resolved, without recourse to war.

The Shared Interests of All Nations

The extreme destructiveness of modern weaponry has made a practical necessity of the moral imperative that we are our brothers' keepers. Contemporary warfare is inescapably suicidal: Aggressors and victims now share a common fate. Security has thus become indivisible: It can no longer be attained at the expense of one's adversaries but only in cooperation with them. Even the most powerful nations are no longer capable of assuring physical security for their citizens. Indeed, it is the most powerful who have come to join the most insecure and to create the most insecurity.

This vulnerability is paralleled in the realm of economics, where trade has become so thoroughly internationalized that no nation can afford any longer to ignore the opportunities in the global marketplace, nor can any nation long remain insulated from its periodic crises. This mutual vulnerability has never been more clearly demonstrated than in the unprecedented plunge of stock prices throughout the capitalist world on Black Monday, October 19, 1987, when in the space of eight hours, the Dow Jones Industrial Average lost 508 points, more than 20 percent of its total value. In nine days of trading, the New York Stock Exchange lost $1 trillion, including $500 billion on the day of the plunge. With the stunning suddenness of an earthquake, exchanges throughout the world immediately collapsed in the wake of the tremor from Wall Street.

Though the socialist world remained insulated in the near term from the turbulence in capitalist financial markets, it is clear that a prolonged economic downturn in the West would also doom efforts by the Soviet Union and Eastern bloc nations to revive their own moribund economies by depriving them of essential investment capital and equipment to rebuild their aging industrial infrastructures. This condition of mutual vulnerability, a product of ever-growing economic interdependence, affirms the fundamentally new reality that economic security, like military security, can no longer be attained by wholly unrestrained competition between nations but must be tempered by a measure of cooperation based on a pragmatic assessment of mutual self-interest.

This mutual vulnerability is echoed and intensified by certain ominous trends in the global environment. Deforestation and desertification, toxic pollution of soils and water, the lethal effects of acid rain, depletion of the ozone layer, and climatic changes induced by the "greenhouse effect" extend across all national boundaries, menacing large parts of the planet at once. Meanwhile the AIDS epidemic continues to spread, threatening to become the twenty-first century's Black Plague. Purely national defenses are helpless to shield against the threats to security represented by these environmental trends. Cooperative efforts engaging the energies of many peoples and nations are essential to address these shared perils.

Despite deep and sometimes irreconcilable differences, all nations share certain fundamental concerns that affect their most vital interests. This foundation of shared interests holds promise for constructing a global system of common security.

The Avoidance of Nuclear War. Even proponents of nuclear war-fighting strategies no longer find it politically wise to suggest that a nuclear war is "winnable." Research into the possible effects of a "nuclear winter" indicates that the aggressor in a nuclear exchange would likely fall victim to the radiation and climatic disruptions triggered by an attack even if the aggressor were not assaulted in return. All nations, regardless of their motives and ambitions, share a stake in avoiding nuclear war.

The Avoidance of Conventional Warfare. Closely related to the prevention of nuclear war is the avoidance of less apocalyptic forms of warfare. Most strategic analysts and other observers understand that any nuclear-armed nation losing a conventional war in which its vital interests are involved would sooner or later—and likely sooner—resort to its ultimate weapon. And with its first use would likely ensue an exchange of nuclear warheads with little or no restraint of any kind. The deadly connection between nuclear and conventional arsenals among the nuclear powers is so intimate that even conventional war between them flirts with apocalypse.[2] It is thus in the interest of all nations, and especially the superpowers, to prevent all conventional armed conflict.

The Prevention of Nuclear Proliferation. During the first generation since the invention of nuclear weapons, the nuclear "club" has remained an exclusive affair, including six nations (the United States, the USSR, Great Britain, France, India, and China) with an acknowledged capability and two more (Israel and South Africa) with a capacity still unacknowledged but widely credited. Seeking membership in the club is a growing host of lesser candidates (among them Brazil, Argentina, South Korea, Pakistan, Iran, and Iraq). A variety of subnational terrorist groups may also attempt to wield greater influence by the blunt and brutal instrument of nuclear terrorism. Although none of these candidates is believed to have crossed the nuclear threshold, it becomes increasingly likely (with the enormous accumulation and often careless handling of nuclear materials) that other nations and groups will achieve their ambition within the next decade. It is clearly in the interest of the great majority of nations to prevent this occurrence, since it would render an already tenuous restraint on nuclear proliferation essentially obsolete.[3]

Reductions in Military Spending. High on the agendas of both the Soviet Union and the United States is the task of reinvigorating their ailing economies. The crushing burden of maintaining immense arsenals and armed forces not only depletes the economic vitality of the great powers but robs essential resources from the reconstruction of their declining industrial bases and the provision of basic needs in the developing world. Military spending in the United States is closely related to decreasing innovation in the civilian sector. This declining capacity for innovation in turn has direct impact on domestic economic efficiency and competitiveness in world markets. It is in the immediate interest of all nations to release themselves from this self-imposed and self-destructive burden. Savings liberated by an effective disarming process would not only shrink the Himalayan mountain of debt now accumulating worldwide, but would release the essential resources—financial, material, and human—now lacking for many new and urgently needed undertakings.

Barriers to Agreement

Why, then, do the great powers fail to act in accordance with what appears to be clearly in their most vital interests? Deeply suspicious of their adversaries, most rival states believe that only the possession of superior armed power and technology (most often in the form of offensive threat) will suffice to deter an enemy presumed to be relentless and unprincipled. "They only understand force," adversaries say of one another. But if each seeks superiority by threatening the other, where does the contest end? "An eye for an eye 'til everyone is blind," say the wise words of an Irish folk song. To allow this attitude to determine foreign policies ensures catastrophe.

Others argue that if it has proven so difficult to reach agreement on the small steps entailed in traditional arms control treaties, it is simply not realistic to propose a far larger step like reducing or eliminating the war-making capability of nations. Despite its apparent logic, we question the wisdom of this argument. The degree to which the international system can be transformed depends less on the size of the proposed step than on whether the idea is sufficiently timely and compelling to marshal the effective political will to enact it. This will, in turn, is influenced by at least two factors: the practicality of the idea (that is, whether it appears capable of doing what it promises) and whether it meets the felt needs of people well enough to elicit their commitment to make it real. Taking a big step with unmistakable boldness strikes an emotional chord that fatally compromised and technically obscure half measures like traditional arms control can never inspire.

Two other barriers to agreement are still more deeply seated. If nations were to restrict or eliminate their ability to wage offensive war against one another, they would also relinquish their capacity to intervene militarily in the internal affairs of smaller nations. The numerous military operations now underway with the direct or indirect sponsorship of the superpowers indicate that the inclination to intervene is still their habit and predilection. Yet they cannot achieve enduring security for themselves without eliminating their own capacity to intervene militarily in the affairs of other nations. This is the trade-off. This is the price that must be paid for security in the nuclear age.

Finally, and most tellingly, most nations continue to operate on the assumption that while the nuclear age requires certain modifications in the system of competitive national armaments by which states have so long governed their relations, it does not require a fundamental system change. But even the most ambitious arms control proposals now under consideration, while lessening the immediate threat of conflict, would not alter the essential dynamics of the present system. Lacking a clear sense of direction, political leaders and policymakers on both sides of the East-West divide have made no sustained effort to develop a concrete idea of where they want their nations and the world to be ten, twenty, or fifty years hence. As Einstein so well observed, everything has changed but our way of thinking.

The Urgent Need to Change the System

No mere modification of the present system of international relations will suffice to carry us into the next century with a reasonable assurance of survival and security. A fundamental system shift is now imperative.

Although it is beyond the scope of this inquiry to define the precise structure and evolution of this system transformation, the outlines are clear. By one means or another, the war-making capability of nations must be progressively restricted and ultimately eliminated, and in its place must be established a wide range of alternative means for playing out those conflicts now carried on by warfare.

James W. Rouse, a successful businessman and chairman of the board of the Enterprise Foundation, made the point in his commencement address at Johns Hopkins University in May 1985 that when faced with finding a solution to a problem, the most sensible starting point is to determine where you want to be when you have succeeded.

> It is a way of thinking that raises up images of what might be—should be—and thereby helps people to see potential that otherwise might not be understood and evokes action that might not otherwise occur. These images generate energy and forestall early compromise with lesser results. Such images are often dismissed as visionary and impractical. And the state of mind that often evokes that response is one of the burdens of our society. It is a state of mind that inhibits movement towards goals that may be widely accepted as valid and important by discounting them in advance as unachievable.

Linking Principles and Pragmatism

What, then, makes for a successful movement? How are "images of what might be" made real? A successful movement for social change requires both an unwavering commitment to first principles and a flexible and pragmatic set of strategies for attaining them. In matters of war and peace, these twin imperatives are all too often found at odds with one another. Popular peace movements are well attuned to visions of a world without war and are fueled in large part by the emotional inspiration of an inchoate yearning for peace. But they have remained chronically vague about the actual means of enacting these visions. Arms control specialists, on the other hand, have based their cautious, incremental approach to peace on meticulous attention to technical detail. But in their assiduous pursuit of the achievable compromise, they have too often lost sight of larger goals and, indeed, may have unwittingly obstructed their realization.

Our approach is to unite the principled and the pragmatic, enunciating a vision and goal sufficiently ambitious to inspire heroic efforts on their behalf while designing strategies sufficiently practical to make their achievement a realistic possibility. Like other great social causes, from antislavery abolitionism to the environmental, civil rights, and women's movements, the movement to render war obsolete possesses a moral and spiritual dimension that campaigns to limit or eliminate particular weapons systems wholly lack. This dimension is vitally necessary if the cause is to attract sufficient energy to overcome lingering resistance to change.

At the same time, we take this apparently utopian premise—the possibility of changing the international system—and subject it to rigorous scrutiny, examining the strengths and weaknesses of each of the alternatives considered here. By this principled and pragmatic approach, we seek to demonstrate that what has long been dismissed as visionary is in fact practical. Given intelligent planning and the essential political will, even so great a goal as the abolition of war is not impossible.

Precedents for a System Change: The Case of Slavery

Given present political realities, a world in which organized warfare is no longer accepted as a human institution may seem too much to hope for. Yet human beings have compiled a long and impressive record of achieving the seemingly impossible, and not just in technical feats. In the eighteenth century the so-called "divine right of kings" was annulled, demonstrating that humankind could progress beyond social barriers that had long been accepted as givens. In the nineteenth century, another, still more significant, system shift occurred when chattel slavery, a practice accepted since the earliest known civilizations, was universally abolished. The transformation was all the more remarkable because the time elapsed between the first widespread questioning of the practice and its universal abolition was little more than a hundred years, in an era when social and historical change occurred at a distinctly slower tempo than it occurs today. And in the single generation since World War II (in fact mostly in the 1960s), the great colonial empires erected by the European powers over several centuries were dismantled in an unheralded but largely nonviolent system shift.

The case of slavery and its abolition is worth pondering for a moment. Like war, slavery had been considered innate to the human condition and was taken by many (though not many slaves, no doubt) to be morally sound. For thousands of years, war was celebrated as the crucible in which all manly virtue is tempered. It is only since the harrowing traumas of two world wars that this worshipful attitude has waned. Even now, after all illusions about its edifying nature have been destroyed in the rubble of its outcome, war is still taken by most people to be "inevitable," a permanent affliction like some incurable social disease.

Slavery in the eighteenth and nineteenth centuries, like war in the twentieth, was integral to the vital economic interests of powerful and entrenched elements in the existing societies. Today it is no secret that certain sectors, regions, industries, and individuals profit enormously in the near term from the exploitative war system of the arms race. In the long term, however, the cumulative cost is extracted from the entire society.

Along with these similarities between the cases of slavery and war, however, there is one crucial difference. Although the elimination of slavery from the United States did not require inventing a replacement (as the free market economy of the northern states already existed and had proven itself more efficient), the elimination of war requires the deliberate development of successful substitute arrangements to ensure the security of nations. The willingness of governments to relinquish their interventionary capabilities will be determined in large measure by the acceptability of a substitute that yields tangible security and economic benefits while leaving nations free to act and exert influence by means other than war.

Just as the abolition of slavery did not mark the end of exploitation (which took other, more devious but still abusive forms), so the elimination of the war-making capabilities of nations would not mark the end of conflict between them. Even after war between the great powers is rendered effectively obsolete, so-called "brushfire wars" at the periphery of the planet's concerns may continue to occur at a lower level of intensity for some years to come, at least as long as weapons can be clandestinely manufactured and supplied. In addition, nations deprived of military means of intervening in the affairs of other nations may choose to wield economic or political weapons with greater force and effect. Perfect justice is no more achievable in social and political systems than in individual human action. But restraining and then eliminating the gratuitous violence of mass organized warfare between nations is still a worthy and ambitious goal, and it may well lie within our reach.

Planning for Peace

Given the precedents of these major social advances and the shared interests of all nations in preventing armed conflict, it does not seem too much to begin planning seriously for the twenty-first century to mark the end of organized warfare between nations. Like the social advances before it, this system shift will not likely be the consequence of any mere technological breakthrough but the result of a political response to popular demand and an accommodation to new realities.

Notes

1. From a letter to Richard R. Simon, April 4, 1956.

2. Although a conventional war between the major nuclear powers would indeed risk "going nuclear," unconventional warfare in the developing world, in the form of so-called "low intensity conflict," has become an increasingly common form of combat between the great powers precisely because it enables them to go to war without risking nuclear confrontation. In Nicaragua, Angola, Afghanistan, and elsewhere, the superpowers train, finance, and provide logistical support for surrogate fighting forces to advance their interests without (excepting the Soviet troops in Afghanistan) exposing their own peoples to risk. Putting an end to this new, clandestine form of international violence may well require measures not yet conceived in most plans for global security systems.

3. Many nonnuclear nations that are parties to the Non-Proliferation Treaty have contended that the nuclear nations have not lived up to their commitment in the treaty to bargain in good faith for the reduction of nuclear weapons. This failure, in their view, undermines the treaty and the commitment of nations to hold to its terms.

PART ONE

The United Nations and Six Alternative Approaches to Global Security

CHAPTER TWO

Introduction to Part One: Beyond the Balance of Power

The system of competitive national arsenals by which the nations of the world now operate is commonly called the "balance of power"—or, as it has been more aptly termed in the case of the superpowers, "the balance of terror." It is an arrangement somewhat more organized than an imagined "state of nature" but a good deal less consciously contructed than a national constitution. The balance of power system can claim a venerable ancestry, having governed a great many relationships between nations in a wide variety of circumstances across the centuries.

But with the advent of "ultimate" weapons, first and foremost in the form of nuclear arsenals, the balance of power arrangement has come under severe strain, its capacity for assuring national security irreversibly diminished. More arms have not produced more security, as history had formerly taught, but ever less. Ironically, the citizens of those nations with the largest arsenals and greatest preoccupation with "national security" have come to feel among the most threatened. We have become unwitting victims of our own fears and our fearsome devices.

Early Efforts to Create a Global Security System

Beginning near the turn of the century with the Hague Conferences of 1899 and 1907 and with increasing frequency since, innovative statesmen and political theorists have sought to conceive a more rational and effective system to govern relations between nations, a system capable of maintaining peace in what will likely always remain a highly diverse community of nations. Thinkers have conceived alternative "world orders" and, in some cases, world governments and constitutions, designed to fulfill certain universally accepted needs and values.[1]

On two occasions—both in the aftermath of worldwide wars—attempts have been made to graft a global security system on the anarchic system of national security by which nations still govern their relations with one another. First at the League of Nations between World War I and World War II, and then at the United Nations in the postwar years, the nations of the world have struggled to achieve a minimal degree of order so as to be able to carry on their disputes without resorting to war. The League was generally considered to have failed. Its successor, the United Nations, has not been dramatically successful either, although its modest accomplishments may be more important than we realize. In any case, the experience of these attempts has taught us much about the problems, though not yet the fullest possiblities of a global security system.

The Era of Arms Control, 1962–1987

Frustrated in their efforts to create an effective global security system, the majority of policymakers and policy analysts seeking ways to reduce the risk of war turned, during the past quarter century, toward the more incremental and apparently pragmatic approach that became known as arms control. Viewing more ambitious goals as utopian and unattainable, the arms control community has argued that ending the arms race may well not prove possible, at least in the foreseeable future, and that therefore the best we can hope to accomplish in the near term is to restrain its excesses and channel new technological developments in more stabilizing directions.

This piecemeal approach to peace has dominated mainstream political discourse for the past twenty-five years. In its early days (particularly during the era of détente in the 1970s), arms control could be credited with a number of useful accomplishments, beginning with the Partial Test Ban of 1963 and continuing through the Non-Proliferation Treaty (1968), the ABM Treaty (1972), SALT I (1972), and SALT II (1979, never ratified but adhered to until 1986). In all, thirteen arms control agreements were completed during the 1960s and 1970s, restricting weapons proliferation, banning and limiting specific weapon deployments, and enhancing crisis stability.

Despite these tangible achievements, the fundamental dynamics of the arms race between East and West have not significantly changed during twenty-five years of earnest arms control efforts. In fact, by every available measure, the arms race has both proliferated and intensified. In the quarter century between 1962 and 1986, military spending worldwide more than trebled, from $300 billion in 1962 to nearly $1 trillion in 1986.[2]

In addition, and still more menacingly, a number of the arms control agreements that have been most useful in restraining competition between the superpowers and preventing the proliferation of nuclear arms to other nations have been breached, abrogated, or abandoned in practice by one or more of the contracting parties, or rendered irrelevant by technical advances not limited by treaties. In November 1986, the United States explicitly exceeded the mandated limits of SALT II in response to alleged Soviet treaty violations. Meanwhile, both nations proceeded with ballistic missile defense research and development programs in de facto violation of the ABM Treaty they had both signed. By every significant measure and by a consistently wide margin, new arms developments have outpaced the development of arms control.

Alternative Security: A Renaissance of Global Thinking

In response to the apparent collapse of arms control in the early 1980s, increasing numbers of academics and public figures during the past several years have begun to reconsider more comprehensive arrangements for global security. Under the general rubric of "alternative security" and "alternative defense," there has been a revival of interest in old and neglected plans as well as a renaissance of creative thinking about new approaches to assuring global security.

Much of this new thinking has begun to coalesce around the notion that global security is best understood as a comprehensive system with mutually supportive components. This approach differs significantly from arms control, which tends to be a patchwork assemblage of proposals and treaties without a higher organizing principle other than stabilizing the arms race. But because terms like "system" are not yet broadly familiar, it may be useful here to establish a few elementary definitions.

Defining a Security System

What do we mean when we speak of a system? In the broadest sense, a system is any set of interconnected and mutually reinforcing structures or patterns that together govern the functioning and direction of a given entity. There is a synergistic relation between these component parts: working together, they enhance one another's performance. Systems spontaneously occur in the natural world on every level, animate and inanimate. The weather, for example, is a system; so is the circulatory network of veins, arteries, and heart in the human body. Neither was organized by a conscious human intelligence. They are simply the natural structure and pattern of being. Less visible but no less influential are the political and social systems human beings construct for themselves at all levels of social organization.

What, then, do we mean by a "security system"? A security system is an integrated set of institutions, structures, technologies, treaties, agreements, and norms of behavior developed to assure security for a given polity. Defining the scope of this community is vitally important in determining whether the system works for all parties concerned or for some at the expense of others. Within the nation-state system, each government defines the community it chooses to protect by the perimeter of its national borders. This definition becomes problematic when a nation chooses to claim interests beyond that frontier or to threaten other nations as a means of defense. A global security system, on the other hand, encompasses the entire human community within its protective circle and seeks to assure security equally to all nations and peoples within it. This subtle but fundamental shift of emphasis distinguishes alternative security thinking from the nation-centered strategies that remain the orthodox approach to global politics.

Intellectually and geographically, the field of alternative security is now expanding so rapidly that is is quite impossible to encompass its richness and variety. Our purpose here is to describe the principal archetypes for the alternative global security systems now most widely under consideration. Classifying so broad and varied a range of proposals inevitably involves a certain simplification and may create somewhat artificial distinctions between systems and strategies that are better conceived as complementary. In chapter 13 we consider how they might be synthesized in a still more effective integrated system.

We have chosen here to concentrate on the military dimensions of national and global security, on what must be done with existing weapons and forces to make them safe enough for our common survival. But we recognize that security ultimately depends on many factors other than the disposition of military forces. Economic stability, for example, is equally essential. In chapter 12 on economic conversion, one vital aspect of this dimension is considered: the difficulties of transition from a war to a peace economy. Improved institutions for conflict resolution and management are also vital; and although some are described in this book, they do not make up its central focus. Finally, there are the intangible social and cultural dimensions of security, habits and attitudes that reinforce war or peace. These aspects of security remain unexamined in this book not because they are unimportant, but because it is impossible to cover so broad a range of considerations without losing focus. Our concentration on the military dimensions of security should not be taken as a statement that these are the only factors that matter. They serve simply as a starting point for considering a still broader range of changes in other realms of human society that must occur if we are successfully to move from the tenuous nuclear cease-fire of the present toward a genuine and enduring peace.

Why have we chosen these alternatives and not others? Certainly others are imaginable, some of them all too much so. The possibility of world tyranny has stirred and haunted the imaginations of novelists and the aspirations of would-be despots longer and more deeply than any of the alternatives surveyed here. Security systems can be benign or perverse, depending on whose security is being assured and at whose expense. With the exception of strategic defense, these alternatives have been chosen with a conscious and deliberate preference for more "just" and nonviolent varieties of order, systems designed to assure security to peoples as well as governments. We take it as a given that lasting peace is not possible without a modicum of rough justice and that an unjust peace may simply be a hidden form of war. But other positive alternatives may indeed be possible, and readers are invited to explore the terrain between and beyond the possiblities sketched here.

The Format of Part One

These security systems vary widely in scope and applicability. Indeed, some are not necessarily systems at all, but strategies or proposals, perhaps components, of a larger system yet to be conceived. Minimum deterrence and nonprovocative defense, for example, are essentially military postures rather than comprehensive political systems. The Clark-Sohn peacekeeping federation, however, is complete enough to be considered as a blueprint for a limited world government in political as well as military dimensions.

We have followed a similiar format in each case, giving first the historical background for the genesis of the idea, then a review of its conceptual foundations, followed by an analysis of its principal features. These particular systems have been selected in order to cover a broad spectrum of possibilities. The United Nations is placed first because it is the only system of global security now in existence and is thus an appropriate starting point, whatever its shortcomings. Then one classic revision of the UN Charter is considered, the Clark-Sohn Plan, which extends the UN's authority and power far beyond their present range to make it a bona fide world government, albeit of a strictly limited nature.

Next, we examine three proposals (minimum deterrence, qualitative disarmament, and nonprovocative defense) that might best be characterized as "advanced arms control," in that whereas they deal primarily with arms and leave aside consideration of most other aspects of international relations, they all cut far more deeply into existing arsenals than do any arms control proposals now on the table between the superpowers.[3] These three candidate systems share a few important characteristics. All seek to lower the level of offensive military capability available to nations as a means of reducing the general level of threat, which proponents of these strategies see as a central driving force behind the arms race. All begin from the assumption that security in the nuclear age must be mutual. Thus they transform the ancient moral imperative of the Golden Rule into a simple, practical necessity: To become secure ourselves, we must also secure the survival of our adversaries.[4] In addition, while they dwell primarily on the disposition of military forces and armaments, all three systems presume an increased use of existing conflict resolution mechanisms (mostly under UN auspices). Moreover, all could be strengthened in their political dimensions by being linked to a much reformed and expanded UN system.

Considered next is civilian-based defense. CBD is likely the most far-reaching of all the systems in its implications for restructuring national arsenals, since it entirely eliminates them. It is also implicitly the most revolutionary in that it requires the reorganization of national and global culture along thoroughly nonviolent lines. Finally, strategic defense is considered here because it is being pursued today by the superpowers and a growing list of other nations and has been proposed as an authentic alternative to the balance of terror.

Stepping Stones

In examining these alternative security systems, it is important to keep in mind that no formal arrangement can claim perfection—that is, no system can ensure that war between nations will never again break out. Perfect invulnerability to war is no more attainable in a political system than is perfect invulnerability to missiles in the most optimal strategic defense. But whereas in the case of strategic defense a leaky shield might well be catastrophic, in a genuine alternative security system even a less-than-perfect shield against war would still represent a lasting benefit to all nations.

It is virtually certain that any world system set up today will not meet all the requirements of the twenty-first century. Conditions change rapidly in response to new technologies of destruction and communication, the internationalization of world markets and business, the startling growth of human population in the developing world, increasingly severe threats to the biosphere, and many other factors. For these and other reasons, any new global institutional arrangements that might be agreed to at this time may seem quite inadequate fifty, seventy-five, or a hundred years from now.

These alternatives should therefore be regarded as stepping stones in an ongoing process of change, the outer limits of which will necessarily be left to future generations. But the adoption of any of these systems would be no ordinary, incremental step forward. It would represent a quantum leap into a new world of opportunities and difficulties, a world in which significant human material and financial resources would be released from destructive purposes and redirected to preserve the integrity of all life.

Notes

1. See, for example, the work of the World Order Models Project (WOMP), including Richard Falk and Saul H. Mendlovitz, *The Strategy of World Order* (3 vols.) (New York: Institute for World Order, 1966).

2. Ruth Leger Sivard, *World Military and Social Expenditures, 1985* (Washington, DC: World Priorities, Inc., 1985), p. 12.

3. Only once in recent years have arms control negotiations between the superpowers strayed beyond the narrow confines of traditional arms control, in the so-called "near-miss" at Reykjavik. Meeting in Iceland in November 1986, General Secretary Mikhail Gorbachev and President Ronald Reagan fleetingly appeared to agree on the elimination of all nuclear weapons (or all ballistic missiles, as the United States later asserted) within ten years. The episode was quickly disavowed by the Reagan administration in the wake of fierce resistance from NATO allies and a far more modest proposition, the elimination of intermediate- and (some) short-range missiles in Europe, was substituted and agreed upon. The rapidity and decisiveness with which the Reykjavik rapprochement was rejected would seem to indicate that mainstream arms control thinking still remains trapped within the fairly narrow confines of minimal restraint rather than considering more comprehensive reductions and system changes.

4. Some world order theorists argue that merely securing the survival of oneself and one's adversaries is not in itself sufficient and that an enduring peace requires the assurance of a measure of economic well-being and social justice as well.

CHAPTER THREE

The United Nations: A Tool Neglected

Of all the strategies and systems surveyed in this book, only the United Nations currently exists. Imperfect and incomplete though it is, the UN provides us with a living laboratory in which to trace the evolution of a concept of security from theory into practice amid the often dismaying realities of global power politics. If the UN has thus far failed to accomplish much of the task assigned it by its founders, a careful study of the sources of its failures—as well as a recognition of its neglected successes—may help us to judge what will and will not work in the various alternatives explored in this book. In the process, it may also help us rescue and revive what is still worth preserving in the UN system itself.

Origins of the United Nations: The League and Its Legacy

The United Nations system was in many respects a child of the League of Nations, the attempt following World War I to organize a global political community sufficient to prevent war. The League is viewed by most historians today as a failed project, and those who designed and conceived the United Nations viewed the UN Charter as a means of remedying the manifest inadequacies of the League's structure. By the time the League was established, the United States had returned to its habitual isolationism and profound suspicion of foreign entanglements. Despite the formidable efforts of President Wilson, the U.S. Senate, in perhaps its most fateful truculence, rejected the League and thus doomed it to ineffectiveness. Because several of the Great Powers of the era did not join the organization, the League could never hope to represent the global community, still less to resolve conflicts.

The United Nations was conceived, designed, and established even before World War II ended. Cognizant of the disarray into which nations fall once necessity no longer drives them together, the UN's founders began thinking about the structure of a new international organization even before the United States entered the war. The structure of the proposed organization gradually emerged during a series of wartime conferences. The Atlantic Charter, signed by Franklin Delano Roosevelt and Winston Churchill in August 1941, declared that all nations "must come to the abandonment of the use of force," but did not explain how. At that juncture, it was still undecided whether the organization would be selective or universal in its membership. Some, like John Foster Dulles, who as secretary of state during the Eisenhower years became a prime architect of the Cold War, advocated an "association of free peoples" more like the North Atlantic Treaty Organization (NATO) than the UN. But the idea that prevailed, in keeping with Roosevelt's own predilection, was to seek a more universal composition.

The Formal Structure of the UN Charter

The United Nations is formally centered around a General Assembly consisting of representatives of each member state in the organization, a Security Council composed of the great powers and a rotating set of other members, a Secretary-General, and a Secretariat to handle administrative tasks. The Security Council, originally composed of the five Big Powers of the era (the United States, the USSR, Great Britain, France, and the Republic of China [on Taiwan]), which possessed permanent seats), plus six rotating seats for other member nations, was expanded in 1955 to fifteen members. Each of the Big Five possessed a veto power over actions of the council.

The Security Council was given the primary authority to deal with all issues concerning "international peace and security," topics on which the General Assembly could "recommend" but could not act. To the Security Council alone was given the power to order military action. In the sole instance where conventional military action was commanded, however, the Security Council only succeeded in acting because one of the two antagonists (the Soviet Union) was temporarily absent from the chambers, having left in protest against the refusal to admit its ally, the People's Republic of China, to the UN.

With the paralysis of the veto-plagued Security Council, the General Assembly undertook a more active role in security issues. Ironically, though this power shift ultimately benefited the middle and smaller nations somewhat at the expense of the Big Powers, it was the United States that initiated the shift in the first instance. Fearing a Soviet veto of the military sanctions it spearheaded against North Korea in 1950, the U.S. government in November 1950 introduced the Uniting for Peace Resolution, which provided that "if the Security Council, because of lack of unanimity of the permanent members, fails to exercise its primary responsibility for the maintenance of international peace and security . . . the General Assembly shall consider the matter immediately with a view to making the appropriate recommendations to Members for collective measures . . . including the use of armed force when necessary. . . ."[1] The General Assembly exercised this power on several important occasions (for example, in the Suez crisis in 1956 and in the Congo in 1960).

The second branch of the UN security system, its administrative apparatus, is the Secretariat and its chief officer, the secretary-general. Although denigrated on occasion by both superpowers when his actions displeased them (Andrey Gromyko once dismissed him as "a glorified clerk"), the secretary-general, especially Dag Hammarskjöld, became a figure of considerable power and influence. The secretary-general's mandate is to draw the attention of the Security Council to any matter that may threaten international security; his independence has often drawn the greatest ire from superpower governments whose own sovereign independence he has sometimes implicitly threatened. Wary of having to contend with a secretary-general whose force of personality might give him the capacity to limit, however little, their own freedom of action, the United States and the Soviet Union have tacitly agreed in recent years to elect to the post men without the compelling public presence and the activist approach that characterized Hammarskjöld.[2]

The International Court of Justice

The judicial branch of the UN security system, the International Court of Justice, is actually a carryover from the League of Nations, where it was known as the Permanent Court of International Justice. A special Committee of Jurists from forty-three nations met in Washington, D.C., just before the UN founding conference and urged that all member nations immediately accept the compulsory jurisdiction of the court. But this view encountered powerful opposition from delegation members of both the Soviet Union and the United States, who made it clear that they could not accept the statute if such a clause was included.[3]

The failure to establish the court's compulsory jurisdiction so weakened its role in events that it has never been more than marginally engaged in the principal conflicts of the postwar years. The decision by the United States to deny the court's jurisdiction in the case brought by Nicaragua in 1984 concerning the mining of its harbors, and its subsequent defiance of the court's judgment, are just the most recent of many occasions in which the voluntary nature of the court's authority has severely curtailed its effectiveness.

Other Mechanisms of Conflict Resolution

Article 33 of the Charter calls upon parties to any dispute to seek a solution first between themselves before bringing it to the Security Council, utilizing any of several modes of conflict resolution: negotiation, inquiry, mediation, conciliation, arbitration, judicial settlement, resort to regional agencies or arrangements, "or other peaceful means of their own choice." Article 34 gives the Security Council the right to initiate an investigation of any dispute to determine whether it "is likely to endanger the maintenance of international peace and security," a right it has exercised through nonbinding "recommendations."

Individual member states may, and often do, bring disputes to the council for consideration under Article 35, but the Charter emphasizes that the Security Council's primary duty is to facilitate and assist the parties in their own efforts to reach agreement, including making recommendations to the parties. The Charter also stipulates that legal (as opposed to political) disputes may be directed by the council to the International Court of Justice, but this procedure has in fact rarely been followed.

If the Security Council determines that a "threat to the peace," "breach of the peace," or "act of aggression" exists, the Charter provides that the council may apply any or all of the following measures: complete or partial interruption of economic relations and of rail, sea, air, postal, and telegraphic services, radio and other means of communication, and the severance of diplomatic relations (Article 41). Such nonmilitary sanctions have rarely been invoked by the council, and despite their ostensibly mandatory nature, such sanctions have never proven fully effective because nations have opted largely to ignore them.

It is hard to gauge the effectiveness of these procedures for peaceful settlement in the UN system. "No one can say what global catastrophes might have occurred if certain controversies had not been successfully dealt with," writes Inis Claude, an international affairs scholar, "or what easy solutions might have been reached even if elaborately institutionalized procedures had not been available. . . . There is general awareness of the failures of the United Nations, but less consciousness of its pacificatory successes, and still less recognition of the possibility that it has prevented some controversies from growing big enough to bring it either blame for failing to solve them or credit for success in so doing."[4]

Collective Security in Theory and Practice

The theoretical foundation of the original UN security system (and of the League of Nations before it) was that at the call of the Security Council, member states would take adequate action to put an end to aggression or unlawful use of force. This arrangement was viewed as the most practical means of assuring peace in a world system of nation states stubbornly committed to remaining sovereign. The framers of the UN Charter studied carefully the flaws in the League's collective security system and sought to strengthen those provisions in their new organization. While members of the League were urged to join in economic and financial measures against violators of the League Covenant, no military measures were provided. The UN Charter, by contrast, establishes a more comprehensive ban on the use of force, imposes mandatory sanctions (economic, diplomatic, and military), and requires member nations to make available contingents from their armed forces for UN use. But in practice, these provisions have proven little more effective than those of the League that preceded them. The weaknesses of the UN security system soon became apparent. In the UN Charter, collective action of any kind, military or nonmilitary, depends on unanimity and consensus. The veto, bestowed on each of the Big Five powers of the Security Council and without which most of them would never have signed the document, assured from the outset that the UN would encounter great difficulty acting at all.

The Cold War froze the machinery of collective action before it was even set in place. The disagreements first erupted in the Military Staff Committee negotiations between the Big Five chiefs of staff, which stretched for fifteen months between 1945 and 1947. The committee was assigned the task of determining, under Article 47, "the Security Council's military requirements [for] the employment and command of forces placed at its disposal, the regulation of armaments, and possible disarmament." Its first task was to implement Article 43 of the United Nations Charter, which defines the arrangements by which the UN system is to keep the peace: "All Members of the United Nations . . . undertake to make available to the Security Council, on its call . . . armed forces, assistance, and facilities . . . necessary for the purpose of maintaining international peace and security." In theory, this arrangement would have guaranteed to the United Nations a powerful collective armed force, under the direction of the Security Council, to deploy against any would-be lawbreaker. But in practice Article 43 has remained inoperative.

To implement this arrangement, the United States proposed a far larger armed force for the UN than any other nation, West or East.

> The United States envisaged a large force with heavy emphasis on mobility and striking power. With regard to ground forces, the U.S. proposed twenty divisions; the French, sixteen; the Soviet Union, twelve . . . It was the estimates for air and naval forces, however, that strikingly revealed the differences between the United States and the other members regarding the kind of forces the Security Council would require. The U.S. proposed an air force more than three times as large as that favored by any of the other permanent members. Its naval estimates included over three times as many destroyers, over seven times as many submarines, and in addition called for battleships, aircraft carriers, and assault craft; none of these were mentioned in the Soviet figures.[5]

The United States sought to persuade the UN to establish "a mobile force able to strike quickly at long range and to bring to bear, upon any given point in the world where trouble may occur, the maximum armed force in the minimum time." The Soviet Union balked at such proposals, arguing that "it would be sufficient for the Security Council to have at its disposal relatively small armed forces." Beneath the Soviets' resistance, no doubt, was a suspicion that these offensive forces might ultimately be turned against them, an apprehension that could not have been abated by a statement by the British representative on the Military Staff Committee, who suggested:

> If any one of the permanent members, guilty of a breach of the peace or of an act of aggression, were to call a halt to the United Nations force, the remainder of the United Nations would be entitled [under Article 51] to take action against that Member. Their forces, already made available to the Security Council, could legitimately be jointly employed to that end for so long as the Security Council failed to take the measures necessary to maintain international peace and security.[6]

Such a strategy of turning the force against one of its own constituents would, of course, have negated the very basis of collective security and would have canceled the Big Power veto on which consent for the Charter was based. It was not collective security but "selective" security, in Inis Claude's phrase, involving security for some at the expense of others. The differences between the U.S. position and that of both its allies and its adversary were more substantial than the disparity in numbers; they envisioned quite different components, deployments, and purposes. Ultimately it proved impossible to reconcile these differences. Discussions of the issues continued for about a year past the issuance of an inconclusive report, after which all further debate on the issues themselves ceased. The committee continues to meet to this day, "but only as a matter of form."[7]

The impasse in the Military Staff Committee consigned Article 43 and its provisions to an oblivion from which it never again emerged. Roosevelt's conception of the "four big policemen" guaranteeing the peace collapsed into the abyss opened by the postwar East-West split. On only one occasion did the UN take collective armed action against an alleged violator of Charter norms—in Korea—and there the operation was more akin to selective than collective security, as it indirectly pitted one superpower and its allies against another and confirmed their antipathy rather than their solidarity.

What made action possible in that instance was the Soviet Union's temporary absence from the Security Council chamber, as the Soviet representative had walked out in protest against the exclusion of mainland China from the UN. In his absence, the United States and its Western allies were able to set in motion arrangements for collective military action against North Korea, which had recently invaded South Korea. Realizing that it could not hope to continue such action when the Soviets returned to the council, the United States introduced the Uniting for Peace Resolution to shift authority for military action toward the General Assembly and thus to circumvent a Soviet veto.

Whatever else it was, the Korean action was not collective security in the sense envisioned by the UN's founders, but was rather an adjunct to the U.S. strategy of "containment," by which the West sought to isolate and neutralize Soviet efforts to spread its influence beyond its large but limited postwar empire. Although a number of other nations contributed token contingents to the Korean venture, the United States committed by far the greatest number and operations were directed entirely by U.S. military personnel. In most respects the Korean action was a conventional military operation, a form of warmaking modeled on the Allied wartime experience but now engaging the two principal allies in indirect combat with one another.

Weaknesses of the UN Security System

In sum, the arrangements of UN security system as conceived in the Charter disintegrated even before they took effect, becoming the first casualty of the Cold War. But even in the absence of such implacable hostility, the system might never have worked as its designers intended. Apart from the Cold War, the UN system faced several obstacles, among them the following:

1. The system could only work if the UN's forces were stronger than any national force. But they could never become so unless nations agreed to reduce their own forces and commit them instead to the international force. Thus emerged a contradiction: "Collective security cannot work

unless states disarm, but states will not disarm until collective security has clearly shown that it merits confidence."[8]

2. The veto power given to each of the Big Five powers at Yalta and San Francisco was undoubtedly a political necessity, since none would have signed the document without it; its result was not only to prevent the Security Council from taking any effective action but to protect from UN sanctions those very nations most likely to abuse their overwhelming military power, the Soviet Union and the United States.

3. The early failure of the Big Powers to agree on a collective security force to keep the peace signaled to other, smaller nations that they could never depend on the UN for their own security. The Charter "provides no firm commitment by any state, and thus offers no potential victim of attack any real assurance of collective assistance."[9]

4. As has been noted by many observers, the UN Charter is a distinctly "pre-atomic" document; indeed, many believe it was rendered almost instantly obsolete by Hiroshima and Nagasaki, which occurred less than two months after the San Francisco drafting conference. Most of all, the UN's framers were thinking primarily about the possible resurgence of Japanese and German militarism and did not foresee the fateful East-West schism.

5. Finally, collective security as conceived by its exponents was a thoroughly militarized means of peacemaking, a strategy of making war to stop war. In retrospect, it seems unlikely that such a punishing strategy could ever succeed in bringing about reconciliation between warring parties.

The Emergence of Peacekeeping

The drafters of the UN Charter did not envision peacekeeping in the sense that it has come to be practiced by the organization over the past thirty years. UN peacekeeping operations were an ad hoc invention born of the necessity of the moment. Nevertheless there were a few historical antecedents, among them the international force dispatched by the League of Nations to supervise a plebiscite in the Saar in 1935. Early arrangements included the Advisory Committee for the UN Emergency Force set up in 1956. Nearly a decade later, in 1965, a Special Committee on Peacekeeping Operations was established.

Peacekeeping as defined and practiced at the UN differs fundamentally from collective security. "Collective security is an adversary, punitive process, not an impartial, cooperative one," wrote Larry Fabian, author of a study of UN peacekeeping, "and its activation was to depend on identification of a declared common enemy, while peacekeeping presences are built on the premises that none exists."[10] Its definition, crafted by some of its practitioners at the International Peace Academy, is "the prevention, containment, moderation, and termination of hostilities between or within states through the medium of third party intervention, organized and directed internationally, using multinational military, police and civilian personnel to restore and maintain peace."[11]

Peacekeeping is, in other words, a form of nonviolent action—a noncoercive activity whose weapon is peaceful interposition and whose principles are nonpartisanship and objectivity. UN peacekeepers are instructed to see themselves not as advocates but as impartial intermediaries, employing measures short of war to damp down local violence, reduce the risks of escalation, and prevent outside intervention. "The stuff of peacekeeping is not a capacity to coerce but an ability to induce compliance with as little coercion as possible."[12]

As a largely nonviolent form of intervention, UN peacekeeping has required of its practitioners a very different set of skills from traditional soldiering—patience, tact, and unflappability under severe provocation. These requirements have encountered some resistance from some tradition-minded military personnel, who see it as weakening a soldier's essential discipline. But in the course of a dozen peacekeeping operations, a body of experience has accumulated, producing a new breed of military personnel, "soldiers without enemies," in Larry Fabian's apt phrase.

> Peacekeepers dress like soldiers, organize like soldiers, live like soldiers, and are equipped like soldiers, but in terms of traditional images of fighting men, they behave in a thoroughly unsoldierly way. They have no deadly foe to destroy or be destroyed by. They fight very little and use their weapons rarely. They prefer compromise to conquest. They substitute persuasion and prevention for punishment, and they apply tact and patience instead of firepower. . . . They are warriors among diplomats.[13]

Three Kinds of Peacekeeping

As practiced at the UN, peacekeeping has been broadly of three kinds.

Peace Observation. Small fact-finding groups have been dispatched to trouble spots throughout the world to report back to the secretary-general and the Security Council in Greece (1947), Palestine (1948), Kashmir (1949), and Lebanon (1958).

Mediation and Reconstruction. UN peacekeeping missions have performed various diplomatic functions, including mediation and arbitration of disputes, while others have engaged in social aid and economic assistance. The most extensive and successful example of such activities has been the UN presence in Cyprus for many years, where a branch of the UN military department deals with local-level social and economic concerns that might otherwise lead to conflict. UN activities on Cyprus include refugee aid, the distribution of goods and services, and medical, agricultural, and educational assistance.

Interposition of Forces. The most common and widespread form of UN intervention has been the interposition of a nonviolent buffer force between the combatants in a dispute to prevent further conflict, as well as to observe ceasefires, maintain demilitarized zones, and prevent external intervention. UN peacekeeping forces have been placed in the Middle East in 1956 and 1973, in the Congo in 1960, and in Cyprus in 1964, among others. In all cases the forces have been given permission to enter, a precondition set by the UN.

In the intractable Middle East conflict, the UN first established the United Nations Emergency Force (UNEF) in 1956, which supervised the withdrawal of Israeli, British, and French forces after they attacked Egypt for nationalizing the Suez Canal Company; UNEF remained for the next eleven years to supervise the peace. The mission, involving some 6,000 men from ten countries, succeeded in part because it enjoyed a rare if reluctant consensus of support from both the United States and the USSR. The value of its presence was unhappily verified when, in 1967, President Gamal Abdel Nasser of Egypt asked UN forces to evacuate and their withdrawal helped precipitate the outbreak of renewed armed conflict between Israel and its Arab neighbors. Following the Yom Kippur War of 1973, a second UN force (UNEF II) supervised the cease-fire and remained in place until 1979.

The largest, costliest, and most complex UN peacekeeping mission was the Congo mission between 1960 and 1964. At its peak, the UN force (nicknamed ONUC, by its French initials) engaged some 20,000 military and specialized personnel. Together they maintained law, order, and essential services during the first four years of the nation's independence from Belgium. But unlike UNEF, ONUC never enjoyed the combined support of both superpowers; indeed, the Soviet Union, which supported one of the warring factions, virulently condemned both the operation and the secretary-general, Dag Hammarskjöld, eventually demanding his resignation. The cost of the mission, more than $400 million, provoked a financial crisis that threatened for a time to destroy the UN itself. Despite these traumatic events, the UN presence in the Congo did stop the bloodshed and achieve the transition from colonial rule to independence in a way that no other institution of less global authority likely could have.

A review of these and other missions demonstrates that despite their somewhat unspectacular results, UN peacekeeping operations have been substantially more successful at keeping the peace without undue bloodshed than were earlier and more partisan efforts at collective security.

Perhaps more importantly, in the instances where they have been utilized, UN forces have succeeded in preventing unilateral intervention by larger nations seeking influence or control, often under the guise of their own multinational but highly partisan collective forces.

Sources of Success

The UN missions that have succeeded share certain characteristics: (1) they have remained largely nonviolent, responding even to severe provocations with a minimum of counterforce; (2) they have always obtained the consent of at least one of the combatants before entering into a conflict, and usually both; (3) they have, on most occasions, enjoyed broad support from the international community (with a few important exceptions, especially in the Congo); (4) they have been widely accepted as impartial, where no national or multinational force apart from the UN would likely be so viewed; and (5) they have sought to adapt themselves to the social and cultural milieus in which they have been placed, establishing a rapport with the local inhabitants that eases the tasks of peacemaking and peacebuilding.

The very success of UN peacekeeping in subduing conflicts has provoked debate in some quarters about whether such intervention in some cases ends up reinforcing an unjust status quo or freezing a conflict in place without resolving it, reducing the outward violence and thus diminishing the sense of urgency necessary to confront the underlying issues. The tragedy of the ten-year UNEF presence on the Egyptian-Israeli border (1956–1967) was that neither nation took advantage of the breathing space opened by the truce to deal with the unresolved political problems. The UN was ultimately blamed for the collapse of the truce, but the failure was really that of the combatants, one of whom (Egypt) ordered the UN out of the region in order to resume hostilities. Practitioners of peacekeeping acknowledge the problem and argue that peacekeeping missions should always be accompanied by concurrent efforts at peacemaking (mediation and diplomacy) and peacebuilding (economic and social aid) in order to avoid simply suppressing conflict and to deal with it instead at its roots.

From the outset, UN peacekeeping forces have been drawn from the smaller and middle nations. The organization of peacekeeping was first achieved through cooperation between the secretary-general, Dag Hammarskjöld, and the Advisory Committee for the UN Emergency Force created by the General Assembly. Hammarskjöld, a gifted Swedish diplomat who served as secretary-general from 1953 until his death in 1961, sought to promote the UN as a conciliator and mediator, practicing "consensual peacekeeping" and "preventive diplomacy."

Several "middle powers" (Canada, the Nordic states, Ireland, India, Austria, and the Netherlands) became the principal source of manpower for UN peacekeeping missions. Of the dozen peacekeeping missions in the first quarter century Sweden participated in ten, Canada in nine, Denmark in eight, and Norway, Ireland, and Finland in seven. Due to their proven partisanship, the superpowers have both been tacitly disqualified from participating in UN peacekeeping missions, although the United States in particular has contributed considerable sums to their upkeep.

There are not now and have never been standing UN peacekeeping forces, trained and maintained specifically for the purpose. The UN has always been obliged to muster its forces on an ad hoc basis, mostly without prior training in the distinctly different arts of peacekeeping. However, in 1964 the Scandinavian countries (Sweden, Norway, Denmark, and Finland) together established a Nordic standby force of some 4,500 volunteers and created a modest training program to prepare them for UN duty.

The Recent Fate of Peacekeeping

Like nearly every other UN activity, peacekeeping has inevitably been affected by the incessant cross fire of East-West animosities. The United States has maintained a consistent policy of excluding the Soviet Union whenever possible from involvement in peacekeeping operations in order to prevent it from gaining strategic influence in the regions of the UN missions. The Soviets in their turn have, until recently, viewed most peacekeeping missions as Western ploys to maintain exclusive control and have on occasion bitterly attacked the secretary-general. During the Congo mission, Premier Nikita Khrushchev demanded the removal of Dag Hammarskjöld and his replacement by a troika of representatives from the East, West, and neutral countries. The USSR and the United States have, however, found sufficient common interest in the Middle East and elsewhere to allow UN missions to go forward.

Recent statements by Soviet leaders indicate that their attitude toward UN peacekeeping operations may be changing. In a widely cited article in *Pravda* in September 1987, General Secretary Mikhail Gorbachev proposed, as an element in a "comprehensive system of international security," wider use of UN peacekeeping forces and military observers to disengage parties in conflict and to monitor cease-fire agreements. He also proposed use of Security Council permanent members as "guarantors of regional security assum[ing] the obligation not to use force or the threat of force . . . " and establishment of a UN-based "multilateral center for lessening the danger of war," including a direct communications link between UN headquarters, the nations constituting permanent members of the Security Council, and the chair of the nonaligned movement.[14]

Although low-key operations have continued in the Middle East and on Cyprus, there have been few new UN peacekeeping ventures in recent years. This lull is unfortunately not due to any decline in international unrest; indeed, if anything, interstate violence is on the rise, with more than twenty wars currently underway. It is, rather, a consequence of the decline of UN influence and the growing tendency of nations to bypass the institution, take matters into their own hands, and settle their arguments by force. Both superpowers have resorted to overt and covert military intervention in open defiance of Charter norms and numerous lesser powers have followed suit.

In some instances, multinational forces have been assembled outside the UN to undertake specific tasks that the organization in its earlier days might have fulfilled. The Camp David Accords between Israel and Egypt, for example, provided for the establishment of a Multinational Force and Observers (MFO) to monitor the terms of the agreement. In this case, the mission has been relatively successful and has aroused no great controversy.

The Lebanon Debacle: Hazards of Bypassing the UN

In Lebanon, however, the consequences of bypassing the UN have been calamitous. In 1983 the Lebanese government asked the UN to enlarge its 6,500-member force then in the country, but Israel, questioning the unit's impartiality, prevented the move. Instead, the United States, France, Great Britain, and Italy together formed a Multinational Force (MNF) that ultimately abandoned any pretense of impartiality and engaged in open combat in support of Christian Phalangists. Answering fire from the shore, U.S. forces shelled civilian neighborhoods in Beirut with 16-inch artillery shells from battleships stationed nearby and conducted bombing strikes from U.S. aircraft carriers. The consequence was a savage round of counterstrikes, including the massacre of 243 U.S. Marines by a truck bomb delivered to the U.S. military compound in Beirut. The Multinational Force withdrew in haste and humiliation. Syrian troops moved in and the Lebanese were left to carry on their civil war without restraint.

The Lebanese case illustrates the inappropriateness of using selective security arrangements with participation by only one political bloc in place of a more universally supported and broadly representative mission. While on occasion such impartiality has been achieved outside the UN system, it is somewhat easier to accomplish within it, where the machinery is already in place. In bypassing the UN's existing apparatus for peacekeeping, nations not only saddle themselves with burdens they are ill-equipped to handle but further weaken the UN's capabilities by denying it the support it needs and deserves to develop into an effective peacekeeping mechanism.

The Unknown UN: Its Specialized Agencies

Although the UN's failures as an institution of conflict control have been widely noted and perhaps overly emphasized, its successes as a global agency for other vital functions have been much underappreciated. Indeed, the specialized agencies (some of which are integral to the UN system while others are independent but associated), which were conceived in the Charter as a secondary function of the organization, have proven more effective than the institutions established to serve its original and primary purpose as a system of war prevention.

The World Health Organization (WHO), the Food and Agriculture Organization (FAO), the High Commissioner on Refugees (UNHCR), the UN Fund for Population Activities, UNICEF, UNESCO, the International Atomic Energy Agency (IAEA), the International Labour Organisation (ILO), the International Monetary Fund (IMF), and other agencies perform invaluable services that are seldom recognized so long as they continue to function but would be sorely missed if they suddenly failed. Coordinated by the Economic and Social Council (ECOSOC) and the General Assembly, the activities of these agencies constitute between 80 percent and 90 percent of all UN programs, performing many services that are not and could not effectively be handled by any other organization. Equally valuable has been the UN's vital but seldom acknowledged role in promoting an orderly process of decolonization in what could otherwise have become a prime source of international conflict.

It is beyond the scope of this book to delineate the nature of the UN's manifold activities beyond its well-known security functions or to suggest ways in which they could be strengthened. But it is important that we recognize and appreciate that much of what the UN does, it does very well. The routine effectiveness of its specialized agencies may cause us to take their performance for granted. In the broadest sense, these agencies contribute significantly to global security.

Conclusion: The Future of the UN Security System

After dominating the UN during its first twenty years, for the next two decades Western nations became an increasingly embattled minority as nearly a hundred newly independent nations joined the organization, identifying their interests as different from and often contrary to those of the West. The Western response to this shift was an accelerating decline in support for the United Nations. Regard for the organization reached so low an ebb in the United States in the early and mid-1980s that politicians and national security planners alike no longer found it necessary to include the UN in their calculations of foreign policy. Many simply ignored its existence and suffered no penalty for doing so.

The frustrations and failures of global security institutions led many strategists in both West and East to retreat to overtly unilateral or competing alliance strategies, to an unequivocal embrace of the balance-of-power system that has proven notoriously unstable over the past century. Thus the UN languished while national military arsenals continued to grow. The liberal internationalism that briefly held sway in the United States in the early postwar years was largely eclipsed by a renewed unilateralism and an obsession with the "the national interest" narrowly defined in opposition to the interest of most other nations.

This was not the first crisis the UN had faced. Indeed, the organization has been repeatedly plagued by life-threatening crises. Yet somehow it has always survived, perhaps because, as Robert Johansen observes, it "has become indispensable before it has become effective."[15] Most unexpectedly, and just at the moment when the UN appeared headed for bankruptcy, the organization gained new stature and importance in 1988 as events placed it at the center of revived efforts to resolve a number of longstanding conflicts around the world. Guided by Secretary General Javier Perez de Cuellar, the UN successfully negotiated a cease-fire in the eight-year Persian Gulf war between Iran and Iraq and arranged for the withdrawal of Soviet troops from Afghanistan. Through the UN's good offices, conflicts in Namibia, the Western Sahara, and Cambodia also appeared in 1988 to be advancing toward long-sought resolutions. So significant were these cumulative achievements that the UN's peacekeeping forces were awarded the 1988 Nobel Peace Prize in recognition of their "decisive contribution toward the initiation of actual peace negotiations."[16]

Even the Reagan administration, which had maintained a consistently hostile stance toward the UN for nearly its entire eight years in office, appeared to begin to alter its policy in the last few months of its term. Having refused to pay certain of its obligatory dues to the organization for several years, the United States stood at least $467 million in debt in regular contributions and an additional $65 million in arrears in its support of UN peacekeeping as of August 1988.[17] On September 26, 1988, President Reagan pledged to pay a small portion of U.S. debts to the UN, $44 million immediately and $144 million under the 1989 budget.[18] Just one month after pledging this payment, however, the

Reagan administration announced that it would continue to withhold $59 million of the $144 million until the Fifth Committee of the General Assembly, which oversees UN finances, approved a new austerity budget. Its earlier pledge to pay was widely understood in retrospect to have been a political gesture to avoid an embarrassing confrontation when Reagan spoke before the General Assembly at the end of September 1988.[19] Two weeks later, Reagan praised the UN's efforts in his valedictory speech to the General Assembly, predicting "a new age of world peace" in which the UN "has the opportunity to live and breathe and work as never before."[20]

It was still too soon to tell whether these sudden and unforeseen successes would mark a permanent reversal in the decades-long decline of the United Nations. Success may have been due in many of these cases less to the UN's interventions than to a cumulative war weariness on the part of the belligerents. Nevertheless, the institution was there at the moment when it was needed and proved effective both as a forum for negotiation and a police officer of the peace. In success as in failure, the UN experience indicates that when nations (and particularly great nations) find reason to use the UN effectively, they can and do, and when they do not find it in their interest to do so, they can cripple the organization through neglect or abuse. Commenting on the numerous peace initiatives of 1988, Stanley Hoffman noted that they tell "a great deal about the sharp limits the international system puts on the successful use of force."[21] Insofar as that lesson was being learned in the late 1980s, the United Nations stood to gain increased use and support in years to come.

Redesigning the Tool, Remodeling the Structure

"It's the poor craftsman who blames his tool," runs the carpenter's old saw. The UN is a tool, or a set of tools—nothing more and nothing less. Emotionally satisfying as it may be to shift the blame to the institution we have created, in fact we have no one to blame but ourselves for whatever it fails to achieve. We designed and constructed it, and then in frustration abused and neglected it. Like any tool, it is only as effective as the ingenuity of our design and our skill in wielding it. We will not improve our skill by blaming the tool, but by practicing how to use it better and by modifying the design to improve its performance. If its failure has been our failure, its success will be a product of our commitment to make it work. It is exactly as good as we make it.

Over the years since the UN's creation, many scholars and theorists have suggested ways of reforming the organization. Some have asserted that it is a hopelessly inadequate structure and that our time is better spent building something new and more substantial than remodeling what's left of this temporary dwelling. A number of the more comprehensive and thoughtful proposals will be surveyed in the next chapter. But it is important, too, to recognize the time, effort, and expense that have gone into creating this institution. These are resources we should not lightly abandon. Flawed as it is in design and construction, and weathered as it has been by the prevailing political crosswinds, there nevertheless remains a foundation on which new rooms may always be built.

We need not be overly concerned with the formal designs of our additions. In the history of the organization, we have been better served by its spontaneous innovations than by its initial organizing principle, armed collective security. Building on what has worked, we may yet construct a shelter sturdy enough to withstand the abuse to which it will surely be exposed.

Notes

1. Leland M. Goodrich, Edvard Hambro, and Anne Patricia Simons, *Charter of the United Nations: Commentary and Documents* (Third and Revised Edition) (New York: Columbia University Press, 1969), p. 122.

2. Hammarskjöld was also chosen because he seemed at the time to be a quiet and uncontroversial man, an impression that was obviously mistaken.

3. Goodrich, Hambro, and Simons, *Charter of the United Nations,* pp. 546–547.

4. Inis Claude, Jr., *Swords into Plowshares: The Problems and Progress of International Organizations,* 3rd ed. (New York: Random House, 1964), p. 209.

5. Goodrich, Hambro, and Simons, *Charter of the United Nations,* p. 324.

6. Ibid., p. 323.

7. Ibid., p. 324.

8. Claude, *Swords into Plowshares,* p. 237.

9. Ibid., p. 246.

10. Larry Fabian, *Soldiers Without Enemies* (Washington, DC: Brookings Institution, 1971), p. 23.

11. Indar Rikhye, Michael Harbottle, and Bjorn Egge, *The Thin Blue Line: International Peacekeeping and Its Future* (New Haven, CT: Yale University Press, 1974), p. 11.

12. Fabian, *Soldiers Without Enemies,* p. 29.

13. Ibid., p. 28.

14. Mikhail Gorbachev, "The Reality and Guarantees of a Secure World," USSR Mission to the United Nations, Press Release no. 119 (September 17, 1987), p. 7.

15. Robert Johansen, "The United States, The United Nations, and A New Code of International Conduct," unpublished ms. (New York: World Policy Institute, 1986), p. 2.

16. Sheila Rule, "U.N. Peacekeeping Forces Named Winner of the Nobel Peace Prize," *New York Times,* September 30, 1988, p. 1.

17. Paul Lewis, "The U.N. Dove: Hobbled by the U.S.?" *New York Times,* August 9, 1988, p. 7.

18. Elaine Sciolino, "Reagan, in Switch, Says U.S. Will Pay Some Old Dues," *New York Times,* September 14, 1988, p. A-8.

19. See Paul Lewis, "U.S. Holding Back Part of U.N. Dues Over Budget Issue," *New York Times,* October 15, 1988, p. 1.

20. "Excerpts from the President's Speech," *New York Times,* September 27, 1988, p. A-6.

21. Stanley Hoffman, "Lessons of a Peace Epidemic," *New York Times,* September 6, 1988, p. A-19.

CHAPTER FOUR

A World Peacekeeping Federation: The Clark-Sohn Plan

Even before the signing of the UN Charter, there were those who believed it could not succeed because it had not gone far enough. In the early postwar years, a strong intellectual and citizens' movement grew up in support of one or another form of world government to modify or replace the United Nations with a more effective structure for global order. At the University of Chicago, Robert Hutchins, Rexford Tugwell, Stringfellow Barr, and a commission of eminent colleagues issued a "Preliminary Draft of a World Constitution," replete with Romanesque flourishes like a Chamber of Guardians, a Grand Tribunal, and a Tribune of the People.[1] The United World Federalists, an advocacy organization founded to promote the idea in mainstream political circles, attracted the youthful energies of such future public figures as Norman Cousins (for many years editor of *The Saturday Review*), Kingman Brewster (later president of Yale University), Alan Cranston (later a U.S. senator), and William T. Holliday, then president of Standard Oil of Ohio.

Grenville Clark and Louis B. Sohn

The most comprehensive and systematic proposal to emerge from all this activity was the so-called Clark-Sohn Plan. *World Peace through World Law*, the document that became the classic formulation of the world federalist structure of government, was the product of a decades-long collaboration between two Harvard lawyers, Grenville Clark and Louis Sohn. Clark was an eminently successful Wall Street lawyer and a patrician New England "public citizen" who, as a self-motivated minister without portfolio, helped shape numerous critical national policy initiatives by dint of his formidable personality, determination, and position. Sohn, younger by a generation, was a Polish immigrant to the

United States who had narrowly escaped an almost certain death at the hands of the Nazis. In appreciation of his good fortune, he has devoted a substantial part of his life to devising strategies to prevent a future war. A young professor at the time of their meeting, he eventually came to hold the most prestigious chair in international law in the United States as Bemis Professor of International Law at the Harvard Law School.

Clark had been the principal force behind the eminent citizens' movement in 1915 that organized training camps in Plattsburg, New York, to drill officers in preparation for the war in Europe, which the United States had not yet entered. Realizing early on that the United States would inevitably become involved and realizing as well the lack of preparation for this eventuality among U.S. armed forces, Clark gathered a select group of his Harvard classmates and other prominent acquaintances to form a Military Training Camps Committee that was responsible for training 80 percent of the officers who eventually directed the American Expeditionary Force in France. This successful private initiative undoubtedly saved thousands of lives in the course of the war and hastened the termination of hostilities. Not until 1917, when the United States officially entered the war, did the U.S. Army reassume responsibility for running the officer training camps.

History appeared to be repeating itself a quarter century later when, in the spring of 1940, Clark surveyed the state of affairs in Europe, where war had once again broken out, and viewed with alarm the chronic unreadiness of U.S. troops to meet what once more seemed to him an inevitable involvement in that conflagration. In April 1940, Clark met with President Franklin Roosevelt, who had been his classmate at Harvard and a longtime friend, to urge FDR to introduce a compulsory military training law. While Roosevelt agreed it should be done, he felt it would never pass the Senate in a renewed climate of isolationism. He declined to publicly endorse Clark's initiative but agreed not to oppose it and privately supported it. Clark, meanwhile, returned to his personal campaign for compulsory service, reconvening many of the original members of the Military Training Camps Association who twenty-five years earlier had initiated the Plattsburg Camps, in the same Nicholas Biddle Room of the Harvard Club, to organize a public campaign for compulsory peacetime conscription in preparation for entering World War II. Clark drafted a bill stipulating compulsory registration of all able-bodied men between the ages of eighteen and thirty-five, selection by lottery, service at $5 a month, and release from the military after one year. This legislation in time became the Selective Service Act. Passed in September 1940 and extended in 1941 by a one-vote majority in the Senate, the act established compulsory registration. Within two months of its passage, some 15 million men had registered under the new law.

"A Federation of Free Peoples"

So it was with a measure of perhaps unconscious irony that Clark found himself, in the last third of his life, campaigning for the abolition of the very armed forces whose training he had done so much to establish in the United States. But the change had already begun even as he was busy organizing the campaign for the Selective Service Act. In 1940 Clark privately published his "Proposal for a Federation of Free Peoples," which renounced the principle of unbridled national sovereignty on which the balance of power system rests and argued instead that security could only be attained by the mutual acceptance of a higher rule of law.

In the language of the era, the term "free peoples" was highly ambiguous, tending (according to one's interpretation) in quite contrary directions. In 1940, Clark conceived the federation as encompassing only those nations with "institutions resting on the consent of the governed," and thus restricted its initial membership to the United States, France, Great Britain, Canada, Australia, the Union of South Africa [*sic*], New Zealand, Ireland, Finland, the Scandinavian countries, Holland, Belgium, Switzerland, "and several of the countries of Central and South America most advanced in the practice of stable, popular government. . . . This is not to say," he hastened to add, "that the Federation of Free Peoples should be highly restrictive in its membership. To the contrary, the policy should be to welcome new members *as fast as they can qualify by being in sympathy with the fundamental purposes of the federation* (original emphasis)."[2]

Stimson: "Go Home and Figure Out a Way"

But it was not until the war was nearly over that Clark received an unofficial commission from his friend, Henry Stimson, Roosevelt's secretary of war, whom Clark had long served as a special adviser. It was Clark to whom the secretary of war had turned in the wake of Pearl Harbor to draft a declaration of war. And when, in late 1944, it became apparent to Stimson that the United States would indeed succeed in making the atomic bomb and so hasten the war's termination, he once again turned to Clark with a new and reverse assignment: "Go home and try to figure out a way to stop the next war, and all future wars." Stimson likely didn't realize, when he delivered his charge, how far Clark would go in his determined pursuit of his assignment, for he not only retired from Washington, D.C., to the family farmhouse in Dublin, New Hampshire, but devoted his entire remaining life of more than two decades to two overriding concerns: world peace and civil rights. In time he produced, in conjunction with his colleague, Louis Sohn, the most comprehensive and thoughtfully considered plan for a world peacekeeping federation ever conceived.

He began his work with a detailed critique of the Dumbarton Oaks proposals that established the framework for the United Nations. He sought to have them amended to reinforce the capacity of the future international organization to act by strengthening the General Assembly and eliminating the Great Power veto. "The underlying defect of the Dumbarton Oaks proposals," he wrote, "is not in their failure to grant ample nominal powers. It is rather that no machinery is proposed whereby the nominal powers can be exercised with any certainty in a time of crisis. . . . I emphasize that we need above all imagination and a creative spirit, capable of a great leap forward in the organization of a world now truly made one by modern invention. The founders of 1787 not only had the vision of this nation but also the practical skill to find the formulae that made it possible. If we cannot fully equal their mature political wisdom, we can at least try to rival their capacity for original and adventurous thought."[3]

Dublin One

Clark viewed with dismay the results of the San Francisco conference, which followed closely the pattern set down in the Dumbarton Oaks proposals. In a letter to the new president, Harry Truman, he insisted that "Sometime, if we are really to have world order, we (and others) will have to modify our ideas about 'sovereignty' and make up our minds to relinquish the unilateral veto as to joining in cooperative action to maintain peace."[4] Then, in a move that echoed his earlier campaigns for military training and conscription, he convened, on his farm in Dublin, New Hampshire, a gathering of some fifty eminent persons to consider how best to salvage and reform the fledgling United Nations. Called "Dublin One" after Clark's local phone number, the conference included Owen Roberts, a former justice of the U.S. Supreme Court, Thomas K. Finletter, a future secretary of the Air Force, and the youthful Norman Cousins, Kingman Brewster, and Alan Cranston.

Clark set the tone for the gathering in his keynote address, later summarized by Cousins:

> He forecast a struggle for the balance of power under conditions of uncertainty and insecurity for both [the U.S. and USSR]. He saw the emergence of a

> world atomic armaments race. . . . He believed the moment in history had come for creating the instruments of workable law . . . a world government which would have "limited but adequate powers. . . . " In short, he proposed world law as the only alternative to existing world anarchy.[5]

Most significantly, Clark delineated an organization of universal membership, in contrast to his earlier proposal, in 1940, for a more exclusive federation of "free" peoples.

It was on this point, and the related issue of sovereignty, that the conference divided, though not irreparably. Justice Roberts, Stringfellow Barr, and three other participants declined to sign the final declaration. Roberts proposed instead "that simultaneously with efforts to attain a world federal government, the United States should explore the possibility of forming a nuclear union with nations where individual liberty exists, as a step toward the projected world government."[6]

The conference's own division thus reflected a growing division in the larger movement for international organization between those (mostly future liberal internationalists) who advocated a more universal and democratic institution and those (mostly future conservative advocates of containment and balance of power strategies) who sought to create an alliance with strong military dimensions between the like-minded nations of the West. While the conservatives ultimately prevailed in the establishment of NATO and its sister and rival alliances in the years to come, it was the internationalists who prevailed at Dublin One, thanks largely to the commanding presence of Grenville Clark. In its final declaration, the conference proposed "that a World Federal Government be created with closely defined and limited powers adequate to prevent war and strengthen the freedoms that are the inalienable Rights of Man."[7]

Four months later, the group, now some sixty persons, including Albert Einstein, met again at Princeton. But the meeting produced little of consequence other than one memorable anecdote that served as a kind of unwitting epitaph for the entire effort. As later related by Supreme Court Justice Felix Frankfurter, the eminent scientist was approached by a participant and asked, "'Dr. Einstein, how is it that the brain of man is able to evolve those wonderful theories and translate them into practice in the world of physics, and yet we stumble along at the razor's edge of the abyss of destruction. . . . Why can't the human brain answer these questions of government and politics?' And the profound Einstein in his lovable, childlike way, the childishness of great profundity, said: 'The answer is very simple: politics is so much more difficult than physics.'"[8]

In most of his previous campaigns, Clark's timing had been impeccable—just far enough in advance of conventional thinking to provide effective leadership but not so far beyond that few would grasp the relevance and validity of his proposals. But in the case of world government, he was evidently generations in advance of his time, if indeed history was even headed in his direction. Then, too, his earlier proposals had reinforced trends already underway, with powerful constituencies in place to support and enact the plans, while his proposal for a world federal government ran contrary to centuries of precedent and in opposition to many of the very institutions that had supported his earlier efforts. In this respect, he found himself in a position of profound and painful irony not unlike Einstein, who spent the last portion of his life arguing for the establishment of governing structures adequate to control the bomb whose invention he was instrumental in proposing.

From *A Plan for Peace* to *World Peace Through World Law*

Dismayed with the lack of progress in his Dublin committee, Clark decided to proceed alone and in collaboration with Louis Sohn. He produced, in 1950, a brief volume entitled *A Plan for Peace.* Even before this book was published, the authors started working on a detailed plan for universal, enforceable, and complete disarmament and for a United Nations strong enough to maintain peace in a disarmed world. Preliminary drafts were widely distributed in 1953 and 1956; some 2,000 comments and criticisms were received and taken into account in the text of the first edition published in 1958 under the title *World Peace Through World Law,* which emphasized the close connection in the authors' thinking between peace and law, and the need for institutions required to maintain law and order.

Later editions, in 1960 and 1967, took into account further comments and criticisms received and the constant changes in international relations, especially the advent on the world scene of many new nations and their interest not only in peace, but also in economic development. The third edition thus contained two alternative models for a new world order: (1) a revision of the United Nations Charter, paragraph by paragraph, with a detailed comment explaining the changes and special detailed annexes on disarmament, a United Nations Peace Force, a judicial and conciliation system for settling international disputes, a World Development Authority, a Bill of Rights, and a novel revenue system to maintain the new institutions; and (2) a Draft Treaty Establishing a World Disarmament and World Development Organization, which would supplement the United Nations and could be established without requiring any changes in the Charter of the United Nations but would nevertheless accomplish all the desired changes in international institutions.

The plan included a variety of institutional components relating to global security:

1. A greatly strengthened General Assembly with authority to direct and control all the organs and agencies of the United Nations except the International Court of Justice, the World Equity Tribunal, and the World Conciliation Board (which would remain altogether independent of political control). The assembly's representatives would be elected initially by national legislatures but eventually by direct popular vote of the entire global electorate, and their apportionment would be based on the population of each nation (originally thirty representatives for each of the four largest, fifteen for the next eight, six for the next twenty, etc.).

2. An Executive Council in place of the existing Security Council, consisting of seventeen members, elected from and by the General Assembly. The council would include a representative from each of the four most populous nations (China, India, the USSR, and the United States), and one from four of the eight next most populous nations. The veto would be abolished, but a majority of twelve of the seventeen members of the council would need to agree on all "important" matters. Unlike the present arrangement, where the Security Council stands legally superior to the General Assembly, the Executive Council under Clark-Sohn would be subsidiary to the assembly, which would now assume primary responsibility for handling issues of international peace and security.

3. A much expanded and strengthened world judicial and conciliation system endowing the International Court of Justice with extensive compulsory jurisdiction over legal disputes between all nations; and supplementing it with a new World Equity Tribunal (with the power to recommend but not to issue binding decisions) to deal with nonlegal disputes between nations; a World Conciliation Board to assist nations in finding agreed solutions for their disputes; and a system of twenty to forty regional tribunals to try individual offenders against the Charter. The International Court of Justice and the World Equity Tribunal would be composed of independent judges elected for life by the General Assembly. Provisions would be made to enforce the judgments of the court; and under certain restricted circumstances, the recommendations of the tribunal would become enforceable, but only after a confirming vote by three-quarters of the assembly, including two-thirds of all the representatives from the twelve largest nations.

4. A permanent UN Peace Force consisting of two components—a full-time standing force of between 200,000 and 400,000 persons and a Peace Force Reserve of 300,000 to 600,000 persons. Forces would be distributed widely throughout the world, mostly in the smaller nations, and the UN would maintain its own bases and supply, research, and development infrastructures. The Peace Force would come under the control of a reconstituted Military Staff Committee, consisting not exclusively of the Great Powers (as in the present Charter) but exclusively of the smaller nations. The Peace Force would be equipped with the most advanced conventional weapons and a small, invulnerable, carefully safeguarded nuclear arsenal but would not possess chemical or biological weapons. It would also maintain the capacity to move men and matériel rapidly to any part of the world in case of need.

5. A United Nations inspection service to police the disarming process and assure that no clandestine rearmament occurred. The Inspection Service would have "complete freedom" of movement into, out of, and within the territory of every nation.

6. A World Development Authority to help finance economic and social projects, primarily in the developing world.

Elimination of "Excess" National Forces

Under the original Clark-Sohn Plan, all armaments and armed forces in all nations (except domestic police to maintain internal order) would have been eliminated during a thirteen-year disarming process. In order to avoid a too long and too dangerous transition period, this timetable was cut to six years, divided into a one-year preparatory period, and ten six-month periods; during each of these ten periods, 10 percent of military forces would be disbanded in every nation and 10 percent of existing armaments and armament-making facilities would be eliminated or converted to other uses. Even those nations not joining the United Nations would be required to disarm since, Clark and Sohn reasoned, any exception would undermine the entire process. "We should face the fact that until there is *complete* disarmament of every nation without exception there can be no assurance of genuine peace."[9]

The forces remaining, then, would be solely the United Nations Peace Force and tightly circumscribed international police forces composed of local police not exceeding eighteen for each 10,000 of population, and central police forces not exceeding seven for each 10,000 of population and in no case more than 100,000. While the United Nations force would be strong enough to overcome one of these national forces, these forces might combine easily into a strong opposition force if the United Nations force should attempt to abuse its powers.

Control of Remaining Forces

Clark and Sohn were both keenly aware of the possibilities of tyranny inherent in the concentration of military power and political authority in a world government and sought by a variety of innovative means to hedge these powers with strict limitations in order to lessen the likelihood of their abuse. Although they invested their reformed UN with a small residual deterrent stockpile of nuclear weapons drawn from discarded national stocks (reasoning that no inspection scheme could be sufficiently rigorous to assure that absolutely none were being concealed), they assigned custody and maintenance of the arsenal to a nonmilitary agency, the United Nations Nuclear Energy Authority.

Moreover, they designated the General Assembly as the sole institution with the authority to order the use of these weapons by the Peace Force, and then only after the assembly had formally declared that nuclear weapons had actually been used or had been imminently threatened against any nation or the United Nations itself. Furthermore, Clark and Sohn stipulated that stockpiles of nuclear materials should be widely dispersed across the planet to avoid the possibility of their usurpation by the nations in which they were located. Hence, not less than 5 percent or more than 10 percent of the total UN arsenal would be situated at any time in any region of the world in which the UN force would be located.

Ultimate control of the Peace Force itself would be similarly vested in civilian hands, through the General Assembly and its special Standing Committee, as well as the Executive Council. While receiving advice from a Military Staff Committee composed of high military officers from five small nations, the Executive Council (acting on the authority of the General Assembly) would retain control over the organization, discipline, training, equipment, and disposition of the Peace Force; it would also map long-term strategic directions and supervise actual operations.

To ensure that the Peace Force would be recruited on as wide a geographical basis as possible, a limit of 3 percent of the total strength of the force would be imposed on the number of nationals of any nation serving in the force at any one time; similar limits would apply to each main branch of the force and the officer corps; and no unit of the force would contain more than fifty persons of the same nationality. As with nuclear materials, the Peace Force itself would be stationed entirely outside the territory of the twelve (or, later, sixteen) largest nations and in such a way that not less than 5 percent or more than 10 percent of its total strength would be stationed in any one of the eleven to twenty regions into which all the territory of the world outside these largest nations would be divided by the General Assembly.

In vesting the ultimate authority to control the Peace Force in the General Assembly, Clark and Sohn sought to remove that power, insofar as possible, from national governments that had so often proven untrustworthy in the use of military force and had invested it in a body elected by the direct vote of the global electorate. By these and many other constitutional designs, they sought to render their peacekeeping federation "tyranny-proof."

Institutions for Conflict Resolution

Under the Clark-Sohn Plan, institutions for the peaceful settlement of disputes would be greatly expanded and elaborated from their embryonic development under the current UN Charter. As noted above, an extensive judicial and conciliation system would be established, including a World Court with compulsory jurisdiction in justiciable matters, a World Equity Tribunal to handle nonlegal concerns, a World Conciliation Board to offer mediation services, and a variety of regional courts to enforce laws relating to the disarming process. The stipulation of compulsory jurisdiction in the court system would greatly strengthen the significance of those bodies in the entire system, for with it world law would become enforceable for the first time, replacing the purely optional present arrangement, where nations can—and do—blithely ignore the World Court's decisions without enduring any serious penalties. Under the Clark-Sohn Plan, moreover, world law would be enforceable on individuals (and corporations) as well as on nations.

In these and other respects, the Clark-Sohn conflict resolution system is considerably more comprehensive than the current Charter and approaches the sophistication and enforceability of national court systems. If such a system were successfully set in place, many conflicts that presently break out in open violence for lack of other means of reconciling or settling outstanding grievances might be prevented in time or resolved without resort to arms.

Disarmament Proposals of the Early 1960s

Although it received appreciative attention in certain circles at the time of its publication, the Clark-Sohn Plan was never seriously considered in the political realm where it would have had to garner support in order for its provisions to be enacted. But the early 1960s were a time, perhaps more than any since the years following World War I and surely more than any time since, when disarmament came closest to being seriously considered by the superpower governments themselves. In 1959 the UN General Assembly passed a resolution declaring for the first time that the principal goal of all arms negotiations under UN auspices was no longer simply the balanced reduction of national arsenals to a more tolerable level of danger and cost but "general and complete disarmament."

The United States in 1960 accepted the idea of general disarmament, but insisted that the reduction of national forces must be preceded by the strengthening of international instruments to prevent national aggression (such as universally accepted rules of law on that subject, backed by a world court and by effective means of enforcement through an international armed force) and by the "development of international machinery to ensure just and peaceful settlement of disputed issues in a disarmed world."[10] This shift of emphasis reflected a move away from the Charter's original collective security arrangements, which left all national arsenals intact and each nation largely responsible for protecting its own territory and interests, and in the direction of the kind of comprehensive security system envisioned by Clark and Sohn (although never with the degree of precision and specificity achieved in their plan).

The McCloy-Zorin Agreements

For the next few years, disarmament was actually a live issue between the superpowers, eliciting detailed proposals and extensive debate. An Eighteen-Nation Disarmament Committee was created to carry on the negotiations. And for a brief time, negotiations did proceed with extraordinary rapidity. In a mere thirty-six days of actual negotiation over a three-month period between June and September of 1961, John J. McCloy, President John F. Kennedy's disarmament adviser, and Valerian Zorin, the Soviet ambassador to the United Nations, reached accord on a "Joint Statement of Agreed Principles for Disarmament Negotiations," which later became known as the McCloy-Zorin Agreements. Endorsing a plan for "general and complete disarmament" of unprecedented scope and depth, they agreed to:

> *(a)* Disbanding of armed forces, the dismantling of military establishments, including bases, cessation of the production of armaments as well as their liquidation or conversion to peaceful uses;
>
> *(b)* Elimination of all stockpiles of nuclear, chemical, bacteriological and other weapons of mass destruction, and the cessation of the production of such weapons;
>
> *(c)* Elimination of all means of delivery of weapons of mass destruction;
>
> *(d)* Abolishment of the organization and institutions designed to organize the military effort of States, cessation of military training, and closing of all military training institutions;
>
> *(e)* Discontinuance of military expenditures.[11]

In addition, the McCloy-Zorin Agreements proposed the creation of an international disarmament organization under UN auspices, whose inspectors "should be assured unrestricted access without veto to all places, as necessary for the purpose of effective verification"; it pointed out that disarmament must be "accompanied by the establishment of reliable procedures for the peaceful settlement of disputes and effective arrangements for the maintenance of peace"; and, in particular, it called for strengthening the arrangements (formulated in Article 43 of the UN Charter) for states to supply men and matériel to the UN for an international peace force to enable the United Nations to "deter or suppress any threat or use of arms" in violation of the Charter.

The Statement of Agreed Principles was submitted to the General Assembly on September 20, 1961, where it was unanimously ratified. Simultaneously, however, an exchange of published letters between McCloy and Zorin made clear that they had not been able to come to an agreement, in the time allotted them, on the issues of inspection and verification, so the sentence that dealt with them had been deliberately omitted. This exclusion was the principal flaw on which subsequent negotiations on a treaty to implement the Agreed Principles ultimately foundered. (In the quarter century since that time, verification capabilities have been greatly enhanced and the Soviet Union has evinced an increased willingness to accept inspection, so the issues that blocked further progress on the Agreed Principles in the early 1960s may no longer be insurmountable.)

Despite the difficulties of inspection and verification in 1961, the Soviet Union and the United States might have worked out a compromise were it not for other developments in the United States that weakened the will of the president. Opposition to implementation of the McCloy-Zorin Agreements built up quickly. It came from the military-industrial complex, as President Eisenhower had foreseen, and it came from within the Kennedy administration itself. Kennedy told McCloy that he had been persuaded that it was politically dangerous to take a stand on the disarmament issue so early in his administration. "I can't afford a defeat," Kennedy told the disappointed McCloy. "I'm afraid you'll have to be more on your own."[12] McCloy knew that without Kennedy's full support, the task was hopeless. He returned to his law practice in New York. The political will of the president was no longer there.

U.S. and Soviet Draft Treaties

Still, the McCloy-Zorin Agreements formed the basis for two draft treaties submitted by the United States and the Soviet Union in 1962 to the Eighteen-Nation Disarmament Committee. The differences between the drafts were more than linguistic; in both approach and underlying philosophy, they were divergent. The Soviet draft proposed a virtually automatic process without any pauses between its three phases and without provisions for delay in case of noncompliance; the U.S. draft proceeded more by trial and error, pausing after each stage to evaluate the success of the regime and not proceeding without proven effectiveness. The Soviet draft began with very large cuts in weapons and forces and diminished with time; the U.S. draft began with small cuts and increased them in later stages. The Soviet draft specified inspection only of weapons eliminated but not of those that were permitted to remain; the U.S. draft insisted on inspecting progressively, zone by zone, the elimination of weapons and weapon-production facilities. The Soviet draft routed complaints of treaty violation to the Security Council, where the veto could easily thwart punitive action; the U.S. draft simply gave either party the right to stop the disarmament process or to abrogate the treaty if it determined that in its view the other had violated the terms of the agreement.

In summary, the Soviet draft treaty did not provide the essential machinery for the peaceful settlement of disputes that would effectively eliminate the impulse to resort to armed intervention. On the other hand, the United States draft contained at least some provisions for gradually improving the machinery for the just and peaceful settlement of all international disputes, for a Peace Observation Corps, and for progressive strengthening of the United Nations Peace Force, which at the end would be strong enough "so that no state could challenge it." While these proposals were not as detailed as the Clark-Sohn proposal and did not tackle such difficult issues as the veto in the Security Council, they clearly followed the trail blazed by the Clark-Sohn Plan. Nevertheless, the negotiations that followed the presentation of the two plans led only to an agreement on a few general provisions and soon were abandoned in favor of nuclear test ban negotiations.

The Decline of Disarmament and the Rise of Arms Control

The superpowers' brief flirtation with disarmament proposals in the early 1960s soon faded, a casualty of many contrary forces, including domestic political constituencies in the United States. Ironically, the success of the Partial Test Ban Treaty in 1963 may have played a role in diminishing public pressures (which had been building in the United States, Great Britain, and elsewhere since the late 1950s) for a more comprehensive settlement. And finally, with the change of presidents following the Kennedy assassination, the new administration quickly became preoccupied with other matters—the Great Society, the war in Vietnam, and a host of other projects and crises. In retrospect, it seems clear that the early 1960s marked not only the beginning but the end of serious interest in comprehensive disarmament.

With the apparent failure of the first tentative probings between the United States and the Soviet Union (or more accurately, failure of the political will to sustain negotiations long enough to produce results), the great majority of politicians, pundits, and academics concerning themselves with questions of international security turned decisively away from complex and comprehensive plans for disarmament and toward the more piecemeal and incremental approaches that became collectively known as "arms control." Viewing disarmament as a utopian goal unattainable in the realm of practical politics and useful for little more than gaining rhetorical advantage in the perennial contest for global public opinion, arms control advocates focused instead on preventing just the most flagrantly irresponsible weapons programs, with the goal of "stabilizing" the arms race but without attempting to terminate it.

With the emergence and ascendancy of arms control thinking, practical consideration of disarmament (and of any more comprehensive proposals for global security) largely vanished from mainstream intellectual circles for the following two decades. The Arms Control and Disarmament Agency (ACDA), founded in 1962 by the Kennedy administration, which had produced a variety of useful studies during its first few years on the political and economic ramifications of disarmament, took an increasingly timid approach to its mandate, until by the 1980s it became more identified with justifying arms increases than with planning for their reduction or abolition. Comprehensive plans for disarmament were viewed as so patently impractical that even the most daring of thinkers abandoned their blueprints and focused instead on critiques of specific weapons systems. Though disarmament continued as a high priority item on the agendas of the UN General Assembly and most peace movements, the pragmatic and objective analysis required to grapple with the inescapable problems of such a comprehensive change was largely eclipsed.

During the past few years there has been a minor revival in systematic thinking about disarmament. Returning to the twin precedents of the McCloy-Zorin Agreements and the Clark-Sohn Plan, political theorist Marcus Raskin has produced a new "Program Treaty for Security and General Disarmament," structured along similar lines. Unlike the Clark-Sohn Plan, which permits the UN Peace Force to possess and if necessary use nuclear weapons, the Raskin Plan specifically excludes from its arsenal all weapons of mass destruction and terror weapons. "The UN will not have a monopoly on violence and will not be able to use force in and of itself to stop the aggression of other nations."[13]

Conclusion: The Near-Miss at Reykjavik

Distant and anachronistic as they have come to seem since 1966, Clark-Sohn and other proposals for disarmament and world government may still have much to tell us about how peace must ultimately be organized. Indeed, in the cyclical nature of politics, these ideas may yet gain broader currency and practicality at some point in the future, though it is hard to say when. In the view of many observers, the superpower summit at Reykjavik in 1986 may have marked a watershed in arms control negotiations. Contrary to all plans and expectations, the two leaders stumbled briefly out of the familiar confinement of incremental arms control and into a stunningly different set of possibilities. Instead of setting limits on numbers of weapons always higher than present stockpiles, they spoke of halving all nuclear weapons within five years, eliminating them in ten.

Many observers at the time saw Reykjavik as a "near-miss" for an historic agreement, thwarted solely by disagreement over a minor detail about testing strategic defenses. Many analysts since have sought to dismiss it as a freak occurrence, an accident, and a strategic blunder. In its wake, West European leaders sought to "repair the damage" by rejecting President Reagan's proposal to eliminate nuclear weapons altogether. They agreed instead to a proposal to eliminate intermediate-range missiles in Europe, not nearly so daring a proposition.

Almost in spite of themselves, the superpower leaders at Reykjavik may have unwittingly altered the terms of the debate in ways that cannot be rescinded. For the first time, strategic analysts are being forced to consider how to cope with the possibility of a world with far fewer nuclear weapons—indeed, perhaps none. One of their early findings is that nuclear arsenals cannot safely be eliminated while large, offensive conventional arsenals of unequal size and strength remain in place, since in the absence of nuclear weapons, "the great equalizer," differences of military power may well become more consequential. For this reason, politicians and analysts alike may need to begin to think about the kinds of comprehensive disarmament so carefully considered by Clark, Sohn, and others a quarter century ago.

Futurologist Herman Kahn, who gained fame for his projections of unthinkable scenarios for nuclear war at around the time the last of these plans were being proposed, sketched a particularly witty scenario to describe the adoption of Clark and Sohn's eminently reasonable plan for peace. Kahn imagined a U.S. president dispatching a copy of *World*

Peace Through World Law to the Soviet premier, inscribed with the following message:

"There's no point in reading this book; you will not like it any more than I did. I merely suggest you sign it right after my signature. This is the only plan which has been thoroughly thought out; let us, therefore, adopt it."[14]

Notes

1. The Committee to Frame a World Constitution, *Preliminary Draft for a World Constitution* (Chicago: University of Chicago Press, 1948).
2. Quoted in Gerald Dunne, *Grenville Clark: Public Citizen* (New York: Farrar, Strauss, and Giroux, 1986), pp. 185–186.
3. Ibid., pp. 49–50.
4. Ibid., p. 153.
5. Ibid., p. 157.
6. Ibid., p. 159.
7. Ibid., p. 158.
8. Ibid., pp. 160–161.
9. Grenville Clark and Louis Sohn, *World Peace Through World Law: Two Alternative Plans,* (3d ed. enlarged) (Cambridge, MA: Harvard University Press, 1966), pp. xxv, xxix.
10. Address by U.S. Secretary of State Christian Herter to the National Press Club, February 18, 1960, reprinted in U.S. Department of State, *Documents on Disarmament,* 1960, p. 44, at 50.
11. "Joint Statement of Agreed Principles for Disarmament Negotiations of the Soviet Union and the United States," September 20, 1961, p. 1.
12. From an unpublished interview in 1981 with John McCloy by Mark Gerzon, author and president of Mediators' Productions, Inc.
13. Marcus Raskin, "Program Treaty for Security and General Disarmament" (Washington, DC: Institute for Policy Studies, 1984), p. 21. Among the plan's unique features is a form of Hippocratic oath for scientific workers "which abjures them from doing research, development, and experimental work on weapons of mass destruction." In addition, the plan calls on each nation to "internalize in its respective laws a *no-surrender* clause which makes it a domestic crime to surrender against an aggressor nation."
14. Dunne, *Grenville Clark,* p. 193.

CHAPTER FIVE

Minimum Deterrence: How Little Is Enough?

As the sole nation with a nuclear capability in the initial years after World War II, the United States pursued a policy of deterrence, by which it sought to prevent the advance of Soviet ground forces on Western Europe by threatening to retaliate with its entire atomic arsenal. At that time, the U.S. nuclear stockpile was extremely small by present standards, reaching a mere 100 small bombs by 1949. With the Soviet entry into the nuclear arms race in September 1949, however, the United States concentrated on enlarging its nuclear forces to deter the Soviets from ever using a nuclear weapon. By 1954, the United States had shifted to a policy of "massive retaliation," defined by Secretary of State John Foster Dulles as the intent to retaliate "instantly" and "massively" against the centers of Soviet military and economic power "by means and at places of our choosing," in response to any future Soviet aggression anywhere in the world.[1] As both nations' nuclear stockpiles grew larger and larger and first the United States and then the Soviet Union deployed arsenals capable of totally decimating its adversary, each nation began to develop nuclear weapons with a counterforce capability—that is, nuclear weapons designed to wipe out enemy strategic forces. In this way, it might be possible in a crisis to launch a preemptive strike on one's enemy without having to fear a significant retaliatory strike. The United States and the Soviet Union continue to develop their nuclear arsenals with this goal in mind, each attempting to make its arsenal more sophisticated and, at the same time, more credible.

An alternative to this sort of extended deterrence is a policy known as minimum deterrence. Minimum deterrence, also known as pure, finite or fundamental deterrence, refers to a nuclear strategy in which a nation (or nations) maintains the minimum number of nuclear weapons necessary to inflict unacceptable damage on its adversary even after it has suffered a nuclear attack. It is a strategy that a nuclear nation could pursue unilaterally or in conjunction with other nuclear nations. To date, nuclear nations that have unilaterally pursued policies approaching minimum deterrence have done so largely because the cost of a more extensive deterrent has been prohibitive. In France, for example, an effective nuclear deterrent is a primary goal of the government, but no attempt is made to keep up with superpower deployments. The French nuclear force is capable of destroying enough major cities in the USSR to make a Soviet invasion or attack unprofitable. In theory there is no reason why this strategy could not be adopted successfully by the superpowers themselves or by either independently. Neither of the superpowers, however, appears willing to pursue a minimum deterrent unilaterally. This discussion, therefore, focuses on minimum deterrence brought about by multilateral negotiations between all the nuclear nations.

The Origins of Minimum Deterrence

The U.S. Navy made the first official minimum nuclear deterrent proposal when it took the position in 1958 and 1959 during the Eisenhower administration that the United States required only 232 Polaris missiles to decimate the Soviet Union. Such a force, according to navy officials, provided "generous adequacy for deterrence alone," as opposed to "the false goal of adequacy for 'winning.'"[2] This calculation was supported in the early 1960s by President Kennedy's science adviser, Jerome Wiesner, who stated that a few hundred survivable nuclear weapons would suffice to deter any potential adversary from attacking the United States. Nevertheless, the U.S. Navy and the Wiesner recommendations were followed by increases in the superpowers' nuclear stockpiles far in excess of these suggested levels.

In the early stages of the accelerated strategic competition of the 1960s, Secretary of Defense Robert McNamara studied the issue of deterrence to establish how much nuclear firepower would be needed to create an ongoing, credible deterrent. At the time there was already concern that escalating competition in nuclear weapons could be both militarily destabilizing and economically debilitating. In view of this concern, McNamara stated in 1965 that a credible deterrent could be maintained regardless of the number of strategic weapons an adversary deployed as long as nuclear forces capable of inflicting "assured destruction" were deployed. McNamara held that an "assured destruction" level required a nuclear force capable of destroying two-thirds of Soviet industry and one-third of the Soviet population.[3] This deterrent force could be achieved, he asserted, with a nuclear force equipped with 400–500 strategic launchers. Such a force could cause enough damage to deter any attack from the Soviet Union (or any other nation), regardless of how much more nuclear weaponry that nation possessed. In other words, even if the Soviets had two, three, four, or more times as many warheads, the United States would still have a sufficient deterrent force.

In theory, Robert McNamara's "assured destruction" established a level beyond which nuclear deployments would be unnecessary. Since 400–500 strategic launchers were seen as a force capable of inflicting unacceptable damage on any adversary, anything beyond this level would be overkill. Unfortunately, arms competition in the nuclear arena soon pushed both superpowers' arsenals well above the level of weapons sufficient to inflict "assured destruction." The United States and the Soviet Union were not content with arsenals capable of devastating one another; instead, each sought to develop more sophisticated nuclear weapons with greater accuracy, more warheads, and greater penetration power—in sum, a war-fighting capability that could destroy the other side's deterrent in a first strike and thus avoid a devastating counterattack.

Although the superpowers continue to modernize their strategic forces with little regard for McNamara's original recommendation concerning "assured destruction" levels, several highly qualified individuals have pursued the concept of minimum deterrence in greater detail.

Recommendations from the Academic and Scientific Community

Perhaps the most significant and comprehensive proposal for a minimum deterrent has been formulated by Harold Feiveson, Richard Ullman, and Frank von Hippel, three Princeton professors who published their ideas jointly in the August 1985 issue of the *Bulletin of the Atomic Scientists.*[4] Advocating that the arsenals of the superpowers be reduced to about one-tenth their current levels, they recommend the complete removal of tactical nuclear warheads, the elimination of most intermediate range nuclear weapons, and an 80 percent reduction in strategic warheads, leaving each side with a total of 2,000 warheads. The 2,000 warheads would be distributed so that 500 could be delivered by land-based ballistic missiles, 500 by submarine-launched ballistic missiles, and 1,000 by long-range bombers.

Each warhead in this scenario is assumed to have a yield of 100 kilotons. Although this yield is relatively low compared to many of the warheads currently in the superpowers' stockpiles, it is equivalent to eight bombs of the size dropped on Hiroshima. As the Princeton Project on Finite Deterrence has pointed out, "such a warhead could destroy, by blast and fire, an area of about 50 square kilometers (20 square miles), containing, in a typical large urban area, about 100,000 people.

Several such warheads in the illustrative arsenal could be targeted against *every* U.S. and Soviet city with a population over 50,000."[5]

Richard Garwin, former director of the IBM Watson Laboratory and a U.S. government consultant on matters of military technology, has proposed a minimum deterrent that would reduce nuclear arsenal levels well below that of the Princeton Project on Finite Deterrence. Garwin advocates reducing the superpowers' nuclear stockpiles to 1,000 each. These 1,000 warheads would then be subdivided into 400 small, fast-burn, mobile, single-warhead intercontinental ballistic missiles (Midgetmen), 400 submarine-launched ballistic missiles (50 little submarines with 8 warheads apiece), and 200 air-launched cruise missiles on 100 long-range bombers.[6] Garwin argues that this scenario would be far more stabilizing than the present U.S. nuclear force structure, even if the Soviet Union were to cheat and conceal or rebuild weapons after agreeing to a minimum deterrent like Garwin's. Although the Feiveson–Ullman–von Hippel proposal and the Garwin recommendations for a minimum deterrent are quite different, neither claims to be the only satisfactory way to structure a minimum deterrent.

Recommendations from Policymakers

When George Kennan first recommended 50 percent reductions in superpower nuclear stockpiles in the early 1980s, his comments had no visible effect on the arms control negotiators of the Reagan administration. But in 1986 when Secretary of State George Shultz and President Reagan began to make public statements about 50 percent reductions of nuclear weapons, the notion of minimum deterrence began to receive unprecedented, official attention. On November 17, Secretary of State Shultz endorsed the idea of a minimum deterrent in the context of dramatic reductions of strategic forces, stating, "Even after the elimination of all ballistic missiles, we will need insurance policies to hedge against cheating or other contingencies. We don't know now what form this will take. An agreed-upon retention of a small nuclear ballistic missile force could be part of that insurance."[7]

Of the leading U.S. officials to have considered minimum deterrence, Robert McNamara, secretary of defense during the Kennedy and Johnson administrations, has treated the idea most thoroughly. In *Blundering into Disaster,* he held that our "ultimate goals should be a state of mutual deterrence at the lowest force levels consistent with stability."[8] McNamara stated that the complete elimination of nuclear weapons is desirable but not feasible. He argued that for the foreseeable future, the superpowers' ability to build a small nuclear force without being detected makes the complete elimination of nuclear weapons impossible. Nevertheless, he stressed that present verification capabilities are sufficient to detect any significant cheating that might take place under a minimum deterrent and that policing a minimum level of mutual deterrence is therefore possible. The number of warheads required to remove the threat of cheating would be determined by the number of weapons that could be built by the Soviet Union without detection. According to McNamara, a comprehensive study of this issue would probably find that a force of a few hundred warheads would be sufficient.

> Two considerations would determine the ultimate size and composition of the deterrent force: that it deter attack with confidence, and that any undetected or sudden violation of arms control treaties would not imperil this deterrence. With tactical nuclear forces to be eliminated entirely, and the strategic forces having five hundred or fewer warheads, the present [world] inventory of fifty thousand weapons could be cut to no more than one thousand.[9]

McNamara stated that the process of moving toward a minimum deterrent can be started immediately at Geneva, but he also recognized that the limited-force goals he advocated are far reaching and will require other nations to participate in the negotiation process. Other nuclear powers that have targeted the Soviet Union, specifically France, Great Britain and China, must be involved in any nuclear reduction agreement that leads to minimum deterrent policies for the superpowers. As Professor Ullman wrote, "Soviet planners would likely see the imbalance of these forces, added to American weapons, as politically unacceptable."[10] Pentagon officials are likely to feel equally uneasy about smaller nuclear powers retaining their full arsenal if the superpowers agree to reduce theirs.

Attaining Maximum Stability

If the nuclear nations negotiate, sign, and implement a minimum deterrent treaty, it can be assumed that all parties will want to be sure it is as stable as possible. There are a number of ways to strengthen stability.

Changing the Structure of Nuclear Forces

Assume that each superpower retains only 500 warheads, a force sufficient to target every city in the Soviet Union with a population over 100,000 twice and still have nuclear weapons remaining to target smaller population centers or more remote industrial centers—clearly a formidable deterrent. Assume also that each of the other nuclear powers retains proportionately fewer numbers. Under these conditions, the most stable minimum deterrent system would be one that includes submarine-launched ballistic missiles with single warheads. Missiles based on submarines are relatively invulnerable both because of their mobility and the lack of adequate technology to detect them once submerged. Although antisubmarine warfare technologies are rapidly being developed in both the Soviet Union and the United States, submarine-launched nuclear missiles assure a retaliatory capability, at least for the moment.

Long-range bombers armed with cruise missiles are also often considered particularly appropriate for a minimum deterrent system because a large portion of a bomber fleet can remain on alert, ready to become airborne. Bombers also offer the advantage of being able to come extremely close to their targets and yet still be recalled. Both of these characteristics would make long-range bombers a stable component in the arsenal of a minimum deterrent system.

On the other hand, missiles with multiple warheads and a high degree of accuracy and penetration power are counterproductive for a minimum deterrent system because they incite first use of nuclear weapons in a crisis situation. Missiles with multiple warheads can hit as many as ten to fourteen targets if used in a first strike. With these sorts of weapons, no nuclear power can afford to wait and see what its adversary will do if it appears that a nuclear exchange is imminent. From a military point of view the only sensible action is to attack first, before a significant portion of one's own nuclear forces is destroyed. This situation puts an unfortunate hair trigger on the use of nuclear weapons, with each side preparing to draw faster than the other.

The longer a missile is in flight or the farther it is positioned from its target, the greater the amount of reaction time it allows during an incoming missile alert. Greater reaction time decreases the need for a destabilizing launch-on-warning policy. For this reason, in most minimum deterrent scenarios long-range, land-based missiles are retained in preference to short- and intermediate-range, land-based missiles, and tactical nuclear weapons are usually eliminated altogether.

Tactical nuclear weapons are the least desirable type of nuclear weapon for a minimum deterrent force. These weapons are now designed to be interchangeable with conventional weapons in order to enhance the credibility of nuclear weapons use in response to conventional aggression. In the process, unfortunately, they also make the use of nuclear weapons more likely. Tactical nuclear weapons in effect blur the line between conventional and nuclear forces, making it easier for a conventional conflict to escalate into a nuclear war. If a minimum deterrent agreement were adopted among the nuclear nations, tactical nuclear weapons would almost certainly be completely eliminated, as they would otherwise be destabilizing to the nuclear forces that remained.

Comprehensive Test Ban

In 1963 the leaders of the United States and the Soviet Union signed the Limited Test Ban Treaty, which prohibited all testing of nuclear weapons above ground, under water and in outer space. President Kennedy hoped that a follow-up treaty could be signed with Premier Khrushchev or one of his successors that would expand the Limited Test Ban Treaty to a Comprehensive Test Ban Treaty, effectively eliminating all testing of nuclear weapons both above and below ground. Although a comprehensive test ban has never been agreed upon, it has long been recognized that such a treaty would have a dramatic effect on nuclear weapons developments and thus the nuclear arms race.

Because testing is the most verifiable stage between the planning and stockpiling of new nuclear weapons, a comprehensive test ban would significantly strengthen a minimum deterrent system. If nuclear weapons are to be limited, preventing tests is a good way to add credibility to the claim that no one is secretly deploying new weapons.

Other Bans

Other prohibitions can strengthen a minimum deterrent system by preventing competition and limiting the threat caused by remaining nuclear weapons. For example, Feiveson, Ullman, and von Hippel support a superpower ban on new nuclear delivery systems as well as agreements restricting deployment of new antisubmarine, antiballistic missile, and antiaircraft technologies to prevent one side from destabilizing the nuclear balance.[11] Without a delivery system development ban there would be a temptation for the superpowers to continue competing by developing ever more sophisticated means of delivering the limited number of weapons they retained. Such a ban, as well as prohibitions on new antisubmarine, antiballistic missile, and antiaircraft technologies, would help assure that no nation would attain a threatening counterforce capability. Unfortunately, in contrast to a comprehensive test ban, many of these complementary prohibitions would be difficult to verify.

Transition Problems

The transition to worldwide minimum deterrence would require agreement among all nuclear nations, not just the superpowers. The reduction of nuclear arsenals during the transition process would most likely involve stages of verifiable, across-the-board percentage cuts. The superpowers alone might initiate the first step in these reductions, but soon after this initial cut (or even before), the superpowers would probably insist that the smaller nuclear nations enter into the reduction process.

Negotiations would be necessary to determine the exact process by which arsenals would eventually be reduced, but agreement on maintaining a reasonable ratio between the nuclear weapons of the superpowers and those of the smaller nuclear nations during the reduction process may not come easily.

An equally difficult transition problem would be how to reach agreement on which nations qualify as nuclear powers. Several countries, most notably Israel and South Africa, are generally believed to be undeclared nuclear nations. It seems clear that either these countries must become part of the overall agreement or open themselves to inspection procedures that would assure the declared nuclear powers that the nations in question do not have nuclear capabilities. The same treatment would apply to any other nation pursuing a nuclear weapons capability.

Strengthening Nonnuclear Forces: A Conventional Buildup

Because the United States presently depends on its nuclear forces to deter both conventional and nuclear aggression, many proponents of minimum deterrence advocate that the United States strengthen its conventional forces in the process of moving toward a minimum deterrent. This position has been most strongly stated by Robert McNamara in *Blundering into Disaster*. McNamara held that Warsaw Pact conventional forces are much larger than NATO conventional forces and that this fact must be taken into consideration if the superpowers agree to shift to minimum deterrence. Favoring a minimum deterrent, McNamara advocated a conventional buildup of NATO forces to assure all NATO countries of their ability to deter conventional aggression by any of the Warsaw Pact nations in the absence of the present nuclear deterrent.

This policy would be extremely costly. Conventional arms are much more expensive than nuclear arms, consuming roughly 80 percent of the U.S. military procurement budget. Thus McNamara advocated a plan for reducing the threat of nuclear weapons and stabilizing the strategic balance in a way that would actually provoke greater arms competition and higher military budgets. An alternative to a minimum deterrent system with enormous increases in conventional weapons is to enter into an agreement to reduce conventional weapons and nuclear weapons simultaneously so that the present approximate parity between the superpowers is maintained and the reduction in nuclear forces does not leave one power with an enormous conventional advantage. Such an approach to defense would go beyond what is normally considered within the scope of minimum deterrence, but many of the problems with minimum deterrence that might be addressed by increasing conventional military expenditures could be more easily addressed through combined conventional and nuclear reductions.

Future Prospects

A minimum deterrent system requires dramatic shifts in national security strategy. The superpowers would have to accept the notion of permanent military parity, give up the drive for superiority, and abandon the pursuit of warfighting or preemptive strike capabilities. Nevertheless, if nuclear arsenals were reduced to a few hundred warheads, the world would witness the elimination of tens of thousands of nuclear weapons. Implementation of a minimum deterrent system would result in a major reduction in mankind's ability to destroy itself. Although minimum deterrence would not eliminate the war-making capabilities of any nation, it could reduce threat and increase stability. Because a minimum deterrent does not directly address conventional weapons, for all but a very few nations no demilitarization is involved in its implementation.

Although it is a policy that could be implemented by only the nuclear nations, minimum deterrence affects the entire world. If adopted, worldwide minimum deterrence would in effect place a global limit on nuclear weapons. In addition, a global minimum deterrent system would require the continuing cooperation of all the nuclear powers and so would undoubtedly greatly inhibit nuclear proliferation. The implementation of a minimum deterrent system would represent such an enormous departure from U.S.-Soviet relations to date that it would foster a new climate in which agreement on other issues would be far more likely.

Notes

1. Quoted in Richard Smoke, *National Security: The Nuclear Dilemma* (Menlo Park, CA: Addison Wesley, 1984), p. 72.
2. Robert S. McNamara, *Blundering into Disaster* (New York: Pantheon, 1986), p. 123.
3. The Harvard Nuclear Study Group, *Living with Nuclear Weapons* (New York: Bantam Books, 1983), p. 156.
4. Harold Feiveson, Richard Ullman, and Frank von Hippel, "Reducing the U.S. and Soviet Nuclear Arsenals," *Bulletin of the Atomic Scientists*, vol. 41 (August 1985), p. 144.
5. Ibid., p. 145.
6. Richard Garwin, "MAD Is SANE Interview with Dr. Richard Garwin," *Cornell Review*, September 1986, p. 10.
7. David K. Shipler, "More U.S. Changes on Arms Proposed," *New York Times*, November 18, 1986.

8. McNamara, *Blundering into Disaster*, p. 122.

9. Ibid., p. 123.

10. Richard H. Ullman, "Nuclear Arms: How Big a Cut," *New York Times Magazine*, November 16, 1986, p. 78.

11. Feiveson, Ullman, and von Hippel, *"Reducing U.S. and Soviet Arsenals,"* p. 148.

CHAPTER SIX

Qualitative Disarmament: Eliminating the War-making Capability of Nations

In the spring of 1932, some sixty nations gathered in Geneva under the auspices of the League of Nations to begin the first global disarmament conference. Being the first of its kind, it could still sustain the belief among the delegates and their respective governments that their deliberations might actually produce a transformed world. In this collective effort to assure that the planet would never again be subjected to the trauma of a world war, a multitude of proposals was considered. Persuaded that the Great War had been precipitated by a runaway arms race, most nations offered proposals that in one fashion or another sought to restrict the war-making capacity of nations. The Soviets put forth a plan for "general and complete disarmament," while the French presented a proposal for an international security force under the League's control. But the conference's deliberations ultimately focused on several proposals based on the principle of "qualitative disarmament," first promulgated by the British and later elaborated by the U.S. delegation.

The Conversion of a Military Strategist

The concept of qualitative disarmament was introduced to the conference by Lord Robert Cecil, an eminent British statesman who had been instrumental in making the League of Nations a reality and in placing disarmament at the top of its agenda. Cecil had compiled the documents for the Geneva Disarmament Conference, and without his expertise and preparations the meeting would probably not have occurred. Presenting the concept to the assembled delegates, Cecil urged them "to decrease the offensive power of armaments, while leaving the defensive power untouched . . . [for] anything which diminishes the power of aggression proportionately to the power of defense necessarily increases the safety of the world."[1]

The principle of qualitative disarmament did not originate with Cecil but with his friend and military adviser, Captain (later Sir) Basil Liddell Hart. Widely regarded as the greatest military strategist of the twentieth century, Liddell Hart had made his reputation in the early years after World War I with a brilliant strategy for utilizing revolutionary trends in warfare toward mechanization and mobility in the service of what he termed "the indirect approach"—concentrating strength against weakness, striking where the enemy is weak, and choosing impregnable positions of defense that tempt the enemy to attack and fail. So shrewd were his tactics that General Heinz Guderian, German strategist of the Nazi blitzkrieg, declared himself Liddell Hart's "disciple in tank affairs," while Field Marshal Erwin Rommel, "The Desert Fox," whose legions vanquished the British in North Africa in the early years of World War II, concluded that "the British would have been able to prevent the greatest part of their defeats if they had paid attention to the modern theories expounded by Liddell Hart before the war."[2]

So it is all the more remarkable that Liddell Hart also authored the theory on which qualitative disarmament is based. "It was the hardest test that had ever confronted me," he wrote in his memoirs in 1931 after being invited by the Committee of Imperial Defence to help formulate an official policy for Great Britain to take to the disarmament conference the following spring.

> For I soon realised that the obvious solution would entail annulling not only the development of tanks as a military tool but the whole concept of reviving the power of the offensive and the art of war, by "lightning" strokes with highly mobile mechanised forces—thus cancelling out all I had done during the past ten years to develop and preach this new military concept. If I propounded the "disarmament" antidote to it, and helped to obtain its adoption at the coming Conference, it would mean strangling my own "baby."[3]

Nevertheless, he did so, transforming himself from a war to a peace strategist through an intellectual and spiritual migration that led him, in his later years, to give serious consideration to the potential of a thoroughly nonviolent defense. In January 1932, Liddell Hart produced a long memorandum entitled "The Problem of Land Disarmament: A Solution—Simple and Complete," outlining his theory. Christopher Kruegler described the theory in the following way:

> As "fractions lead all too easily to friction," with endless quibbling over numbers of weapons, he advocated a qualitative rather than quantitative

> approach to disarmament. The problem, as he saw it, was to make armies non-aggressive by rendering them incapable of attack but eminently capable of defense. . . . Liddell Hart was so convinced that he had hit on the solution to the problem that he wrote to Philip Noel-Baker that he was prepared to "stake his reputation" on the prediction that no offensive would ever prevail if these conditions were met. "By these restrictions you could reduce armies to the state of men in armour without swords. The idealist may regret to see men going about in armour, but the realist can perceive that the process is innocuous, if still expensive. And gradually the humour of it may become apparent, thus leading to it being discarded."[4]

World War I had demonstrated to many strategists that certain weapons were advantageous to the defense while others benefited the offense. During the first four years of the war, rifles, machine guns, and light artillery so strengthened the defense that neither side along a 400-mile front had been able to take more than a few hundred yards, and then only at immense human cost. In the latter phase of the war, however, new technologies were introduced, involving what Liddell Hart called "defense-breaking weapons"—bombs dropped from aircraft, heavy artillery, tanks, submarines, large battleships, aircraft carriers, and poison gas. It was these new offensive innovations above all that Liddell Hart and Cecil sought to eliminate.

The principle of reducing offensive weapons to increase the relative effectiveness of the defense was ultimately adopted by the British government and initially supported by the British foreign secretary, John Simon, who is credited with having coined the term, "qualitative disarmament," to describe the process. Simon was responsible for engineering passage of a unanimous motion committing the conference to that principle. But ironically, it was also Simon who, by some accounts, ultimately sabotaged his own earlier efforts and arranged a slow death for the idea.

The Hoover Plan

Just as the British initiative began to lose momentum, President Herbert Hoover in June 1932 presented to the conference a U.S. plan for comprehensive qualitative disarmament. Citing the Kellogg-Briand Pact of 1928 "which can only mean that the nations of the world have agreed that they will use their arms solely for defense," President Hoover proposed that "this reduction should be carried out not only by broad general cuts in armaments, but by increasing the comparative power of the defense through decreases in the power of attack." He then proposed "the abolition of all tanks, all chemical warfare, and all large mobile guns; the abolition of all bombing planes, the total prohibition of all bombardment from the air; and reduction by one third of battleships and submarines, and by one quarter of aircraft carriers, cruisers and destroyers."[5]

Moreover, the plan left open the possibility of additional reductions of naval armaments in later years. In these and other respects, the U.S. plan closely adhered to the principle of qualitative disarmament. Had the conference adopted it, the United States alone would have been required to eliminate 300,000 tons of naval vessels, over 1,000 large mobile guns, 900 tanks, and 300 bombing aircraft.

The Hoover Plan was widely acclaimed at the conference, garnering nearly unanimous endorsement, and for a time it looked as if it might carry the day. Even nations that might have been expected to voice disapproval appeared supportive. The French and Soviet delegates spoke in favor, as did the delegate from Mussolini's Italy, much to everyone's surprise and Il Duce's fury. Perhaps most astonishing was Germany's warm endorsement of the plan. Perceived by many nations as the most likely cause of a new arms race, the German government had openly expressed its discontentment with the restrictions placed on its military forces by the Treaty of Versailles.

As a condition of the peace settlement, Germany had been required by the Allies to accept a strict prohibition on weapons deemed offensive by the victorious powers, in order to assure them that the Germans would never again be physically capable of launching a successful attack against the Allies. In effect, then, the Germans had been forced to engage in unilateral qualitative disarmament. Chafing at being held to these restrictions while the Allies freely rearmed, the German government viewed the Hoover Plan as an opportunity to place similar restraints on all other nations and thus to regain equality among them.

According to Philip Noel-Baker, a Nobel Peace Prize laureate who was deeply involved with the Geneva conference and who has written extensively on the subject, it was John Simon, the British foreign secretary, who ultimately killed the Hoover Plan. Under pressure from conservatives in Britain, Simon issued a counterproposal that involved some arms reductions but left enough offensive weapons in place to effectively void the principle of qualitative disarmament that he himself had been instrumental in introducing to the conference. Although the delegates from the United States made clear that they preferred the Hoover Plan, they nonetheless were supportive of Simon's alternative. Still, Franklin Roosevelt, who succeeded Hoover in early 1933, returned to the original principle in his opening statement to the conference in May 1933, demonstrating both his comprehension of and his commitment to the concept. "If all nations will agree wholly to eliminate from possession and use weapons which make possible a successful attack, defenses will automatically become impregnable, and the frontiers and independence of every nation will become secure."[6]

A few weeks after making this statement, President Roosevelt offered to apply to U.S. armed forces the offense-eliminating provisions in Part V of the Treaty of Versailles enforced on the Germans, if other governments would agree to the same restrictions. Despite this second bold attempt by a U.S. president to generate a major agreement, no further progress was made. During eighteen months of debate, Germany had already begun to rearm, and although the British later made several concessions, they were not sufficient to regain lost momentum. Germany became increasingly set on rebuilding its own arsenal regardless of what agreements other nations might reach. With Hitler's accession to power, the outlook for the conference grew still more bleak. Germany left the conference on October 14, 1933, and shortly after announced that it was renouncing its membership in the League. The chance to achieve qualitative disarmament in an era when arsenals were still relatively limited in size and complexity had been irretrievably lost.

Yet it is important to note that the principle itself was not unworkable, even though certain persons of influence worked successfully for its defeat. Writing nearly thirty years after the event, Liddell Hart declared that had the Hoover Plan been accepted, "as it nearly was," the tanks and bombers that fueled the Nazi blitzkrieg would likely never have been produced, and if produced in secret would surely have been detected by League inspectors. And without the blitzkrieg, he asserted, World War II itself could have been prevented.[7]

The Recent Revival of Interest: Randall Forsberg, "Confining the Military to Defense"

Qualitative disarmament was then forgotten for half a century while other options were pursued. During this time, the notion of defending one's country by maintaining offensive military forces superior to one's potential enemies predominated among both political leaders and military strategists. But with the advent of nuclear parity between the superpowers in the 1960s, the inescapably suicidal outcome of this offensive strategy became evident to many. In recent years, this situation has begun to force a fundamental shift in defense theory from unilateral offense to common defense.

In the 1980s alternative defense strategists converged on the notion of turning toward defensively oriented armed forces as a means of reducing the perception of threat that they believe fuels the arms race. A small but significant set of proposals has gained currency in recent years delineating the concept of a multilateral, phased process of dismantling the war-making capability of nations, a negotiated treaty or treaties by which all nations agree simultaneously to eliminate all weapons with an offensive capability and to leave in place only those that are mutually accepted as being strictly defensive.

The notion of designing an entire global disarmament process around shedding the offense and leaving in place only the defense was first reintroduced into the debate by Randall Forsberg. Author of a nuclear freeze proposal that gained widespread public support in the United States during the early 1980s, Forsberg spent four years at the Stockholm International Peace Research Institute (SIPRI). She then returned to the United States to propose, first in a speech in 1981 and later in an essay, a comprehensive plan for disarmament entitled, "Confining the Military to Defense as a Route to Disarmament," published in 1984. Reminiscent of the theory of qualitative disarmament first proposed by Liddell Hart and Cecil at the 1932 Geneva Disarmament Conference, her proposal outlines a step-by-step plan for the elimination of all offensive weapons in a series of seven stages.

> The main functions of armed forces today are deterrence, defense, aggression, intervention, armed repression, and armed revolution. Of these, the function most compatible with achieving and maintaining a stable peace is *defense*. If all countries maintained military forces solely for the purpose of defending their national territory, only conventional, short-range forces that provide air, coastal, and border defense would be needed. Aggression, intervention, and armed repression would then cease. Without armed repression, there would be no need for armed revolution. And without aggression, intervention, repression, and revolution, war would never be initiated.[8]
>
> By gradually confining the role of conventional military forces to defense, more and more narrowly defined, we can move safely towards a world in which conventional forces are limited to short-range, defensive armaments, in which international institutions provide an effective nonviolent means of resolving conflict, and in which nuclear weapons can be abolished.[9]
>
> *Step 1:* Stop the production of U.S. and Soviet nuclear weapons and shut down their nuclear-weapon production facilities. . . .
>
> *Step 2:* End large-scale military intervention—the maintenance of military bases and the use of troops, air forces, or naval forces—by the industrialized countries of the northern hemisphere in the developing countries of the southern hemisphere. . . .
>
> *Step 3:* Cut by 50 percent the nuclear and conventional forces of the NATO and Warsaw Pact nations, plus those of China and Japan.
>
> *Step 4:* Strengthen the economic development of Third World nations, promote civil liberties in all countries, and improve international institutions for negotiation and peacekeeping.

> *Step 5:* Abolish all military alliances and foreign military bases and restructure conventional military forces to limit them to short-range border defense, air defense, and coastal defense.
>
> *Step 6:* Abolish nuclear weapons.
>
> *Step 7:* Eliminate national armed forces altogether and replace them with international peacekeeping forces.[10]
>
> Each of the steps is designed to create a plateau of stability which can be maintained for an extended period of time. And each is aimed at eliminating the least defensive, most aggressive, escalatory, and provocative aspects of the military forces and policies that remain in existence at each stage of the process. In addition, each step is designed to encourage simultaneous change in the institutions of military policy and armed forces and in the attitudes that underlie the acceptable uses of force.[11]

In more modest formulations, this approach to disarmament has received extensive support within the international scientific community. The Hamburg Proposals, issued in November 1986 by the International Scientists' Peace Congress, delineate a set of ten steps toward disarmament "based on the recognition that the security of each side is linked to the security of its adversary."[12] Included are a comprehensive nuclear test ban, a ban on the production of fissile materials, deep cuts in nuclear arsenals, prohibition of all space weapons, deep reductions and restructuring of conventional forces along nonaggressive lines, and disengagement of forces along sensitive frontiers in central Europe.

Similar proposals have been advanced by Soviet leaders and policymakers as part of the "new thinking" campaign of General Secretary Mikhail Gorbachev.[13] In an article published in *Pravda* on September 16, 1987, Gorbachev outlined what he called "a comprehensive system of international security," extending the sphere of common security well beyond military and political arrangements to include economic, ecological, and humanitarian considerations. In its military dimension, this comprehensive security system would adopt the principle of "reasonable sufficiency."

> These notions presuppose such a structure of the armed forces of a state that they would be sufficient to repulse a possible aggression but would not be sufficient for the conduct of offensive actions. The first step to this could be a controlled withdrawal of nuclear and other offensive weapons from the borders with a subsequent creation along borders of strips of rarefied armaments and demilitarized zones between potential adversaries. While in principle we should work for the dissolution of military blocs and the liquidation of bases on foreign territories and the return home of all troops stationed abroad.[14]

Perhaps in response to its growing political and moral appeal, President Reagan professed a commitment to the idea of shifting the preponderance of superpower arsenals and strategies from offense to defense. Seeking to justify his Strategic Defense Initiative, he stated that his ultimate goal in developing ballistic missile defenses was to eliminate the offensive nuclear missiles they are intended to repel. Critics of the program question both the feasibility and wisdom of the undertaking, arguing that while claiming to replace offense with defense, in actuality it simply adds a better defense to a better offense to create a still more lethal strike force. But the fact that the principle is being invoked to justify the largest military project in world history is a powerful testament to its political and moral appeal.

In a still tentative and uncertain fashion, an implicit consensus appears to be growing among political forces across a broad range of interests and beliefs in many nations, a consensus on the process around which to organize disarmament. At the same time, a clear majority of citizens and leaders remains profoundly skeptical of proposals to simply "do away with" all weapons and base their security arrangements entirely on trust of their adversaries. Qualitative disarmament provides a means to address both concerns at once, by moving decisively to dismantle the "war machine" (that is, those components in national arsenals more suited to attack than to protection) while preserving and indeed reinforcing those elements more suited to protection than attack.

Common Security Through Qualitative Disarmament

Closely related to the concept of qualitative disarmament is another, more encompassing principle that has also emerged in recent years among innovative strategists and policymakers in both the West and the East—the idea of common security. Although expressions of the principle vary in their particulars, all of the approaches share a common understanding of the fundamentally revolutionary circumstance in which the existence of weapons of apocalyptic destruction has placed the human community. Recognizing that in the nuclear age war spares neither victims nor aggressors, advocates of these approaches renounce strategies of unilateral advantage seeking to defend one's territory by threatening others and seek instead to assure security for each nation by assuring it equally to all.

This concept goes by many names in many places. Although common security is the term most frequently used in the West, it has also been called alternative security, mutual security, shared, cooperative, organic, and whole earth security. In the East, a slightly different lexicon has been used to describe essentially the same idea—terms like comprehensive, universal, equal, all-embracing, and worldwide. However they are formulated and expressed, these strategies all share the commonsense principle that peace and security can no longer be attained at the expense of one's adversaries but only in concert with them.

The idea of common security first achieved broad circulation in the West in a report entitled *Common Security: A Blueprint for Survival,* issued in 1982 by the Independent Commission on Disarmament and Security Issues (better known as the Palme Commission for its chairman, the late Swedish prime minister, Olof Palme). The commission brought together sixteen eminent statesmen and women, present and former high government officials from the Western alliance, the Eastern bloc, and the Third World. Cyrus Vance, U.S. secretary of state under President Carter and a member of the commission, wrote in the Prologue: "There is one overriding truth in this nuclear age—no nation can achieve true security by itself. . . . To guarantee our own security . . . we must face these realities and work together with other nations to achieve common security. For security in the nuclear age *means* common security. . . . On this issue, there should be no divisions between left and right."[15]

The commission enunciated several principles of common security:

1. All nations possess a legitimate and equal right to security.
2. Military force is not a legitimate instrument for resolving conflicts between nations.
3. Policies seeking unilateral advantage must be renounced. Security can only be attained by common action.
4. The principle of parity must be accepted in rival relationships and attempts to achieve military superiority forsworn. "The basic aim must be to establish security at the lowest possible level of armaments."[16]
5. Arms reductions should be qualitative as well as quantitative, eliminating weapons that are most threatening first. "In making such reductions, particular attention should be paid to those types of weapons which raise the greatest concern on either side, as these carry the greatest danger of leading to war."[17]

This last point is noteworthy. While the Palme Commission report did not specifically enunciate a process for qualitative disarmament, it recognized the elimination of weapons that threaten as an essential component of any effective system of common security and a key element in its implementation.

Since the publication of the Palme report, the concept of common security has rapidly proliferated in both East and West. In the Eastern bloc, the idea has gained momentum during the past few years in the wake of the "new thinking" campaign of Soviet General Secretary Mikhail Gorbachev. As Gorbachev wrote in his 1987 book, *Perestroika: New Thinking for Our Country and the World*: "The nations of the world resemble today a pack of mountaineers tied together by a climbing rope. They can either climb on together to the mountain peak or fall together into an abyss. . . . [This] new political outlook calls for the recognition of one simple axiom: security is indivisible. It is either equal security for all or none at all."[18]

The INF Agreement and Strategic Arms Cuts: First Steps Toward Qualitative Disarmament?

The prospective U.S.-Soviet treaty to eliminate all short- and intermediate-range nuclear missiles from Europe (the so-called INF Agreement) is a small but potentially significant step in the direction of qualitative disarmament. Its significance rests less with the scale of the change than its direction. This agreement represents a historic departure from arms control as it has been proposed and practiced by the superpowers for the past twenty-five years. Instead of "controlling" arms (largely by setting limits above current levels, as in SALT II), this agreement proposes to eliminate altogether certain specific classes of weaponry.

In this case, the weapons are also distinguished by being exceptionally advanced (having been deployed only since 1983) and exceptionally offensive in orientation. The Pershing IIs, SS-18s, SS-19s, SS-20s, and cruise missiles to be dismantled under the treaty are all designed to reach their targets exceedingly quickly, leaving effectively no time for confirmation of attack and consideration of options for response. Pershing missiles are capable of reaching their westernmost targets in Eastern Europe in a mere six minutes. The absence of adequate warning and response time in this class of missiles forces both military establishments inevitably toward launch-on-warning postures. The elimination of these hair-trigger systems from superpower arsenals is an advance on its own merits. But in eliminating two entire categories of advanced offensive nuclear weapons, the agreement establishes the precedent that qualitative distinctions are essential to disarmament and the most threatening weapons in national arsenals should therefore be eliminated first.

In late 1987, U.S. and Soviet negotiators also revived negotiations on a proposal first tabled at Reykjavik, Iceland, during the Reagan-Gorbachev summit of 1986 to reduce both strategic (long-range nuclear) arsenals by 50 percent. Affecting as it likely would all missiles based on U.S. and Soviet soil, as well as on bombers and submarines at sea, such a strategic arms agreement would vastly reduce the offensive capability of both nations and would thus represent a giant step in the direction of qualitative disarmament. Moreover, negotiations to eliminate all chemical weapons over a ten-year period, underway for the past eighteen years in Geneva, were reported in late 1987 to be nearing completion. Given the clearly offensive character of chemical warfare, the abolition of this entire category of weapon systems would advance the planet still further in the direction of qualitative disarmament.

Remaining Military Forces

In its pure form, qualitative disarmament would permit the deployment and stockpiling of only those weapons that are deemed suitable for defensive operations and that are therefore not threatening. Mobility, range, and logistics of supply are three of the most critical factors in determining the offensive or defensive capability of particular weapons or weapon systems. Arms anchored in fixed positions, such as fortresses, fixed shore batteries, and minefields, have no mobility, and as long as they are deployed within one's own borders, can do no harm to an adversary who does not choose to attack. All artillery, of course, would have to be positioned far enough back from each nation's borders so that it could prevent foreign forces from invading but otherwise could not penetrate any other nation's territory.

It is clearly impossible to draw wholly unambiguous distinctions between those weapons that are useful for offensive military operations and those that are not. For example, one nation could attack another with the small arms permitted for maintaining internal order. Or mines permitted along borders could conceivably be dropped by civilian aircraft in the harbors of another nation (as occurred in the March 1984 case of the mining of the Nicaraguan harbor at Corinto by the U.S. Central Intelligence Agency). Even a kitchen knife is potentially a lethal weapon. But the weapons permitted to remain under qualitative disarmament should not be of sufficient number or capability to enable nations to mount major offensive operations. And a strengthened capacity for nonviolent peacekeeping under international control could be especially useful in policing the peace in a disarming and disarmed world.

It is important to realize that a minimum nuclear deterrent within qualitative disarmament would be a very different proposition from a minimum deterrent linked to existing or enlarged conventional forces. Proposals by Robert McNamara and others (see chapter 5) to drastically reduce nuclear arsenals while fortifying conventional military forces (but not necessarily in the defensive mode) differ fundamentally from qualitative disarmament, which links vastly reduced nuclear arsenals with vastly reduced conventional forces, all configured in a distinctly defensive posture. The political atmosphere in a world in which both nuclear and conventional arsenals have been so radically reduced would likely be very different from today and might well provide opportunities that do not now seem feasible. In time, confidence in the system might well grow to the point where the remaining nuclear arsenals would seem superfluous and they, too, could be entirely eliminated. In her proposal, Forsberg views the maintenance of nuclear arsenals as fundamentally incompatible with the principles of qualitative disarmament and minimum deterrence as a purely transitional phase on the way to a wholly nuclear-free security system.

Control of Remaining Forces

Unlike a global peacekeeping force, qualitative disarmament leaves control of those forces permitted to remain entirely in the hands of individual national governments. Each nation retains complete authority over the use and disposal of its forces and armaments during and after the elimination of offensive weapons. In this important respect, qualitative disarmament does not require the transfer of sovereignty from national to global authority that is unavoidable under arrangements like the Clark-Sohn Plan. Given the extreme sensitivity of nations to any explicit abridgement of their sovereignty, the fact that qualitative disarmament leaves control of all remaining forces entirely in the hands of each nation represents a considerable advantage in gaining political acceptance.

While all nations would retain control over their remaining forces, qualitative disarmament would require that all nations relinquish their capability of intervening militarily in the internal affairs of other nations. This restriction would apply equally to any global security system requiring nations to give up their war-fighting capability. The deprivation of this capacity would, however, constitute an unprecedented gain for most smaller nations. This is the price the larger powers must pay in return for the security benefits and vast savings on global armaments expenditures. Whether or not nations give up their war-making capability may well hinge on how the larger powers perceive this trade-off.

Conflict Resolution Mechanisms

Although qualitative disarmament does not specifically include mechanisms for resolving conflict, it would not be implemented in a vacuum. Existing mechanisms for conflict resolution like those of the United Nations system would continue to operate and there is no reason why additional mechanisms could not be added when necessary. The disarming process is in itself an indirect mechanism of conflict resolution. Once nations become involved in the reduction process of qualitative disarmament, they begin to receive its rewards both in reduced levels of threat and reduced levels of expenditure. In this way, every nation would be predisposed to avoid conflicts that might imperil mutual gains, a cooperative incentive that might grow as the reductions progress.

Conclusion: A Minimalist Approach to Global Security

In its diverse formulations through the years, qualitative disarmament offers a minimalist approach to world order. Recognizing that nations are profoundly reluctant to relinquish all independent means of shielding themselves from harm and to yield sovereignty on the most critical issues of security to any body other than themselves, the proponents of qualitative disarmament seek to make only those minimal changes they believe are essential to assure a durable peace—eliminating the warmaking capability of all nations by eliminating all weapons capable of effective offensive operations while strengthening all systems designed solely for protection.

Notes

1. Quoted in Philip Noel-Baker, *The Arms Race* (New York: Oceana Press, 1960), pp. 395–396.

2. Quoted in B. Liddell Hart, *Strategy: The Indirect Approach*, 2d ed. (New York: New American Library, 1974), frontispiece.

3. B. H. Liddell Hart, *Memoirs* (London: Cassell, 1965), pp. 183–185. Quoted in Christopher Kruegler, "Liddell Hart and the Concept of Civilian-Based Defense" (Ph.D. diss., Syracuse University, 1984), p. 68.

4. B. H. Liddell Hart, *Papers* (Liddell Hart Centre for Military Archives, King's College, The Strand, London, U.K.), 1/546, Liddell Hart to Noel-Baker, January 4, 1932. As cited in Kruegler, "Liddell Hart," pp. 68–69.

5. Quoted in Noel-Baker, *The Arms Race*, p. 398.

6. Ibid., p. 400.

7. B. H. Liddell Hart, *Deterrent or Defence?* (New York: Praeger, 1960), pp. 250, 254. For a frankly partisan account of the conference and its results, see Philip Noel-Baker, *The First World Disarmament Conference 1932–33, and Why It Failed* (New York: Pergamon Press, 1979).

8. Randall Forsberg, "The Freeze and Beyond: Confining the Military to Defense as a Route to Disarmament," *World Policy Journal*, vol. 1, no. 2 (Winter 1984), p. 310.

9. Ibid., p. 288.

10. Ibid., pp. 314, 315, 316, 317.

11. Ibid., p. 314.

12. "The Hamburg Proposals for Disarmament," International Scientists' Peace Congress, November 14–16, 1986. *Bull. Atomic Scientists*, vol. 42, No. 1 (Jan.-Feb. 1987), p. 52.

13. See Bernard E. Trainor, "Soviet Arms Doctrine in Flux: An Emphasis on the Defense," *New York Times*, March 7, 1988, p. 1.

14. Mikhail Gorbachev, "The Reality and Guarantees of a Secure World," *Pravda*, September 17, 1987; reprinted in Press Release No. 119, USSR Mission to the United Nations, p. 5.

15. Independent Commission on Disarmament and Security Issues, *Common Security: A Blueprint for Survival* (New York: Simon and Schuster, 1982), p. vii.

16. Ibid.

17. Ibid., p. 10.

18. Mikhail Gorbachev, *Perestroika: New Thinking for our Country and the World* (New York: Harper and Row, 1987), pp. 140, 142.

CHAPTER SEVEN

Nonprovocative Defense: Protection Without Threat

During the 1980s a growing number of alternative defense theorists in Western and Eastern Europe, North America, and elsewhere have begun designing a variety of military and nonmilitary strategies deliberately weak in offensive capability and exceptionally strong in purely defensive strength. Concerned by what they view as the unnecessarily threatening and provocative nature of nuclear deterrence, these strategists seek to reassert the vanishing distinction between defense and offense, protection and threat. They reason that by eliminating, insofar as possible, all the components essential to mounting offensive operations, nations thus remove much of the impetus that fuels the arms race—fears fed by the perception of threat.

Variously termed "nonoffensive defense," "just defense," "defensive defense," and "nonprovocative defense," these strategies first gained currency in Western Europe, where they have spread with remarkable rapidity during the mid-1980s. Meanwhile interest has grown in North America and other parts of the West, and increasingly since the advent of "new thinking" under Mikhail Gorbachev, in the Soviet Union and other Warsaw Pact nations. The British Labour party has endorsed a policy of nonoffensive, wholly nonnuclear defense and has pledged to enact it if returned to power.[1] The West German Social Democratic party has also expressed support for nonprovocative defense concepts and Foreign Minister Hans Dietrich Genscher has proposed a phased restructuring and reduction of NATO and Warsaw Pact forces to reflect a more defensive emphasis.[2] For their part, Soviet strategic analysts have advanced the concept of "reasonable sufficiency," connoting, in the words of Gorbachev, armed forces "sufficient to repulse a possible aggression but . . . not . . . for the conduct of offensive actions."[3]

Nonprovocative Defense and Qualitative Disarmament

Although qualitative disarmament is by no means at odds with theories of nonprovocative defensive, the two concepts differ in three significant respects. First, qualitative disarmament is a universal plan, ultimately involving all nations without exception, as any less-than-universal arrangement would leave nonparticipants with the freedom and capacity to inflict unacceptable damage on those nations abiding by the agreement and would thus erode their willingness to remain committed to it. Nonprovocative defense, by contrast, can be undertaken unilaterally by any individual nation to the extent that it wishes, thus obviating the need for negotiations.

Secondly, qualitative disarmament seeks to secure agreement on the elimination of a much broader range of weapons than nonprovocative defense before any reductions can occur. Nonprovocative defense analysts leave in place a large arsenal with diverse capabilities and strategies for repelling an invader. A few even encourage the proliferation of defensive weapons, reasoning that the world cannot have too much pure protection; others are more circumspect. Qualitative disarmament leaves in place at the end of the process a bare minimum of armaments with sharply restricted range and mobility.

And finally, as generally conceived qualitative disarmament is initiated by the superpowers and requires their support to succeed. Nonprovocative defense can be initiated by any nation that so chooses and can be pursued as far as feels comfortable, and even retracted in part if events require. One could easily conceive of leaders of smaller nations starting the process, since they harbor fewer global ambitions and their strategies are already more nearly defensive in character than those of the great powers. One could also imagine that the superpowers would be the last and most reluctant to try the arrangement. In this sense, qualitative disarmament is a "top-down" approach and nonprovocative defense a more "bottom-up" approach to similar goals.

Defense in Depth

In proposing such strategies, alternative defense theorists hark back to a venerable tradition of so-called "territorial defense" with roots in the citizen militias of the eighteenth and nineteenth centuries, as well as to more recent precedents in partisan and guerrilla warfare. "Territorial defense," wrote Adam Roberts, a prominent authority on the subject, "is a system of defense in depth; it is the governmentally-organized defense of a state's own territory, conducted on its own territory. . . . [It] is based on weapons systems, strategies and methods of military organization which are better suited to their defensive role than to engagement in major military actions abroad."[4]

The Swiss Model of General Defense

Although no nation currently configures its forces precisely as they are being proposed by the strategists of nonoffensive defense, a number of nations provide models suggestive of the general direction toward which such strategies would lead. Switzerland has for centuries practiced a defense policy of armed neutrality in which all physically and mentally able men between the ages of twenty and fifty are enlisted in a citizen militia totaling one-tenth of the entire population. Switzerland is thus able to maintain a small professional corps of officers (less than half a percent of the population) at modest expense while being capable of mustering a force of some 650,000 men (80 percent of the male population) to a state of high readiness within 48 hours of an alert. Soldiers keep their small arms, ammunition, and uniforms at home and participate in mandatory training exercises with their local units each year.

In its choice of weaponry, such as tank traps, antitank and antiaircraft systems, the Swiss army reflects its emphasis on defensive forces. Its tanks have a short operational radius and are not equipped for advances deep into enemy territory, but it maintains light vehicles suited to mountain defense. The Swiss have reinforced their defenses with a complex system of demolition points, between 3,000 and 6,000 strategic assets (bridges, roads, tunnels, mountain passes) wired to be destroyed in the case of invasion in order to impede the advance of encroaching armies. Artillery and aircraft are concealed deep inside mountains to assure their survival and small arms are hidden in barns and households. The Swiss air force is likewise configured for defensive purposes. Emphasis is placed on short-range fighter planes and helicopters capable of maneuvering easily among the Alps, while long-range aircraft and heavy bombers are deliberately excluded.

Swiss soldiers are routinely trained in the locales where they are expected to fight in the event of an attack. They thus gain intimate familiarity with the terrain, the hazards and the opportunities of their home territory, a strategic advantage matched only by guerrilla forces. This training produces an efficiency that conventional military forces generally lack, especially foreign troops invading the unfamiliar territory beyond their own borders. The remaining population participates in the "general defense" by maintaining an extremely extensive network of civil defense installations, providing medical services to the wounded, keeping the economy operating at an essential minimum, and engaging in nonviolent resistance in regions of the country that are occupied by hostile forces.

While maintaining a manifestly robust defensive military capability, deterring by "dissuasion" rather than threat, the Swiss also practice more positive incentives to dissuade potential aggressors from attacking. Seeking to make themselves indispensable to friends and foes alike, the Swiss provide their good offices for a wide range of financial transactions (a service with negative as well as positive impacts on international politics), diplomatic negotiations, and humanitarian aid efforts. Switzerland thus not only raises the costs of potential aggression by preparing a resolute and unrelenting resistance but also reinforces the benefits to other countries of maintaining peaceful relations with the Swiss by providing needed services to all who choose to use them.[5]

Sweden's Total Defense

Sweden provides a second model of a defense system with some applicability to nonoffensive strategies. Like Switzerland, Sweden embraces a kind of armed neutrality, but unlike the Swiss, the Swedes do not maintain a vast citizen militia. Instead, they keep a larger standing army that is still distinctly defensive in character. Swedish government officials harbor no illusions that the defense Sweden has prepared is capable of withstanding the concerted assault of a superpower. But they consider that scenario highly unlikely, given what they regard as Sweden's strategic marginality. Instead, the Swedish plan is to deter and if necessary defend against incursions carried out by an aggressor primarily intent on other, more significant strategic assets. Adam Roberts terms this strategy "marginal cost deterrence," in which the defense need not be powerful enough to defeat any aggressor intent on conquest but simply sufficiently resistant to make it too costly for him to try. Instead of the "worst case scenario" that dominates strategic thinking on most military staffs, the Swedes rely on a "most probable case" analysis and prepare accordingly. In the words of the Swedish Defense Staff, "The defense has to be so strong that the costs to defeat Sweden are out of proportion as compared to the strategic advantages which an aggressor might attain."[6]

In recent years, the Swedish government has studied perhaps more seriously than any other country in the world the possibility of integrating a component of civilian-based defense in its "total defense" strategy. Already the Swedes have what may be the world's most extensive civil defense shelter program as well as a well-planned strategy for "economic defense," including the stockpiling of food, various strategic materials, fuel, and heating oil. Sweden supplements its defensive capabilities with an active peace policy, consistently promoting disarmament and development at the UN and other international fora and generally seeking to be an exemplary global citizen.

Yugoslavia's General People's Defense

A third system of territorial defense studied by theorists interested in nonoffensive defense strategies exists in Yugoslavia, whose "general people's defense" combines a sizable standing army, a fallback capacity for partisan and guerrilla warfare, a people's resistance taking many forms and involving the entire population in a variety of tasks, and a "no surrender" clause in its national constitution. Deriving from its wartime experience conducting partisan warfare against the Nazis and its confrontation with Stalin in the early years after World War II, the Yugoslav defense effort is defensive less by design and principle than by necessity. The Yugoslavs gave pause to the Soviets despite the obvious inferiority of their military power, largely by virtue of their equally obvious determination not to be conquered. In addition to a multilayered military defense, the Yugoslavs have developed a broad range of nonmilitary forms of resistance, including moral, political, and psychological resistance techniques and economic and cultural resistance. These nonmilitary strategies closely resemble the tactics advocated by proponents of civilian-based defense, although the Yugoslavs themselves emphatically reject confining themselves to purely nonviolent means of defense.

Characteristics of Nonprovocative Defense

As conceived by its proponents, nonprovocative defense incorporates many of the strategies, military and nonmilitary, employed by the Swiss, Swedes, and Yugoslavs. Among the salient features of most such proposals are the following:[7]

1. A greatly decreased dependence on nuclear weapons. Some strategists, like those represented on the Alternative Defence Commission in Great Britain, specifically reject both national possession of nuclear weapons and the option of taking cover beneath the nuclear umbrella of a superpower patron.[8] Others accept maintaining a purely retaliatory minimal deterrent force as part of a reformed alliance.

2. A rejection of forward-based conventional defense plans being implemented in NATO during the 1980s (deep strike, AirLand Battle strategies), emphasizing instead defensive strategies restricted to one's own territory and specifically abjuring the intent or capability to strike beyond it.[9]

3. An emphasis on developing and exploiting recent advances in weapons technologies favoring the defense over the offense—precision-guided munitions, electronic sensors, buried exploding hose, minefields at the borders, and the like.[10]

4. An emphasis on decentralizing and dispersing the defense to reduce vulnerability and increase the difficulty of disabling it. Most strategists favor arming many small squads of soldiers with advanced small arms (antitank weapons, for example) and dispersing them widely throughout the region to be defended, using advanced communications technologies to keep in touch with one another.[11]

5. After initial hesitation, most alternative defense theorists now include civilian-based defense in their strategies (see chapter 8, Civilian-based Defense), either as a fallback or as an integral component. In order to avoid widespread loss of life and property, some theorists suggest declaring urban areas off-limits to military resistance and confining resistance in those sites to nonviolent techniques.[12]

6. An emphasis on efforts to remain separate from disputes between other nations, to maintain internal strength and unity through social justice, and to play a useful role for other countries as long as left in peace.[13]

Restructuring the Alliances Toward Defense

Though as conceived these strategies could be independently initiated, alternative defense theorists have also designed them to apply to an entire alliance and indeed, to *both* alliances as part of a comprehensive plan for tension reduction and common security. Support for the concept of nonprovocative defense on a cross-alliance basis has been expressed by former high-ranking military officers in both the NATO and Warsaw Pact alliances. A group of retired generals and admirals from the two alliances has met annually for the past several years to discuss how best to reduce competition and enhance cooperation between the two. At its 1987 Vienna meeting, the group formulated a "common security policy for Europe" proposing, among other actions, the establishment of regular contacts between top commanders in the political and military wings of both alliances and the formation of joint working groups to study how best to implement a mutually nonprovocative defense system. Soviet military officers in the group have proposed "the elimination by mutual agreement . . . of such offensive weaponry as tactical long-range bombers, tactical missiles, long-range artillery, [and] large armored formations; in other words, a restructuring qualitatively of the armed forces of both sides."[14]

During the late 1980s this concept gained a measure of attention within the policymaking establishments of both East and West. U.S. ambassador to NATO Alton Keel reported in 1987 that the alliance has initiated studies to identify the most destabilizing elements in both arsenals and to consider "restructuring" as well as reducing those forces.[15] For its part, the Warsaw Pact's Political Consultative Committee offered, in the long-stalled talks of Mutual and Balanced Force Reductions (MBFR) in May 1987, to accept larger cuts than NATO in certain conventional forces in order "to rectify the imbalance that has emerged." The Warsaw Treaty Organization (WTO) committee also called for discussion of a proposal for "reciprocal withdrawal of the most dangerous, offensive types of weapons from the zone of direct contact of the two military alliances."[16]

A similar proposal was made by Polish leader General Wojciech Jaruzelski in spring 1987 and elaborated in an interview with the *Washington Post* in November 1987.[17] Recalling a plan for mutual disengagement of NATO and Warsaw Pact forces first put forth by Polish diplomat Adam Rapacki in 1967, Jaruzelski called for the "gradual and mutually agreed withdrawal" of both nuclear and conventional weapons from Poland, Czechoslovakia, East Germany, and Hungary, within the Warsaw Pact, and from West Germany, Belgium, the Netherlands, Luxembourg, and Denmark within NATO. He also proposed negotiations specifically aimed at reshaping both Eastern and Western European military strategies into clearly defensive arrangements.[18]

Two Soviet strategic analysts, pursuing the concept of "reasonable sufficiency," have envisioned a process that does not require negotiation for its implementation. A. A. Kokoshin and A. V. Kortunov describe an arms race in reverse (reminiscent of U.S. psychologist Charles Osgood's GRIT strategy of 1962),[19] a de-escalation process in which unilateral gestures of restraint in the deployment of offensive weaponry on one side encourage reciprocal restraint on the other.

> On each given level of military counterforce, one of the participants can allow itself unilateral restraint in the further building up of arms, while at the same time, can have at its disposal a sufficient arsenal for warding off a possible threat (in the case of conventional arms) or for plotting an effective retaliatory strike (in the case of nuclear arms). This restraint, in turn, lowers the level of reasonable sufficiency for the second side, which at this time obtains the possibility not only to undertake the analogous steps of the first side, but to go still further without fear of endangering military-strategic stability. In such a way, where there would be a place for original escalation, either unilaterally or in accordance with the measures of organized military forces, the traditional mechanisms of the arms race (action-reaction) would apply in reverse to the opposing side.[20]

Although nonprovocative defense has received considerable attention from alternative security analysts in the United States as well, U.S. policymakers to date have been slower to pick up on the new strategic concept. But in a September 1987 speech to the American Association for the Advancement of Science, Congressman Les Aspin, chairman of the House Armed Services Committee, sketched a plan for reconfiguring NATO forces so as to fortify their purely defensive capabilities and thus to enhance conventional stability in Europe "in the world after INF." Aspin proposed both unilateral and negotiated measures. Through the use of barriers, antitank weapons, close air support, light infantry, in-depth and operational armored reserves, he argued, "there is strong reason to believe . . . that we can achieve a much higher degree of conventional stability."[21] Meanwhile, stability can be further enhanced by negotiated "reductions and limitations on armored forces—primarily tanks. . . . If we can get [the Soviets] to restructure their forces by building-down their tank forces, then a successful first-strike would be that much more difficult for them to carry out."[22]

> Conventional stability can change the nature of conventional war away from memories of World War II where blitzkrieg attacks gave hope of quick, relatively painless victory. Stability will create a new vision—the militarily unappealing prospects of a World War I scenario, where attacks on trenches extracted massive casualties with little gain. . . . At that point, we will have created a world where conventional war gives the attacker little hope of victory, and diplomacy will become a far more rational alternative to crisis resolution.[23]

Questions About the Strategy

Would nonprovocative defense effectively eliminate the war-making capability of nations? As conceived and intended by its proponents, nonprovocative defense does greatly impede the war-making capabilities of those nations that adopt it while leaving intact both national sovereignty and the capacity to defend and protect one's own territory. The real question is whether the arsenals that remain in place, and the infrastructures and industries supplying them, can be depended upon not to revert to an offensive orientation. What would prevent such a development?

It may not be sufficient to shift military strategies while leaving in place the same anarchic system of global conflict management now in effect between nations, a system whose inadequacy so often tempts nations to resort to armed force to settle their disputes. The unilateral decision by a nation to reconfigure its arsenal to become purely protective has the virtue of being an independent action requiring no agreement from anyone else. But by the same token it has the defect of being easily reversible, either in response to a perceived threat from a still-offensive enemy or by the decision, explicit or covert, to "break out" of the nonprovocative defense posture.

Fear of "breakout" is the quintessential nightmare of strategic planners, and in response to it policymakers sometimes choose to break out themselves, tacitly or explicitly abrogating treaties of restraint. The U.S. government's decision to exceed the limits of the SALT II Treaty in November 1986 was justified as a response to alleged Soviet cheating, although the charges were never independently verified. Under a purely voluntary regime of nonprovocative defense, any nation could walk away from the arrangement at any time, and its bad example could trigger the defection of others.

Some observers question whether citizen armies as advocated in nonoffensive defense strategies would unduly militarize the politics and culture of those nations adopting them. Responsibilities now delegated to a relatively limited number of professional officers and enlisted personnel would be far more widely distributed throughout the society, so that military training would extend to a very large portion of the population and could well become a mandatory component of the standard educational curriculum. Some critics of the Swiss defense system argue that despite its neutrality, Switzerland remains one of the more militarized cultures in Europe. Moreover, although Switzerland, Sweden, and Yugoslavia clearly do not pose grave threats to their neighbors, larger nations similarly armed might pose a substantial potential threat to smaller nations nearby.

One of the many ironies surrounding nuclear weapons is that they permit the great majority of citizens in nuclear-armed nations to forget entirely about the defense of their homelands, consigning the task to a relative handful of military personnel. In renouncing the nuclear option as well as the standing army, proponents of nonoffensive defense reassign this burdensome concern to ordinary citizens, likely requiring the reinstatement of a universal conscription system as well as a variety of nonviolent resistance strategies involving every citizen.

Finally, it must be asked whether nonprovocative defense could be effectively applied on a global scale. How would it differ from the distinctly unstable system of competitive conventional defenses that characterized the balance of forces prior to World War II? Being avowedly protective in nature, such a global system would at least theoretically be incapable of sustaining effective aggression. But the only way to prevent misuse of the remaining arsenals would be to erect a global security system around them, including rigorous national and international verification measures to assure that their orientation remains purely protective and a wide variety of nonviolent processes and institutions to handle conflicts previously settled by war.

Notes

1. Alexander Mcleod, "Britain's Labour Party Spells out its Non-Nuclear Defense Plan," *Christian Science Monitor*, July 30, 1984, p. 20.

2. *Non-Offensive Defence (NOD)*, no. 8 (February 1988), pp. 8–9. This newsletter is edited by Bjorn Moller and contains reviews of current research in this field, especially in Europe. Available from the Centre of Peace and Conflict Research, University of Copenhagen, (Centre of Vandkunsten 5, 1467 Copenhagen K, Denmark).

3. Mikhail Gorbachev, "The Reality and Guarantees of a Secure World," *Pravda*, September 17, 1987; reprinted in Press Release No. 119, USSR Mission to the United Nations, p. 5.

4. Adam Roberts, *Nations in Arms: The Theory and Practice of Territorial Defense* (London: Oxford University Press, 1974), p. 34.

5. For a detailed description of the Swiss model of general defense, see Dietrich Fischer, "Invulnerability Without Threat: The Swiss Concept of General Defense," *Journal of Peace Research*, vol. 19, no. 3, pp. 205–225. Reprinted in Burns H. Weston, ed., *Toward Nuclear Disarmament and Global Security: A Search for Alternatives* (Boulder, CO: Westview Press, 1984), pp. 504–532. For a more literary account, see John McPhee, *La Place de la Concorde Suisse* (New York: Farrar, Straus, and Giroux, 1984).

6. Press Department of the Swedish Defense Staff, *The Total Defense of Sweden*, Stockholm, 1963, p. 2.

7. See Note 2.

8. See the Alternative Defence Commission, *Defence Without the Bomb* (London: Taylor and Francis, 1984).

9. See Dietrich Fischer, *Preventing War in the Nuclear Age* (Totowa, NJ: Rowman and Allanheld, 1984).

10. See Frank Barnaby and Egbert Boeker, *Defense Without Offence: Non-Nuclear Defense for Europe* (Bradford, U.K.: Bradford University School of Peace Studies, Peace Studies Paper No. 8, 1982 and published in London by Housmans, 1983). See also Ben Dankbaar, "Alternative Defence Policies and Modern Weapon Technology," in Mary Kaldor and Dan Smith, *Disarming Europe* (London: Merlin Press, 1982).

11. See Horst Afheldt, *Verteidigung und Frieden* (Munich: Hanser Verlag, 1976).

12. See Hans-Heinrich Nolte and Wilhelm Nolte, *Ziviler Widerstand und Autonome Abweher* (Civilian resistance and autonomous protection). (Baden-Baden, West Germany: Nomos, 1984). See also Wilhelm Nolte, Jan Oberg, and Dietrich Fischer, *Winning Peace* (London: Taylor and Francis, forthcoming).

13. See Johan Galtung, *There Are Alternatives!: Four Roads to Peace and Security* (Chester Springs, PA: Dufour Publishers, 1984).

14. See Michael Harbottle, "European Security and the Concept of Non-Offensive Defence" [unpublished]. A report on the meetings of retired military officers from NATO and WTO alliances to a conference on "European Security and Non-Offensive Defence," sponsored by the International Union of Scientific Workers and held in Varna, Bulgaria, October 18–21, 1987.

15. *Defense and Disarmament News*, vol. 3, no. 1 (August–September 1987) (Brookline, MA: Institute for Defense and Disarmament Studies), p. 8.

16. Ibid.

17. See "Memorandum of the Government of the Polish People's Republic on Decreasing Armaments and Increasing Confidence in Central Europe," Warsaw, July 17, 1987. See also Michael T. Kaufman, "Polish Chief Offers Plan for Arms Disengagement," *New York Times*, May 9, 1987, p. 3.

18. For a discussion of other Eastern bloc thinking along these lines, see Gerard Holden, "After INF: A New Warsaw Pact Military Doctrine?" *ADIU Report* (University of Sussex, U.K.), November–December 1987.

19. See Charles Osgood, *An Alternative to War and Surrender* (Champaign: University of Illinois Press, 1962). Osgood proposed "an arms race in reverse," "a graduated and reciprocated, unilaterally initiated, tension-decreasing system" in which nations could safely take small, independent actions in the direction of disarmament and peace as a means of generating a momentum and eliciting reciprocal moves on the part of their adversaries. Knowingly or not, President Kennedy made use of just such a strategy in a series of moves originating with his well-known "Strategy of Peace" speech at the American University on June 10, 1983, and cluminating in the Limited Test Ban Treaty. See Amitai Etzioni, "The Kennedy Experiment," in *Western Political Quarterly* (Spring 1967), reprinted in *Securing Our Planet* (Los Angeles: J. P. Tarcher/St. Martin's, 1986), pp. 40–50.

20. A. A. Kokoshin and A. V. Kortunov, "Stability and Change in International Relations," reprinted by the American Committee on U.S.-Soviet Relations, p. 13.

21. Les Aspin, "Looking at the World After INF," news release, September 29, 1987, p. 9.

22. Ibid. p. 12.

23. Ibid., p. 9.

CHAPTER EIGHT

Civilian-based Defense: The Strength of Bare Hands and Stubbornness

As an ad hoc strategy for resisting perceived injustices of all kinds, nonviolent action has been practiced for hundreds—indeed, thousands—of years. Perhaps most ingenious of all was the Greek playwright Aristophanes' stratagem in *Lysistrata,* in which the indignant women of the warring city-states of Athens and Sparta conspired to deny their warrior mates their amorous affections until the men ceased their tiresome combat. Though apocryphal in that instance, the strategy was enacted in historical fact nearly two millennia later (without knowledge of the Aristophanes play) by the women of the Iroquois Indian nation.[1] But only in the past thirty years has the theory of nonviolence been applied to the problem of national defense. Termed "civilian-based defense" by its foremost proponent, Gene Sharp, this thoroughly nonmilitary form of national security has also gone by other names in other places—including "social defense," "civilian resistance," and "nonmilitary defense." Civilian-based defense is so named because, unlike other techniques of national defense that depend on a professional corps of officers and enlisted personnel to carry out the defense of the realm, it depends primarily on the will and ability of ordinary citizens to resist encroachments on their sovereignty, without recourse to violence.

Proposed in the first instance as an option for individual states to supplement and ultimately supplant their dependence on armed forces for national defense, CBD is not generally conceived as a global system applied to all nations in place of all present means of defense. Since the great preponderance of thinking on the subject has focused on the defense of individual nations confronting the present armed world, we will first examine its theory and practice as a national defense. With this background, we will then explore the possibilities and problems of considering CBD as a global system—first as an independent strategy, thoroughly replacing all other forms of national defense, then as a complement to other, compatible alternative systems.

Sources of Nonviolent Power

The insight on which nonviolent resistance is based is the seldom-recognized truth that all power, regardless of its apparent permanence and invulnerability, ultimately depends on the consent or acquiescence of the governed; and once that cooperation is withdrawn, any power, no matter how savage or imperious, must inevitably falter. Nonviolent power does not depend upon the adherence of its practitioners to a particular moral order or set of principles (like pacifism), but simply on their stubborn and unyielding refusal to be dominated by any force or authority other than themselves.

As delineated by Gene Sharp, civilian-based defense makes use of a wide variety of methods by which people under threat of attack can resist a would-be foreign invader or an internal coup d'état and render themselves ungovernable without resorting to the use of armed force. These methods are grouped in three broad classes of resistance: (1) protest and persuasion (including parades, marches, and vigils); (2) noncooperation (including boycotts and strikes); and (3) intervention (including fasting, nonviolent occupation, and the establishment of a parallel government). Which of these techniques are employed depends on the particular circumstances of the incursion.

The Importance of Preparation

Sharp cites dozens of historical cases of nonviolent resistance that have enjoyed varying degrees of success, from the failed but remarkably resilient Czechoslovak resistance during the Prague Spring of 1968 to Poland's Solidarity movement of the early 1980s and the ultimately victorious Philippine revolution of 1986. In no instance was there prior preparation or training of any kind; yet even in its absence the resistance was remarkably skillful and enduring. How much more effective might such resistance have been if a foundation of careful planning and strategy had been developed beforehand? How effective would armed resistance be if the defending army had never before handled its weapons or drilled as a group and was obliged to devise a purely ad hoc defense?

Sharp emphasizes that to succeed, civilian-based defense must, like armed force, be fully prepared in advance of the event. Indeed, he states that planning for nonviolent defense "would probably be more complex than planning for military defense."[2] The entire populace would need to be informed and educated in the principles and purposes of CBD. Specific occupational groups expected to engage in advanced aspects of the resistance would be given extensive specialized training. But the resistance would not be led from above in the manner of traditional military hierarchies. In order to succeed against a merciless aggressor who would likely seek to "decapitate" the resistance movement by killing or imprisoning its leadership early in the struggle, the citizen defenders would need to disperse authority widely and depend largely upon themselves and one another for support, relying in part on plans set in place before the actual event. Much responsibility for the resistance would devolve upon citizens trained to fulfill certain prearranged functions in the resistance.

Defense at Every Village Crossroads

Unlike a traditional military defense, which seeks both a frontal defense of the nation's borders and a forward defense (more rightly termed "offense") that projects itself into enemy territory, civilian-based defense cannot defend a nation's borders or project power beyond them. It concentrates instead on a defense in depth, preventing not invasion but the successful consolidation of power by an alien authority. In this respect, CBD bears a certain resemblance to territorial or nonoffensive defense, in that both seek less to erect an impermeable shield against invasion than to make the society and its institutions "indigestible" to any would-be tyrant. Any potential aggressor would face the prospect of relentless resistance and could never relax to enjoy the spoils of his conquest. "There are no white flags of surrender in civilian-based defense," wrote Sharp. George Kennan captures well the spirit of such resistance (speaking in a somewhat different context) in describing a defense "at every village crossroads":

> The purpose would be to place the country in a position where it could face the [enemy] and say to it: "Look here, you may be able to overrun us, if you are unwise enough to attempt it, but you will have a small profit from it; we are in a position to assure that not a single . . . person likely to perform your political business will be available to you for this purpose; you will find here no adequate nucleus of a puppet regime; on the contrary, you will be faced with the united and organized hostility of an entire nation; your stay among us will not be a happy one; we will make you pay bitterly for every day of it; and it will be without favorable long-term prospects."[3]

Deterrence by Resistance

Unlike a nuclear-based security system, which cannot defend but only deter by threat of massive retaliation, civilian-based defense restores the defensive function to a nation's citizens. But can it also effectively deter aggression, so that the likelihood of attack is diminished and the gritty necessities of actual resistance are avoided? Yes, argues Sharp, CBD can indeed deter attack, not by threat of retaliation, as in the case of nuclear weapons, but by raising the costs of aggression to the point where they do not justify the expense. And nations adopting CBD as a national defense policy would deliberately make obvious to all potential adversaries the nature and extent of their preparations for resistance as a means of giving pause to any putative plans for aggression such enemies might entertain.

Of course, this kind of deterrence presumes a rational adversary, and adversaries have not historically proven always rational. But nuclear deterrence also requires a modicum of rationality, as a madman might choose to push the button even knowing that he was committing suicide in so doing. One of the great redeeming features of CBD's deterrence by resistance is that it returns defense to its proper place in strategy and abjures all capabilities to attack. This policy and posture thus unambiguously reassure all other nations that no harm will come to them if they do not themselves threaten harm.

Facing Down Nuclear Blackmail

CBD has effectively persuaded some observers of its potential in deterring and defending against conventional land-based invasions of national territory, but many remain skeptical that it can meet the challenge of nuclear blackmail by a nation merciless enough to simply annihilate its adversary by remote control and thus avoid the sticky logistical problems of asserting its authority over a stubborn and rebellious populace. Strategists of civilian-based defense have thus far devoted relatively little attention to this scenario,[4] but they offer several arguments in support of their contention that CBD defends and deters at least as well, and perhaps better than, conventional or nuclear defenses against nuclear threats.

In the first place, argue CBD strategists, nuclear-armed nations feel most threatened by those nations that target them with nuclear weapons and do not generally target nations that do not possess such weapons. In fact, the Soviet Union has repeatedly offered to neutral nations in Europe a pledge not to target them with nuclear weapons if those nations will themselves pledge not to acquire them. Thus nations adopting CBD could, if they choose, conclude such agreements with all possessors of nuclear arsenals. Such pledges could, of course, easily be overridden in the heat of conflict. But even apart from such treaties of nontargeting, nations adopting CBD as a defense policy would be so unambiguously nonthreatening to nuclear nations that they would be unlikely to provoke attack by reason of having incited fear in their would-be adversaries. But would the removal of their own threatening posture invite aggression by making them appear vulnerable?

In the event that a nuclear nation did in fact threaten a nation using only CBD, the defending nation would need to "learn not to blink"—not to be intimidated by such tactics. As social philosopher Kenneth Boulding points out,[5] threats are most effective as long as they don't need to be carried out. Once the bluff is called, much of the leverage of the threat is expended and the cost of fulfilling the threat becomes more apparent. As Boulding argues, following through on threats can ultimately become as costly to the threatener as to his victim.

The spectacle of one nation threatening another that so clearly does not threaten it might so tarnish the public image of the offending country in the world community that the political cost to the threatener who must continue to live in that environment might not prove to be worth the benefits he could expect to derive from making the threat. Unhappily, there are all too many instances in history when outlaw nations have chosen to defy the opprobrium of the global public despite the political costs, as has been seen most recently in the South African minority government's treatment of its black majority.

It remains an open question whether a thoroughly nonviolent response to aggression would prompt more united and effective action from the global community. The defending people or nation could widely publicize the threat and mount a campaign to elicit an international response—universal condemnation and ostracism, total economic, diplomatic, and cultural boycotts of the outlaw nation, even blockades of vital goods—until the threat is rescinded.[6] The would-be threatener would have little to gain from following through with his threat if it meant creating a wasteland of the territory he sought to control, for nothing of value would remain for him to exploit.

The Phased Transition to CBD

Recognizing that few, if any, nations would be willing to shift from a wholly military to a wholly nonmilitary defense in a single, sudden transformation, Gene Sharp envisions a gradual phased process of transition he terms "transarmament."[7] Initially, he suggests, a component of CBD training would be added to the existing military defense as a supplement. Then, as confidence in the technique grows, the military components would gradually be supplanted and the nonviolent element would eventually predominate and replace all dependence on armed force.

This scenario is an accommodation to political realities in those several European nations (including Sweden, the Netherlands, Great Britain, Belgium, and France) where governments or private groups have recently sponsored pilot studies of CBD.[8] In most cases, that CBD might have a useful role to play in a total defense effort, although CBD may not fully replace existing dependence on military arsenals and strategies. Theorists of nonoffensive defense have often included CBD as either an integral component of their policies or as a fallback strategy in case military defenses fail.

Forces Remaining and Who Controls Them

Civilian-based defense has never yet been fully considered as a global security system by any major theorist, so many of the questions relevant to evaluating such systems have still to be asked of CBD. What forces would remain and of what kind? Who would control them? We can only extrapolate from the theory of CBD as it has so far been enunciated by its leading strategists. It is important to acknowledge, in any case, that most theorists of nonviolent defense have not only not proposed CBD as a global security system but do not envision it being adopted by all nations at a set moment in time. Instead, they see the technique being tested first by individual nations, perhaps initially as a supplement to existing military defenses. Then, as it proves its effectiveness, CBD might eventually supplant conventional military strategies in a given nation, and the example of its success might encourage other nations to try the strategy themselves. The evolutionary perspective implicit in this gradualist approach differs markedly from the process designed by Clark-Sohn and some other theorists of global security, who envision all nations simultaneously adopting a comprehensive security system.

On the basis of existing theory, we must presume that no armed forces of any kind would remain in a global CBD security system, neither national nor international, offensive nor defensive. No nation would possess any of the weapons with which armed forces are normally equipped, and no global police force would exist to "enforce the peace" in place of national armies. The degree of disarmament presumed in a global CBD security system extends well beyond anything envisioned in classic proposals for "general and complete disarmament." There is even a question as to whether small arms would be permitted to remain in a CBD security system because as the only weapons still in existence they could become more, rather than less, important than they now are. The sole remaining forces would be the well-trained but wholly unarmed citizenry of each nation, organized on an independent basis, and its primary weapon would be its collective determination to remain free. Each nation would retain control over its own unarmed forces, and within each national contingent each individual would presumably retain control over his or her own participation in the collective defense effort.

Institutions of Conflict Resolution

Conceived as a national defense strategy, CBD does not address itself to minimizing and resolving conflicts by any of the variety of means available through the United Nations and other institutions. But neither does it specifically preclude them, and their nonviolent orientation would seem to fit well with CBD. Indeed, the entire strategy would be greatly strengthened by coupling a national capacity for self-defense by wholly nonmilitary means with increased use of machinery for global dispute resolution.

Eliminating the War-making Capability of Nations

Does civilian-based defense eliminate the war-making capacity of nations? There can be no question that CBD effectively eliminates any capacity to attack or wage offensive operations of any kind in those nations that adopt it as a defense policy. It is quite impossible to use the techniques of CBD for any purpose other than the defense of one's own territory, institutions, and values. A global security system based on the universal adoption of CBD would likely be far more stable than the present system, because no nation would retain the capacity to wage war.

Evaluating CBD as a Global System

But there are many reasons, some obvious and some less so, why among the security systems reviewed in this volume, civilian-based defense is probably the least likely to be adopted as a global alternative. Among them are the following:

Political impracticality. As far as the concept of world government has diverged from the mainstream of political acceptability in recent years, CBD remains a somewhat familiar if unlikely option, with a considerable tradition of theory. As a newer concept, civilian-based defense does not yet possess such a heritage or base of political support. As a national defense in place of traditional military preparations, CBD has been actively discussed only in relatively limited circles since the 1960s, and remains largely unknown as yet to the majority of politicians, intellectuals, and the general public.

A number of nations, most of them in Western Europe, have recently considered the possibility of supplementing their existing military defense preparations with a component of CBD, but only a few governments have taken the step of adopting such plans, and none has seriously considered wholly replacing its military defenses with nonviolent strategies. In the absence of such precedents, it seems very unlikely that nations would universally agree to relinquish their military defenses and replace them with nonviolent defense preparations.

Extraordinary requirements. The success of nonviolent defense depends to a great degree on the commitment and discipline of its practitioners, who are not an elite cadre but the entire populace of each nation. The intensity of this commitment would no doubt vary widely from one country to another, depending on a wide variety of factors, including the allegiance of the citizens to both the national culture and the current regime and their faith in the efficacy of nonviolent defense. Some theorists of CBD believe that although the strategy might work well in a small homogeneous culture with advanced institutions and a long-standing tradition of peaceable behavior (like the Scandinavian countries), it might work considerably less well in large, ethnically diverse nations riven by schisms of culture and politics and burdened with traditions of violence and militarism.

In any case, there is no doubt that CBD is extraordinarily demanding of ordinary citizens, placing the principal responsibility for national defense on their shoulders rather than those of a small professional corps. It is an open question whether citizens would be able to summon the requisite will to undertake a sustained national defense, with all the sacrifices a nonviolent defense in particular would entail.

Militarizing culture? Ironically, in shifting the burden of defense from a professional corps to the citizenry at large, CBD obliges the average citizen to consider and prepare for eventualities he now has the luxury of ignoring. Drilling an entire populace in defense against a theoretical aggressor might produce some unintended negative effects, breeding a paranoia and defensiveness for which there may be no basis. Equally troubling to governments is the possibility that the capacity of citizens for cooperation in resistance to invasion could also be turned on the government itself if it were perceived to be overstepping its legitimate authority. Would a government with limited legitimacy and little popular support wish to place such a "weapon" in the hands of its own people?

Lingering Doubts About the Efficacy of Nonviolence. Despite considerable historical evidence that nonviolent action can indeed be effective against aggression and tyranny, the impression persists that it cannot succeed against a truly merciless and determined aggressor. Mohandas Gandhi succeeded, it is argued, because he was dealing with the British, a "civilized" people who would not descend to barbaric measures; he would not have succeeded with tyrants. This skepticism lingers in the face of the experience of the Danes and Norwegians in resisting the Nazis, Czechs, and Poles in resisting the Soviet Union, and the Filipinos in overcoming Ferdinand Marcos. In all these cases, the aggressors could not be termed extraordinarily merciful and yet, without prior preparation, the resisters achieved remarkable results. Still, it is the ultimate defeat of the Czechs and Poles that is generally emphasized, while the indisputable success of the Filipino people in the revolution of 1986 has been erroneously characterized by many observers since the event as a military coup aided by widespread civilian support.

This ingrained skepticism about the efficacy of nonviolent action is reinforced by ancestral habits of violent behavior and a contemporary fascination with violence, both of which span widely divergent cultures. Many who deplore the resort to force in political relations regretfully conclude that violence is an inevitable occurrence and force the sole final arbiter between nations. Changing this habit of mind will take both deliberate education and an accumulation of successful experience in social change without undue violence. This shift in expectations will take much time, measured more likely in generations than in decades. Its prospects will be greatly enhanced by two concurrent contemporary trends: the increasing inability of armed force to achieve the ends for which it has traditionally been used, and the increasing effectiveness of nonviolent action in confronting and overcoming armed force.

The Philippine Revolution: The People Protect the Army

At no time in recent history have both trends been more startlingly juxtaposed than in the February 1986 Philippine revolution. There the global public was treated to a spectacle with few parallels in the annals of war and revolution. Sequestered in Camp Crame, a military base outside Manila, defecting military forces headed by Defense Minister Juan Ponce Enrile and Lt. Gen. Fidel Ramos came under attack by forces loyal to President Ferdinand Marcos, and hundreds of thousands of unarmed Filipino civilians interposed themselves between the forces to protect the rebel soldiers.

"Tens of thousands of people . . . filled the street and successfully halted a column of armored vehicles that were headed toward the headquarters of the resistance. Direct appeals from members of the crowd to the soldiers caused them to retreat and bolstered the morale of the resistance movement."[9]

"Young men and women handed flowers and candy to soldiers. They planted daisies inside the barrels of their rifles. Priests and nuns knelt before the marines in the . . . tall weeds and prayed. 'This is something new,' said Col. Jose T. Almonte. 'Soldiers are supposed to protect the civilians. In this particular case, you have civilians protecting the soldiers.'"[10]

"The world saw and recorded a people who knelt in the path of oncoming tanks and subdued with embraces of friendship the battle-hardened troops sent out to disperse them and annihilate the military rebels," declared Corazon Aquino in the aftermath of President Marcos' abdication and flight from Malacanang Palace. "All the world wondered as they witnessed, in the space of two months, a people lift themselves from humiliation to the greatest pride."[11]

More recent events in the Philippines, including the rise of violent right-wing vigilante groups, a succession of coup attempts against the Aquino administration, and the continued growth of the Communist insurgency, have since dimmed the glory of Philippine "people's power." All are reminders that the habit of violence is persistent and deep seated, in the Philippines as elsewhere, and is not dispelled by any single series of events, however promising at their moment of inception. A more permanent transformation requires breaking an ancient addiction to violence, a project entailing much time and massive effort. Still, events like the Philippine revolution, the Solidarity trade union movement, the U.S. civil rights movement, and others demonstrate that nonviolence possesses a power of its own whose potency we have yet to measure and whose discovery may one day prove itself equal in historic significance to the splitting of the atom.

At the height of the Solidarity union movement in Poland, Lech Walesa spoke to a CBS interviewer in November 1981:

> Gentlemen, victory can be achieved by various means. It can be gained with tanks and missiles, but I think that one wins better with truth, honesty and logic—in running the economy, in everything. And just take our example, and note that we have not fired a single shot. And we do not know what other means would have to be employed here to win such a victory as ours, except without firing a single shot. I think that the 20th and 21st century should be modeled on a struggle such as the one we have demonstrated. This is a new weapon. Well, not a new one. Actually, an old one. But it is very effective, and tailored exactly to the needs of the 21st century.[12]

Conclusion

Civilian-based defense stands little chance of being adopted in the foreseeable future as anything approaching a global security system. But its proponents have never proposed it as a system to be adopted universally at a particular moment in time, rather as an incremental approach to be taken up by one country and then another. Moreover, as a component in a more comprehensive system, integrated with other strategies of defense and institutions of dispute resolution and global governance, it could indeed become a useful and effective strategy, a vital element in the nonviolent reconstruction of global politics.

Notes

1. In the early seventeenth century, women of the Iroquois tribe determined to refuse intimate relations with their mates until they ceased their warring ways. Believing that women alone possessed the secrets of birth, the Iroquois braves eventually succumbed, an event one historian terms the first successful feminist rebellion. See Stan Steiner, *The New Indians* (New York: Harper and Row, 1960), p. 220.

2. Gene Sharp, *National Security Through Civilian-Based Defense* (Omaha, NE: Civilian-Based Defense Association [Association for Transarmament Studies], 1985), p. 22.

3. George Kennan, *Russia, The Atom, and the West* (New York: Harper and Bros., 1958), p. 62.

4. One organization that has devoted significant attention to the scenario of nonviolent defense against nuclear threats is the Center for the Study of Conflict (5842 Bellona Avenue, Baltimore, MD 21212), Richard Fogg, Director.

5. See Kenneth Boulding, *Ecodynamics: A New Theory of Social Evolution* (New York: Sage Publications, 1972), Chapter 7.

6. For a classic statement of the strategy of defense against nuclear weapons by nonviolent resistance, see Stephen King-Hall, *Defense in the Nuclear Age* (Nyack, NY: Fellowship of Reconciliation, 1959). Written by a son and grandson of British admirals and himself a naval officer of impeccable credentials, King-Hall proposed that Britain renounce not only its own nuclear deterrent but essentially all weaponry and confront any would-be nuclear-armed adversary with the simple determination not to be conquered. Commenting on King-Hall's proposal, Sir B. H. Liddell Hart, the military strategist (see chapter 6), wrote, "It is remarkable, and deeply significant, that a man so combative by temperament and heredity should become a leading advocate of nonviolent resistance. Moreover, events have proved his foresight about the trend of warfare." In *Deterrence or Defense?* (New York: Praeger, 1960), p. 220.

7. The term "transarmament" has also been used by some theorists of nonoffensive military defense to refer to the transition from offensive military postures to purely defensive strategies and policies. The term originated in the 1930s with Kenneth Boulding, was used by nonviolent theorist Theodor Ebert in the 1950s, and was appropriated by Gene Sharp and other nonviolent strategists in 1964 to refer specifically to the transition from military to wholly nonmilitary forms of defense. Sharp asks that for the sake of terminological clarity, all future use of the term be confined to the definition he has given it.

8. See, for example, "Complementary Forms of Resistance: A Summary of the Report of the Swedish Commission on Resistance," Swedish Official State Reports (SOU 1984).

9. "Troops Rush Anti-Marcos Crowd, But Some Defect," *New York Times*, February 24, 1986, p. 4.

10. Clyde Haberman, "A People's Army Confronts the Foe, With Only Flowers for Firepower," *New York Times*, February 24, 1986, p. 4.

11. "Text of Aquino's Statement: 'All the World Wondered,'" *New York Times*, February 27, 1986, p. 6.

12. Lech Walesa, speaking on a CBS News Special Report, "Two Voices of Poland," November 2, 1981, 11:30 to midnight EST, with Walter Cronkite.

CHAPTER NINE

Strategic Defense: Armor or Apocalypse?

During the 1980s, strategic defense[1] has become the most prominent and divisive security issue between the superpowers. Weapons under development for strategic defense have become among the most controversial in the U.S. defense budget. In Reykjavik, Iceland, in autumn 1986, when President Reagan and General Secretary Gorbachev appeared on the verge of an unprecedented agreement to eliminate all ballistic missiles from their arsenals, it was on the issue of strategic defense that negotiations ultimately foundered. The significance of strategic defense is attested to by the huge outlay of financial and human resources that the United States and the Soviet Union have channeled into research and development, by the issue's vast media coverage in the United States, and by vigorous official and public debate in the West concerning the advantages and disadvantages of such a program. Because of its significance in arms control negotiations and military policy, it is a subject without which any discussion of security alternatives would be incomplete.

Despite its importance, however, strategic defense remains an addition rather than an alternative to the present situation of military competition. Although theoretically strategic defenses could be part of a system to reduce or eliminate arms competition, at the moment they are an integral part of East-West rivalry. In this chapter various interpretations and criticisms are examined in order to sketch out the dimensions and the obstacles involved in pursuing strategic defense; we will look in particular at the U.S. Strategic Defense Initiative.

Background

For nearly three decades both the United States and the Soviet Union have sought to develop weapons to defend themselves against ballistic missile attack. Beginning in the early years of development, questions arose concerning the feasibility and desirability of such defenses. Early antimissile defense technologies were primitive and inadequate. Because the targets that missiles present are small, distant, and extremely fast, attempting to intercept a ballistic missile once it is launched is like trying to shoot one bullet into another already in flight. Although both superpowers sought to escape their vulnerability to ballistic missiles, both also recognized that the pursuit of such defense could become extremely destabilizing.

The ABM Treaty

Reluctance to encourage a "use 'em or lose 'em" strategic posture, together with an acknowledgment of the relatively primitive technologies available at the time and a general skepticism about the long-term possibilities for achieving an effective antiballistic missile (ABM) defense, led the two superpowers to enter into treaty negotiations through the Strategic Arms Limitation Talks (SALT I) to prohibit both nations from deploying such defenses. Such a treaty, it was reasoned, would ensure that both superpowers would continue to be deterred from using their nuclear arsenals because both would retain the capability of inflicting unacceptable damage on their adversaries. The ABM Treaty of 1972 limited the superpowers to just two ABM sites apiece (further restricted to one in 1974). This effectively eliminated the possibility of deploying nationwide strategic defense systems. SALT I limited as well the number and type of interceptor missiles, launchers, and radar that both sides might deploy at their sites.

Despite the treaty, both the United States and the Soviet Union have quietly continued to pursue technologies to defend against strategic weapons. Although research was somewhat curtailed by the ABM Treaty, both governments realized the strategic advantages of possessing such a defense, and each feared the other might "break out"—develop new, ostensibly defensive technologies that could then be rapidly deployed in tandem with existing offensive systems to attain a significant military advantage.

The Strategic Defense Revival

In February 1982, after months of advance circulation in the federal bureaucracy, a study advocating a space-based missile shield, known as High Frontier, was released by the Heritage Foundation. It met with considerable criticism. Bruce W. MacDonald, an analyst at the State Department, issued a secret memorandom listing problems with High Frontier that were likely to make the proposal "unworkable." The

Department of Defense announced in another document, "It is the unanimous opinion of the Air Force technical community that the High Frontier proposals are unrealistic regarding the state of technology, cost and schedule." A joint study by the air force and the army made clear on March 31, 1982, that "the concept, as proposed, is not technically feasible for near term application using off-the-shelf or under-development hardware." On November 24, 1982, Secretary of Defense Weinberger wrote of High Frontier, "We are unwilling to commit this nation to a course which calls for growing into a capability that currently does not exist. With the substantial risks involved we do not foresee 'cheap and quick' solutions to support the shift in policy. . . . "[2]

Despite the generally critical response to High Frontier, President Reagan's interest in strategic defense was sparked. Soon information asserting that the Soviet Union was making significant investments and advances in strategic defense technologies began to appear,[3] and Reagan, generally approving of increased military research and development, was drawn to the moral (and thus political) appeal of offering the U.S. public a "purely defensive" shield to replace the morally repugnant alternative of Mutual Assured Destruction. Moreover, the prospect of such an "astrodome defense" appeared to promise a return to the cherished invulnerability of Fortress America that two broad oceans had provided for nearly two centuries—indeed, until the advent of the ICBM. Thus, the Reagan Administration spawned a widespread reappraisal of defenses against strategic weapons, and little more than a year after defense officials had privately castigated the High Frontier proposal for an antimissile shield constructed of weapons on platforms in space, they were contradicting themselves and joining the president in publicly promoting the very same idea. Although Caspar Weinberger took a completely different position after President Reagan insisted the United States must produce a space shield—not surprising considering the additions to the defense budget that the change in position would require—every other statesman still living who had previously held the office of secretary of defense (six in all) remains skeptical.

The Strategic Defense Initiative

Questions concerning the feasibility and desirability of strategic defenses were renewed after President Reagan made his famous "Star Wars" speech on March 23, 1983. In that speech he posed his own question: "What if free people could live secure in the knowledge that their security did not rest upon the threat of instant retaliation to deter a Soviet attack, that we could intercept and destroy strategic ballistic missiles before they reach our own soil or that of our allies?"

After his speech the president ordered increased study of the issue, appointing a commission headed by James Fletcher, director of NASA, to identify the most promising technologies for further research. The Fletcher Commission "produced a pessimistic report, curiously prefaced by an enthusiastic and optimistic introduction, the only part of the report usually read by most non-experts. Asked about this Mr. Fletcher made the astounding statement that it has [sic] not been written by anyone on the committee. By whom then? 'Someone in the White House,' he replied."[4] In this way the Reagan administration qualified the report's doubts and simultaneously gave its strategic defense program, known as the Strategic Defense Initiative (SDI), the appeal of commission approval.

The Soviet Strategic Defense Program

After the ABM Treaty was signed in 1972, the United States continued to research ABM technologies but dismantled its one allowed ABM system, having decided that it was too ineffective and costly. The Soviets, however, continued to upgrade their ABM site within the limits of the treaty. Since the announcement of SDI by President Reagan, the Soviet Union has been adamantly opposed to all U.S. efforts concerning the initiative despite continued efforts of its own.

Soviet directed-energy programs have been in existence since the 1960s and have been funded more heavily than U.S. programs, although the results of the two countries' programs are roughly equivalent, according to the Joint Chiefs of Staff.[5] The Soviet Union has developed a rocket-driven generator and a segmented mirror, leading officials to conclude that it has the capability to generate and store the power needed for a laser weapon. It is also possible that the Soviet Union has the capability to develop the optical system necessary for laser weapons to track and attack targets. However, the Joint Chiefs of Staff hold that the United States leads the Soviet Union in computers, guidance systems, optics, and telecommunications.[6]

The Soviet Union has repeatedly called on the United States to stop its research in the area of strategic defense, but putting aside the Reagan administration's interest in pursuing these technologies, the Soviets' own vigorous research pursuits and the inadequacy of present verification capabilities for a ban on research have made such an agreement impossible. Former National Security Adviser Robert McFarlane said Soviet comments concerning SDI were a "masterpiece of chutzpah" because the USSR is pursuing "the largest research program on earth."[7] The Reagan Administration holds that its own program is a sensible and required response to Soviet ballistic missile defense efforts. There are, however, important differences between the U.S. and Soviet programs.

> Despite their protestations that they have no SDI-type program, the Soviets clearly have taken an interest in strategic defense, investigating new technologies as well as conventional systems. However, Soviet strategic defense work is not directly analagous to SDI in that 1) the Soviet effort encompasses a broader range of systems than does SDI, including air defense and civil defense, which the United States has not thought worth the required investment; 2) much of the Soviet effort has been devoted to BMD technologies that were current when the ABM Treaty was signed, whereas SDI emphasizes new technologies; 3) in the political arena, Soviet defensive programs and SDI play different roles: Soviet programs are not the focus of an announced policy to change the strategic order, as is SDI.[8]

Diverse Definitions of SDI

The proclaimed objectives of the Strategic Defense Initiative are diverse. It has variously been defined as a project to create an impermeable shield against nuclear missiles, to develop a partial shield for the enhancement of nuclear deterrence, to reduce and stabilize strategic stockpiles, and to develop new technologies useful to commercial as well as military applications. In addition, it is unofficially promoted as a means of competing successfully with the Soviets economically, as it has become increasingly pointless for the superpowers to compete militarily. Each of these definitions of SDI is discussed briefly below.

An Impermeable Shield

President Reagan initially spoke of SDI as a means of rendering nuclear weapons "impotent and obsolete." This objective would require a space-based defense that no missile could penetrate, effectively removing the threat of destruction and mutual vulnerability and making a world without nuclear deterrence once again possible. As a technical venture of unparalleled complexity, such an appealing and visionary concept is inspirational and encourages the pursuit of new frontiers. But the Strategic Defense Initiative has engendered widespread controversy and skepticism in the scientific community.

Many computer specialists, including some who have done consultation work for the Strategic Defense Initiative Organization (SDIO), have questioned whether software requiring 10 million to 30 million lines of computer code[9] to be error-free can be relied upon, especially since the system cannot be effectively tested for reliability by any means other than a full-scale nuclear war. If a machine makes one error every 100 times it performs its function, it is 99 percent effective. If twenty-five machines, each 99 percent effective, together perform a function then the machine's effectiveness is reduced to approximately 78 percent ($0.99^{25} \cong 0.78$). If this notion is expanded to a megasystem run by computers operating on millions of lines of software commands, the difficulties facing the Strategic Defense Initiative become obvious.

Several experts have resigned from their jobs at the SDIO because they feel the organization has been more interested in tests that exaggerate SDI's progress to assure its momentum than in valid experiments that reliably demonstrate what can be achieved.[10] David L. Parnas, a member of the Strategic Defense Initiative Organization's Panel on Computing in Support of Battle Management, wrote when he resigned, "If you gave me the job of building the [software] system, and all the resources I wanted, I could not do it. . . . I don't expect the next 20 years of research to change that fact." Parnas holds that his views are scientific, not political judgments, based on "more than 20 years of research on software engineering, including more than eight years of work on real-time software used in military aircraft. They are . . . based on characteristics peculiar to this particular effort, not objections to weapons development in general."[11]

As was reported to Senators Proxmire, Johnston, and Chiles after key scientists involved in SDI research were interviewed by members of the senators' staffs, years of research have not produced a single big break that would make deployment of a comprehensive defense more feasible before the turn of the century than it was in 1983 when the increased research efforts began. Members of the senators' staffs who conducted the interviews wrote that there was concern among SDI scientists that long-term research with the most potential might be scrapped because of pressure for early development and that experiments might degenerate into "a series of sleazy stunts" (as a senior scientist at Lawrence Livermore National Laboratory stated) in order to retain public support and government funding.[12] The report, *SDI: Progress and Challenges*, indicates that the results of SDI research have made the program's difficulties more evident, that these problems are greater than previously anticipated, and that the Strategic Defense Initiative Organization has slowed its research due in part to lack of technical promise and not, as some members of SDIO held, because of congressional budget cuts.[13]

> Congress should maintain a certain degree of skepticism over claims of tremendous advances in SDI research. Hard questions should be asked about what any so-called "spectacular breakthroughs" really accomplished and how far the research was actually advanced compared to the task at hand. So far, SDI has moved ahead by inches. We still have miles to go. . . . Congress

> should be concerned about the priority shifts SDIO has made in its program. They appear to indicate that, contrary to public pronouncements, SDIO still does not have a firm idea of how a strategic defense system might be implemented. Nevertheless, Congress is being asked to pour billions of dollars into the program based on assumptions that the direction of the program is clear. Congress should question why SDIO is rushing to arrive at a development decision by the early 1990s. Comprehensive ballistic missile defenses would not become fully operational until nearly two decades from now. Congress should be made fully aware of the serious risks involved in making a premature decision on whether to develop strategic defenses. Moreover, Congress should inquire as to whether additional time for research will result in a sounder development decision. . . . After completing this review of the SDI research and the defensive systems being envisioned, we are struck by myriad uncertainties and unknowns at every turn in the program.[14]

Both the Federation of American Scientists and the Union of Concerned Scientists have issued strong statements against SDI, and roughly 6,500 scientists and scientific educators have pledged not to accept SDI funds.[15] A National Academy of Sciences (NAS) survey found that 78 percent of scientists who responded to the poll doubted SDI could produce a survivable and cost-effective strategic defense within twenty-five years. Further, only 4 percent felt that "the odds of success were better than even"[16] that an effective defense for the U.S. population could be achieved within twenty-five years.

The American Physical Society (APS), the nation's largest professional society of physicists, released a 424-page report on April 22, 1987, which revealed that "the performance of most of the crucial technologies [of SDI] would have to improve by factors ranging from 100 to more than a million, a scaling up that may or may not be achievable."[17] Whereas previous skepticism about SDI technologies had focused on computer software problems and assumed that many other technologies not now available were promising, the American Physical Society report casts doubt on whether other technologies, especially lasers and particle beams, are going to be effective in the foreseeable future.

The report, which was accepted by advocates and critics of SDI alike as "the most detailed and credible examination of the [SDI] technology since the Strategic Defense Initiative began in 1983,"[18] was produced by the most authoritative panel of scientists yet assembled to study the issue, including fifteen scientists from government weapons laboratories, Nobel Prize winners for laser work, and scientists who held high-level military research positions. The American Physical Society report was prepared and reviewed by some of the nation's most prominent scientists who received full cooperation from the Strategic Defense Initiative Organization and the Department of Defense, including the use of classified materials.[19] One significant conclusion of the report was that many space-based platforms will need to be powered by nuclear reactors, thus contradicting claims that SDI could be a nonnuclear program.[20]

> The power requirements for "housekeeping", i.e. the requirements for a space platform to control altitude, to cool mirrors, to receive and transmit information, to operate radars, etc., is estimated to be in the range of 100–700 kw of continuous power. This would require a nuclear-reactor-driven power plant for each platform, necessitating perhaps a hundred or more of these nuclear reactors in space. These needs require solving many challenging engineering problems not yet explored. Cooling of large space-based power plants is a very difficult task.[21]

Another conclusion of the APS report placed "deployment of any advanced anti-missile system well into the next century."[22] The implication of this assertion is that any interim deployments will be at best simple modifications of ABM systems proposed and rejected in the 1960s.

A short statement issued by APS two days after it released its larger, more comprehensive report summarized the following points:

1. The development of an effective ballistic missile defense utilizing DEW [directed energy weapons] would require performance levels that vastly exceed current capabilities.
2. There is insufficient information to decide whether the required performance levels can be achieved.
3. A decade or more of intensive research would be required to provide the technical knowledge needed for an informed decision about the potential effectiveness and survivability of directed energy weapon systems.
4. The important issues of system integration and effectiveness depend critically on information that does not now exist.[23]

On the basis of these points and its longer report, the American Physical Society concluded its statement in the following way:

> In view of the large gap between current technology and the advanced levels required for an effective missile defense, the SDI program should not be a controlling factor in U.S. security planning and the process of arms control. It is the judgment of the Council of the American Physical Society that there should be no early commitment to the deployment of SDI components.[24]

A Partial Shield

As the technical difficulties of creating such an impermeable shield have become increasingly apparent, official promotion of this grand vision has been largely replaced by discussion of how a space-based defense would enhance, rather than replace, nuclear deterrence. A permeable shield, even if 99 percent effective, cannot effectively protect civilians. If even 1 percent of either superpower's missiles were to penetrate the other's strategic defense system, tens of millions of people could be killed in the blasts alone. Thus, SDI has become a defense of ballistic missiles rather than people,[25] a partial shield that could be used to strengthen deterrent forces by protecting missile bases and command, control, and communication systems. While SDI would likely fail to provide adequate protection of civilian populations in the event of an attack, it could prove somewhat more effective in shielding the weapons themselves from attack.

This shift in definition is significant. The new objective is diametrically opposed to the former objective: Instead of shifting from offensive to defensive weapons, as was the original intention, SDI's purpose under the new definition is to maintain and enhance offensive forces by adding defenses to them. These defenses would not provide a "leak-proof" shield but would help assure that in the event of a preemptive strike by the Soviet Union, U.S. intercontinental ballistic missiles for retaliation would survive. In moving to this new definition of SDI, proponents recognize the inevitability of "leaks," a euphemism for the possibility of millions of deaths if the system is ever used.

A number of prominent officials and ex-officials support this new definition of SDI, among them Zbigniew Brzezinski, President Carter's national security adviser; Max Kampelman, the present chief U.S. arms control negotiator; and Henry Kissinger, President Nixon's secretary of state. To these supporters, even partially effective strategic defenses would cause the Soviet Union to be more uncertain about the success of any attack it might plan. Thus, it is argued, deterrence would be enhanced by U.S. strategic defenses even without a comprehensive or leak-proof shield. But as former Secretary of Defense Robert S. McNamara has made clear, "this assumes that the Soviet military's sole concern is to attack us and that any uncertainty in their minds is therefore to our advantage. But any suspicion they may harbor about our wishing to achieve a first-strike capability . . . would be inflamed by a partially effective defense. Moreover, there are much cheaper and less dangerous ways [than SDI] of achieving the same objective."[26]

The Council of the American Physical Society drew a similar conclusion when it issued a statement including the following three points:

1. Even a very small percentage of nuclear weapons penetrating a defensive system would cause human suffering and death far beyond that ever before seen on this planet.

2. It is likely to be decades, if ever, before an effective, reliable, and survivable defensive system could be deployed.
3. Development of prototypes or deployment of SDI components in a state of technological uncertainty risks enormous waste of financial and human resources.[27]

These points make clear some of the major drawbacks of a partial shield, but it would be wrong to assume in the light of these points that a partial shield was nevertheless feasible. Even Lowell Wood, the scientist in charge of Lawrence Livermore Laboratory's O Group of SDI scientists, has not gone so far as to assert the technical feasibility of strategic defense.

> To do so I believe would be intellectually dishonest. Whether or not strategic defense will be technically feasible a half-dozen years hence will become generally known only a half-dozen years hence. And anyone who presumes to tell you now what will be true that far away in this complicated area is frankly a confidence man. If he isn't reaching for your wallet he probably wants your vote or your political contribution, which is a more popular form of theft against which the law provides no protection.[28]

Facilitating Strategic Reductions

In its search for a new and more credible vision for the Strategic Defense Initiative, the Reagan administration has most recently created a new definition of SDI—to make massive reductions in strategic forces more feasible and stable. According to this definition, SDI is necessary so that Soviet cheating can have no militarily significant effect once nuclear arsenals are enormously reduced. If this is its real purpose, however, SDI need not be concerned with deployments in the near future. Further, the development of strategic defenses by one side in advance of its adversary would create an environment in which significant reductions would destabilize the strategic balance and the adversary would be unwilling to carry through with its reductions. In addition, if strategic arsenals are reduced and one of the superpowers deploys strategic defenses before the other, it might risk a preemptive strike while its adversary's retaliatory capability was relatively minimal.

A Means of Developing Technologies

Some proponents of Star Wars reject the notion that strategic defense will either replace or reinforce deterrence but support the program as a means of developing important new "spin-off technologies" for commercial use, particularly in the fields of lasers, computers, particle beams, and space.

Unfortunately, the spin-off theory overlooks two critical issues. Investing in military research as a means of producing civilian sector innovations is extraordinarily wasteful and inefficient in comparison to direct funding of civilian sector research and development. Although military research once returned more than its cost to the private economy in the form of consumer goods improvements, the process has now reversed. The Packard Commission on the reorganization of the Department of Defense reported in 1985 that "military research is now so exotic and so slow in reaching fruition that it offers little commercial use. In fact, the Pentagon is now a 'net user' of commercial research."[29]

Although they may recognize that the civilian sector benefits of SDI might be more efficiently and cheaply attained if pursued directly instead of as a by-product of a military program, proponents of SDI hold that research in many areas would be unlikely if it were not for military spending.

> Weapons research, they say, has been a key element in technological progress throughout history, and has nearly always produced byproducts of immense value to mankind. Costly though World War II was in human suffering and destruction, for example, wartime research bequeathed a cornucopia of consolation prizes to the survivors, including plastics, synthetic textiles, antibiotics, jet aircraft and nuclear energy.[30]

However, to the degree that funding of military research and development does succeed in producing technologies with commercial spinoff possibilities, the second flaw to the spin-off theory is that these technologies are frequently classified because of their military significance and are therefore not made available for civilian applications.

> "Most of the technology in SDI just doesn't have any equivalent application in the commercial sector," says Arvid G. Larson, principal at Booz Allen and Hamilton, Inc. and a consultant to SDI. Furthermore, by shifting resources to military projects, he argues, SDI may actually impair business R&D. "Megaprojects like SDI take some of the most sophisticated and best people away from commercial R&D," says consultant Edward E. David, White House science adviser to President Nixon. . . .
>
> "There have been spinoffs from military technology in the past," says Booz Allen's Larson, "but SDI does not fall into that category." For example, experts doubt that laser weapons could be turned to industrial use. "These lasers are fun to look at and talk about," says Wolfgang H. Demisch, aerospace analyst at First Boston Corporation, "but there sure as hell aren't going to be direct spinoffs. . . . " David, Nixon's science adviser, says, "Researchers

are being drawn into aerospace and computer-related fields, and in the meantime our manufacturing technology is going to the dogs."[31]

Economic Warfare

Although economic warfare has never been used as an official rationale for the Strategic Defense Initiative, many proponents of the program in the United States and Western Europe view it as a means of placing severe pressure on, if not ultimately bankrupting, the Soviet economy without resorting to armed conflict. Advocates of this strategy remain confident that with its vastly greater wealth and productivity, the U.S. economy can support the unprecedented expense of mounting a strategic defense far more easily than the moribund Soviet economy.

Nevertheless, Soviet authorities have consistently demonstrated their determination to keep pace with U.S. military developments regardless of the cost to their domestic economy. Although the Gorbachev regime has placed great emphasis on improving the supply and quality of consumer goods, the Soviet government can be expected to defer such improvements if it feels this is necessary to assure its military security. U.S. society, by contrast, may politically resist enormous sacrifices for the sake of a military project of uncertain effectiveness and no immediate payoff. Furthermore, despite its considerable relative strength, the U.S. economy is already showing signs of strain, and information from the Central Intelligence Agency indicates that the Soviet Union has and will continue to have the ability to direct resources toward military competition, at an accelerated pace if necessary. Faced with hard times, it is easier politically for the Soviet government to dictate a hard line to its citizens than it is for the U.S. government to persuade its people to voluntarily accept the equivalent.

Problems Facing SDI

The final outcome of the Strategic Defense Initiative remains unclear. Already, however, SDI has focused attention on various problems with the deployment of proposed strategic defense systems. These problems apply equally to the creation of a comprehensive shield to protect against all strategic weapons and to the creation of a partial shield to protect U.S. retaliatory forces against an ICBM attack.

Robert Bowman, former head of the Air Force Systems Command Space Division, has said in reference to the various "Star Wars" schemes:

> All have staggering technical problems. All are likely to cost on the order of a trillion dollars. All violate one or more existing treaties. All are extremely vulnerable. All are subject to a series of counter-measures. All could be made

impotent by a series of alternative offensive missiles and therefore would be likely to ignite the numerical arms race in offensive weapons. All would, if they worked, be more effective as part of a first strike than against one. Most important, all would be extremely destabilizing, probably triggering the nuclear war both sides are trying to prevent.[32]

Cost

Even if we put aside the issue of the technical feasibility of an effective space-based shield against ballistic missiles, there is the question of cost. Current estimates of the ultimate price of the system over a twenty-year period reach in excess of $1 trillion, depending on the system envisioned.[33] At the low end of the estimates, Lt. Gen. (Ret.) Daniel O. Graham, director of High Frontier and chairman of the Coalition for the Strategic Defense Initiative, said that the United States can deploy "a light defense against ICBMs for the entire country, all of populated Canada and a large part of Mexico . . . in five years for $3 billion. . . . Such a defense would be adequate to defend the population from at least the accidental launch of a few missiles."[34] Robert Jastrow, a physicist at Dartmouth College, founder and director for twenty years of NASA's Goddard Institute for Space Studies, and author of *How to Make Nuclear Weapons Obsolete*, said a more sophisticated defense based on "smart bullets"—slugs of metal guided by computers and heat-seeking devices—could be deployed in five years at a cost of $50 billion.[35] More recently Jastrow, joined by three other scientists, reassessed this estimate in a report for the George C. Marshall Institute, advocating a similar strategic defense system at an estimated cost of $121 billion.[36]

Paul Nitze, chief arms control adviser to the President, has repeatedly stated that strategic defenses must be cost-effective—that is, they must be less expensive to deploy than it would cost the Soviet Union to counter them with new offensive missiles. The Soviets have pledged to build whatever offensive ICBM force is necessary to overwhelm this new defense. But such offensive countermeasures at present cost far less than defenses deployed to repel them. As Edward Teller once said bluntly, "I believe we should not deploy weapons in space. . . . To put objects in space is expensive. To destroy space objects is relatively easy."[37]

In December 1986, the Soviet Union announced that it planned to develop countermeasures to SDI that could "at a relatively modest cost and with relatively simple technology . . . neutralize the proposed space-based weaponry or force the United States to spend unacceptably large amounts of money on it."[38] A report from the Council on Economic Priorities estimates that countermeasures "would cost 3 percent to 10 percent of the estimated costs of SDI deployment. The costs [of Soviet countermeasures] . . . would be comparable to the cost of our SDI research program alone."[39]

SDI: Progress and Challenges, prepared for several members of the Senate Defense Appropriations Subcommittee, stated that the SDIO receives funding equivalent to the technology-based research and development programs of all the armed services combined.

> The FY1987 budget request would more than quadruple the SDI budget in just four years. Despite the magnitude of this request, SDIO has yet to produce a definite set of systems architectures, which can be tested against a generated and realistic set of threat scenarios. In fact, there appears to have been no consensus reached on the range of threat scenarios these deployment options might be expected to face. . . .
>
> Furthermore, it is disturbing that despite a tripling of its budget the past three years, the SDIO has been unable or unwilling to develop any cost estimate for deployment and maintenance of a comprehensive strategic defense system. SDIO's statement that it will estimate what these defenses *should* cost is not enough. Congress needs to know what these defenses *will* cost.[40]

Much attention has been given to the astronomical costs of building a sophisticated, layered defense capable of intercepting missiles in their boost (or initial), postboost, midcourse, and reentry phases of flight. Even if this was feasible and affordable, the cost of lifting satellites into orbit is still prohibitive. General Abrahamson of SDIO has estimated that it costs $1,500 per pound to shoot materials into orbit. He acknowledges that this is approximately ten times too expensive, given the enormous number and weight of satellites needed. (Robert Mozley of the Stanford Linear Acceleration Center has made a study of the cost of orbiting materials and feels that General Abrahamson's figure is roughly half what it actually costs at present to put materials in orbit. Thus current dollar per pound lift costs may be closer to twenty times too expensive.)[41]

Finally, relatively little attention has been given to the maintenance of a system once it is in place. The electrical power needed for drive-directed energy weapons, like particle beam accelerators, is approximately one gigawatt (or one billion watts).

> This power could be provided by large chemical or nuclear rocket engines and generators, deployed at considerable distances or otherwise decoupled from the DEW platforms in order to avoid mechanical disturbances and effects of exhaust gases. This may require complex power transfer systems comprising cables, microwave systems, etc. Correspondingly, chemical fuel consumption would be more than five tons per minute of operation per platform.[42]

In addition to the direct costs of SDI, there are indirect costs in terms of the scientific brain power being diverted from other pressing endeavors. This loss is already evident. The U.S. nonmilitary space program, for example, is in an unprecedented state of decline. Because of the enormous funding for SDI, the National Aeronautics and Space Administration (NASA) is finding, on the one hand, that resources for its programs are becoming increasingly scarce and, on the other hand, that military influence and control over its own programs is mounting. The long-term ramifications of this trend may well be devastating. By letting U.S. nonmilitary space ventures lose vitality, policymakers are forfeiting the economic, political, and scientific benefits that would most likely result from a space exploration program. The cost lies also in allowing adversaries to gain advantage in areas that the United States is not addressing sufficiently. The Soviet Union seems well aware of this fact, and may well outperform the United States in space in years to come.

> The space gap is already a reality. The Russians conducted 90 percent of all space activities during 1986, according to the industry magazine *Aviation Week and Space Technology*. The Soviet Union's space station is now operational. A number of unmanned space science missions are being prepared for launch. A new booster, the equal of our abandoned Saturn V, sits on a launch pad.[43]

Finally, as potentially the most expensive project in world history, SDI raises important questions about the impact of unprecedented spending on an economy already burdened with record debts and an ailing industrial infrastructure.

Vulnerability

Orbiting strategic defense structures are relatively easy targets to destroy by comparison to the weapons that they are intended to destroy and that might be used against them. As the head of the U.S. negotiating team for arms control talks, Paul Nitze, has stated, no strategic defense is worthwhile as long as the space-based structures it depends upon remain highly vulnerable. In fact, it is downright dangerous. Both the United States and the Soviet Union have lasers capable of "blinding" photoreconnaissance satellites and the capability to deploy space mines that could destroy any existing satellite. They would cost a fraction of the expense of the space structures required for a strategic defense system. Moreover, SDI space structures would most likely operate in low orbits for maximum efficiency, where they would be most vulnerable to attack. Ironically, technology developed for SDI will be more effective to destroy rather than to protect these structures because

1. strategic defenses must handle many targets at once while weapons to counter strategic defenses can be more selective;
2. weapons against strategic defense may need to harm only part of the system to incapacitate it, but strategic defenses cannot remove the threat of counterweapons without the assurance of a much higher "hit" rate;
3. weapons against strategic defenses can attack at any time, while strategic defense weapons must respond to the timing of the adversary's attack; and
4. strategic defenses will be located in space rather than on friendly territory, where the weapons used against them will be based.

Estimates on the number of satellites needed for an effective space-based shield are high, compounding the problem of vulnerability. Aside from antisatellite weapons that home in on their targets, space debris will also cause severe problems for satellite survival. Space debris occurs naturally but can be inexpensively created intentionally to devastate satellite systems of far greater value. The American Physical Society's 1987 report concludes, on the basis of extensive technical analysis of SDI, that the survivability of the space-based system is "highly questionable" given that countermeasures that go beyond present capabilities "may be less difficult and costly to develop."[44]

> Any strategic defense system depending on ground based lasers, or on other ground based facilities which cannot be extensively proliferated, must be effective in defending against more threats than just ballistic missiles [including cruise missiles and sabotage]. . . . If a DEW [directed energy weapon] falls short of ballistic missile defense requirements, it may still be a credible threat to space-based assets. Space-based platforms move in known orbits and can therefore be targeted over much longer time spans than ballistic missile boosters, post-boost buses or re-entry vehicles. The defense platforms may have key components that are more vulnerable than the boosters and the re-entry vehicles. . . . X-ray lasers driven by nuclear explosions would constitute a special threat to space based sensors, electronics and optics.
>
> Since a long time will be required to develop and deploy an effective ballistic missile defense, it follows that a considerable time will be available for responses by the offense. Any defense will have to be designed to handle a variety of responses since a specific threat can not be predicted accurately in advance of deployment. . . . A DEW system designed for today's threats is likely to be inadequate for the threat that it will face when deployed.[45]

The irony of the issue of vulnerability is that SDI has undermined arms control negotiations and past agreements and may continue to do so, while at the same time it appears extremely probable that any space-based defense will only become survivable by means of a treaty.

Loss of Human Control

Computers must be used to recognize, verify, track, and destroy missiles in the first three to three and one-half minutes after launching. After this "boost phase" the missiles' warheads separate, and the number of targets is significantly increased. Further, each target is only a few feet long, travels at approximately four miles a second without an easily identifiable fiery plume, and is protected by a heat shield capable of withstanding the friction of atmospheric reentry. Each can also be hidden among a large number of accompanying decoys that cannot be distinguished from real warheads with existing technologies. This situation can be aggravated by speeding up the missiles' boost phase, reducing it to last only 100 to 150 seconds.

Thus, space-based strategic defenses pose an unfortunate choice. Either computers recognize, verify, track, and decide to attack incoming missiles, or human control of this process is required. Human control, however, negates the effectiveness of the system. Necessary decisions made without the help of computers allow attacking missiles enough time to be well on their way and make them much harder to intercept. But relegating these processes to computers could be even more devastating.[46] This problem is emphasized by the record of existing early warning systems. Between 1977 and 1984 the U.S. early warning system generated 20,784 false indications of incoming missiles.[47] A crisis could occur because of faulty computer chips, mistakes in programming, mechanical failures, human error, or a wide range of other possibilities. Recognizing these dangers, several top computer experts have resigned from SDI software development, believing that its goals cannot be attained.[48]

A 900-page Congressional report from the nonpartisan Office of Technology Assessment evaluating SDI's computer technology capabilities concluded that it would most likely suffer "a catastrophic failure." Release of the report was prevented in the early part of 1988 by the Strategic Defense Initiative Organization (SDIO) because it was critical of the program, "said an expert who asked not to be identified."[49] The report stated that software problems would make even an early deployment system of existing technologies unworkable.

> Ashton T. Carter, a physicist who is Associate Director of the Harvard Center for Science and International Affairs and a Defense Department consultant with extensive knowledge of SDI, said that he had seen the report and that it offered further evidence of why the system should not be deployed. . . .

> "This is just another carefully done study of SDI that brings the whole thing into question," Mr. Carter said. "What is different about this report, which is one of the most extensive ever done, is that it focusses on the near-term, early deployment of the Phase I system."[50]

Satellite Security

The development of strategic defenses will inevitably affect the security of existing satellites, as almost any advance in technology to intercept and destroy missiles will also be an advance in the technology of antisatellite weaponry. As U.S. satellites are generally more sophisticated and expensive than their Soviet counterparts are, and as the Soviet Union is already in the habit of replacing its satellites much more frequently than the United States does, any space competition that will increase the vulnerability of space-based technology is likely to undermine the U.S. advantages in the deployment of satellite technology. Although neither superpower may be successful in deploying an effective shield against ICBMs, both may well develop more threatening antisatellite weapons in the process of pursuing other space weapons. In effect, both superpowers might create a situation where the survival of their technology was less likely, but given the differences between Soviet and U.S. satellites, this may well be a situation in which the United States has more to lose.

Other Problems

Furthermore, in concentrating on defenses against ICBMs, SDI does not counter the threats posed by nuclear weapons delivered by other means—bombers (including so-called stealth technologies), shorter range missiles, and most menacing of all, cruise missiles. Undetectable in flight by radar and largely unverifiable by existing means of surveillance, such weapons are being rapidly introduced into the U.S. and Soviet arsenals. In addition, countermeasures like the miniaturization of nuclear weapons pose far less of a problem than the many difficulties involved in deploying an effective strategic defense. Thus, the proposed SDI defenses are rapidly being rendered obsolete by our own simultaneous development of less detectable weapons and more effective means of delivering them.

SDI's Effect on the War-making Capability of Nations

Although theoretically missile defenses might limit the vulnerability of those nations that deploy them, they would do nothing to limit the war-making capability of any nation. Research alone for strategic defense requires increases in expenditures and intensifies military competition, and testing and deployment of such systems launches the arms race into the new arena of space, establishing the war-making potential of nations for the first time in the realm beyond the earth. Once anchored there, it might prove as resistant to removal as the enormous arms establishment already entrenched on earth.

Focused on the singular threat of ICBMs, strategic defense does not address security in a broad sense and thus does not constitute a comprehensive alternative to the present system. Not only does it fail to meet the threats posed by new offensive technologies and existing conventional weaponry, but it creates its own new threats as well. If perfected for the interception of enemy missiles, rail gun, particle beam, and laser technologies may need little adaptation for use as offensive weapons. Indeed, the only way to make an offensive weapon more threatening than existing nuclear missiles would be to create a comparable weapon with greater speed and precision. This is exactly what strategic defense technologies intend to achieve.

Even prior to the deployment of any strategic defense system, the development period would be increasingly offensive in character. This point is underlined by recent reports of increased funding for U.S. Air Force development of advanced decoys and zig-zagging missiles capable of penetrating "any defense the Soviet Union can develop."[51] While the Defense Department is seeking to render Soviet missiles obsolete with the Strategic Defense Initiative, the air force is simultaneously seeking to "assure that American missiles never meet the same fate."[52] It seems clear, therefore, that the pursuit of antiballistic missile defenses entails increased competition in offensive weaponry, hence increased potential for warmaking. This is not surprising, as the weapons being developed under SDI are not defensive weapons in the sense that they do not have limited mobility and might be capable of effectively attacking a nation's economic lifelines or overcoming a nation's defensive forces and weaponry.

The pursuit of strategic defense can thus be interpreted either as a modification of the current system of threat-based deterrence, Mutual Assured Destruction (MAD), or as an effort to break out of this discomforting position to reestablish invulnerability while continuing to threaten one's adversary. Indeed, many observers have speculated that it is ultimately not part of a war-ending strategy but part of a war-fighting strategy.

Richard Garwin, an IBM physicist and long-time consultant to the Department of Defense, put his finger on the underlying difficulty of basing security on the development of new technology: "No matter how optimistic you are, how much of a technology fan, you cannot conclude that the 'Star Wars' program will succeed, because technology is useful in defeating the system as well."[53]

Soviet Opposition

Initial Soviet insistence that the United States abandon SDI as a precondition to an arms agreement led some observers to ask, "If SDI can't possibly succeed, why does the Soviet Union so fear and oppose it?" The Soviet leadership has no doubt that both land-based and space-based U.S. defenses can easily be developed by the SDI program to dramatically improve the effectiveness of a preemptive strike. If the United States launched a preemptive nuclear strike on the Soviet Union, a strategic defense system, even if capable of knocking out only a few of the Soviet missiles fired in response, might still significantly diminish the Soviet retaliatory capability once it had suffered a first strike.

That SDI is threatening even as an ostensibly "defensive" addition to an offensive arsenal is reinforced by former Secretary of Defense Caspar Weinberger's comment that "Soviet deployment of such advanced technologies, in concert with the Soviet Union's massive offensive forces, would make this a far more dangerous world than it is now."[54] If this is true, the Strategic Defense Initiative combined with existing U.S. offensive forces presumably is leading to a more dangerous world as well.

Of even greater concern to the Soviets is the likelihood that the project may produce new offensive "space-strike" weapons, which by themselves might prove still more threatening to the Soviet Union than existing nuclear missiles. The Soviets also fear that the United States views weaponry development as a strategy for waging economic as well as military warfare. They are aware that many U.S. proponents of SDI see it as a means of forcing the Soviet Union to compete in high technologies in which the Soviets are chronically weak, to their ultimate economic disadvantage.[55] Even if the Soviet Union does not face dire economic consequences in its efforts to compete with SDI, the program could increase pressures on the USSR and act as part of an economic containment policy to force the Soviet Union to look inward rather than out. If the Soviet Union attends to growing economic problems domestically and thus diminishes its activities outside its borders, its influence as a world power might be reduced. Soviet fear of this possibility is not diminished by the fact that SDI might be the least productive way to go about achieving this end.

The pressing question to be answered now concerning strategic defense research is not whether or not any of its objectives can be successful, but to what degree financial and human resources should be allocated to it and what checks and balances can be built into this pursuit to prevent costly deployments prior to significant strategic defense developments that are essential if strategic defense is to enhance security rather than increase the threat of nuclear war. As Senator Sam Nunn has stated:

> In this respect, I am concerned that the Administration's current and projected funding levels for SDI threaten to absorb an inordinate proportion of defense dollars allocated to research and development. Since 1981, basic research and development of new technology applications have declined from 16 percent of the Defense Department's Research, Development Testing, and Evaluation funds, to 8.7 percent in the Administration's budget request for Fiscal Year (FY) 1987. This decline coincides with buildup of the SDI program. The proposed funding level for SDI next year is larger than the entire R&D budget for the Department of the Army. I believe that the Administration's SDI funding profile in the Five Year Defense Plan is excessive in light of the absence of a basic system design for this program, and disturbing indications of basic disagreements within the Administration as to the program's goals.[56]

Ironically, many SDI proponents find something comforting about this criticism. All the disagreements and controversies concerning funding levels for the SDI program have served the purpose of distracting critics of the Reagan Strategic Modernization Program from criticizing its major components, including the MX missile, the B1 bomber, and the air-launched cruise missile.[57] Each of these programs nevertheless has serious defects (particularly the B-1 bomber) worthy of strong criticism.[58]

Given the costs of strategic defense research and development, let alone the costs of deploying a space-based defense shield, it is essential that other proposals for transforming the present security system be investigated. Further, investigating other ways in which the present security system might evolve requires immediate action. Military projects that are well funded tend to gain a momentum of their own that precludes attention to alternatives and leads to deployments even if they do not satisfy the initiatives' original or revised goals.[59] The Strategic Defense Initiative fits this description and the changing justifications for it are symptoms of an ailing program that has already become considerably entrenched.

Notes

1. Although the term "strategic defense" has been broadly defined as defense against any weapons capable of destroying the sources of military, economic, or political power within a nation, in current parlance it usually means specifically defense against intercontinental ballistic missiles (ICBMs). This may include

shelters for protection against strategic weapons (civil defense) but more frequently refers just to technologies for destroying missiles in flight.

2. William J. Broad, "Space Weapon Idea Now Being Weighed Was Assailed in '82 (Papers Show Early Concern at 'Star Wars' Idea)," *New York Times,* May 4, 1987, p. B10.

3. For several years the Pentagon and Manfred Hamm of the Heritage Foundation have promoted an awesome description of emerging Soviet strategic defense technologies. The Pentagon's 1985 edition of *Soviet Military Power* implies that Soviet programs are, if anything, much more extensive than those of the United States. See also, "Red Star Wars," *The Wall Street Journal,* April 10, 1985, and "Soviet Strategic Defense Programs," *Aerospace,* vol. 23, Fall-Winter 1985, pp. 2–7.

4. Jerome B. Wiesner and Kosta Tsipis, "Put 'Star Wars' Before a Panel," *New York Times,* November 11, 1986, p. 23.

5. Jeanette Voas, *The Geneva Negotiations on Space and Nuclear Arms: Soviet Positions and Perspectives,* Congressional Research Service, Library of Congress, February 14, 1986, pp. 14, 15. See also The Organization of the Joint Chiefs of Staff, *Military Posture for FY1986,* p. 17.

6. Voas, *Geneva Negotiations,* p. 16.

7. Ibid., p. 13. See also Robert C. McFarlane, *U.S.-Soviet Relations in the Late 20th Century,* U.S. Dept. of State Current Policy No. 733, p. 2.

8. Voas, *Geneva Negotiations,* p. 16.

9. Ware Myers, "The Star Wars Software Debate," *Bulletin of the Atomic Scientists,* February 1986, p. 32.

10. William J. Broad, "Science Showmanship: A Deep 'Star Wars' Rift," *New York Times,* November 11, 1986, p. 1. See also Charles Mohr, "Scientist Quits Anti-Missile Panel, Saying Task is Impossible," *New York Times,* July 12, 1985, p. 7.

11. Myers, "The Star Wars Software Debate," p. 31.

12. Douglas Waller, James Bruce, and Douglas Cook, *SDI: Progress and Challenges,* staff report submitted to Senator William Proxmire, Senator J. Bennett Johnston, and Senator Lawton Chiles, March 17, 1986, pp. 1, 3, 4.

13. Ibid., p. 2.

14. Ibid., pp. 3, 4.

15. Malcolm W. Browne, "The Star Wars Spinoff," *New York Times,* August 24, 1986, Sec. 6, p. 69.

16. "Doubt Cast on Missile Shield," *New York Times,* October 31, 1986, p. A36. See also *The Strategic Defense Initiative—A Survey of the National Academy of Sciences,* December 17, 1986. The survey also indicates that NAS members, the preeminent leaders of U.S. science, believe, by a margin of eleven to one, that SDI research does not warrant the $3.5 billion per year appropriation to which Congress had just consented at the time the report was released.

17. "Top Physicists Express Doubt About 'Star Wars' Weapons in Study," *New York Times,* April 23, 1987, p. A6.

18. David E. Sanger, "Missile Defense: New Turn in Debate," *New York Times,* April 24, 1987, p. A8.

19. The members of the American Physical Society Study Group on the Science and Technology of Directed Energy Weapons were Nicolas Bloembergen (cochairman), Harvard University; C.K.N. Patel (cochairman), AT&T Bell Laboratories; Petras Avizonis, Air Force Weapons Laboratory; Robert Clem, Sandia National Laboratories; Abraham Hertzberg, University of Washington; Thomas H. Johnson, U.S. Military Academy; Thomas Marshall, Columbia University; Bruce Miller, Sandia National Laboratories; Walter Morrow, Lincoln Laboratories, MIT; Edwin Salpeter, Cornell University; Andrew Sessler, Lawrence Berkeley Laboratory; Jeremiah Sullivan, University of Illinois, Urbana; James C. Wyant, University of Arizona; Amnon Yariv, California Institute of Technology; Richard N. Zare, Stanford University; A. J. Glass (principal consultant), KMS Fusion, Inc.; L. Charles Hebel (executive secretary), Xerox PARC. The Review Committee included: George E. Pake (chairman), Xerox Corporation; Michael A. May, Lawrence Livermore Laboratory; W. K. Panofsky, Stanford University; Arthur L. Schawlow, Stanford University; Charles H. Townes, University of California, Berkeley; Herbert F. York, University of California, San Diego.

20. "Top Physicists Express Doubt About 'Star Wars' Weapons in Study," p. A6.

21. *Science and Technology of Directed Energy Weapons*, Report of the American Physical Society Study Group, April 1987, Executive Summary and Major Conclusions, p. 11.

22. Sanger, "Missle Defense: New Turn in Debate," p. A8.

23. Statement adopted by the Council of the American Physical Society on April 24, 1987.

24. Ibid.

25. Some people have suggested that a partial shield should be pursued to protect people from terrorist use of nuclear weapons where protection from an enormous arsenal would not be required. It is, however, ridiculous to assume that a terrorist group would be likely to go to the trouble and expense of delivering its warheads by ballistic missile.

26. Robert S. McNamara, *Blundering into Disaster* (New York: Pantheon, 1986), p. 98.

27. Statement adopted by the Council of the American Physical Society on April 24, 1987.

28. Lord Zuckerman, "Reagan's Highest Folly," *New York Review of Books*, April 9, 1987, pp. 37–38. From a transcript of a public debate held at the University of California, Berkeley, on October 9, 1986.

29. Quoted in Glenn R. Pascall, "The Impact of Defense Spending on the American Economy," Business Executives for National Security Education Fund, March 1986, p. 10.

30. Browne, "The Star Wars Spinoff," p. 20.

31. Fred V. Guterl, "Star Wars Is Bad For Business," *Dun's Business Month*, September 1986, pp. 56–58.

32. Helen Caldicott, *Missile Envy: The Arms Race and Nuclear War*, revised ed. (New York: Bantam, 1986), pp. 46–47.

33. See Charles E. Bennett, "The Rush to Deploy SDI," *Atlantic Monthly*, vol. 261, no. 4 (April 1988), p. 60, which states that it may cost $1 trillion just

to launch an SDI system and quotes Louis Marquet, former SDI deputy director of technology, as saying that $100 billion will be needed just to reach the starting line for production of an early deployment system.

34. Daniel O. Graham, "SDI Does Not Aim for Perfection," *Defense News*, September 22, 1986.

35. Robert Jastrow, "SDI Results: A Defense in Five Years," *Washington Times*, August 8, 1986.

36. J. Gardner, E. T. Gerry, R. Jastrow, W. A. Nierenberg, and F. Seitz, "Missile Defense in the 1990s" (Washington, DC: George C. Marshall Institute, 1987), p. 8.

37. Quoted in Bennett, "The Rush to Deploy SDI," p. 58.

38. Phillip Taubman, "Moscow Planning Anti-'Star Wars'," *New York Times*, December 18, 1986, p. 5.

39. Alice Tepper Marlin and Rosy Nimroody, "'Star Wars' Benefits Are an Illusion with Mirrors," *New York Times* (Letters to the Editor), November 14, 1986, p. 26.

40. Waller, Bruce, and Cook, *SDI: Progress and Challenges*, pp. 2, 4.

41. Zuckerman, "Reagan's Highest Folly," p. 40.

42. *Science and Technology of Directed Energy Weapons*, pp. 11, 12.

43. Don Eyles, "Moscow Is Gaining an Edge in Space," *New York Times*, April 21, 1987, p. A31.

44. "Space Weapon Idea now Being Weighed Was Assailed in '82," p. B10.

45. *Science and Technology of Directed Energy Weapons*, pp. 12, 13.

46. See P. M. Boffey, W. J. Broad, L. H. Gelb, C. Mohr, and H. B. Noble, *Claiming the Heavens: The New York Times Complete Guide to the Star Wars Debate* (New York: Random House, 1988), which discusses the problem of writing programs that cannot realistically be tested and debugged. Robert Taylor, former head of computer research for the Defense Advanced Research Projects Agency, is quoted about the feasibility of the required programming: "It can't be done." John Backus, inventor of FORTRAN, states that "a single error in either their program or ours could cause an unprovoked attack and initiate a devastating computer-controlled war."

47. "Accidental Nuclear War: A Rising Risk?" *Defense Monitor*, Vol. 12, no. 3, (Washington, DC: Center for Defense Information, 1986), p. 1.

48. Philip M. Boffey, "Software Seen as Obstacle in Developing 'Star Wars,'" *New York Times*, September 16, 1986, p. 15.

49. Warren E. Leary, "'Star Wars' Runs into New Criticism," *New York Times*, April 25, 1988, p. A8.

50. Ibid.

51. Philip M. Boffey, "Research Success Marks Recent Days for 'Star Wars,'" *New York Times*, February 9, 1985, pp. C1, C8.

52. Ibid.

53. Ibid.

54. Caspar W. Weinberger, *Annual Report to the Congress*, FY1986, pp. 56–57.

55. Flora Lewis, "Soviet SDI Fears," *New York Times*, March 6, 1986, p. 27.

56. Letter from Sam Nunn, April 2, 1987.

57. Ron Lehman expressed this view to Richard Garwin, Len Meeker, and Jonathan Dean when they visited him in the old Executive Office Building (personal communication, Richard Garwin, May 29, 1987).

58. See Molly Moore, "Serious Problems Could Cripple the B-1 Bomber for Years," *International Herald Tribune,* August 11, 1987, pp. 1, 6.

59. See Bennett, "The Rush to Deploy SDI," which gives a detailed description of how the initiative has been transformed into the rapid development of a system of existing technologies with the intent by the Department of Defense to make it "Congress-proof," regardless of scientific or strategic merit, by converting defense dollars into job-based political support.

PART TWO

Keeping the Peace: Issues Common to All Approaches

CHAPTER TEN

Verification: Substituting Information for Weapons

Under every system of alternative security considered in this book, adequate machinery for verifying compliance will be essential to the success of the arrangement. Without confidence in the reliability of its data concerning reductions in the weapons stockpiles of its adversaries, no nation will accept the dismantling of its own arsenal. Conversely, if each party to an agreement is able to verify to its own satisfaction that all parties are heeding its terms, all will be that much more committed to continuing the process.

Verification procedures serve three principal functions: to deter violations and ensure treaty compliance; to detect any variations from agreed arms limitations; and to promote public confidence in arms control and disarmament agreements. The machinery of verification encompasses a broad array of capabilities and arrangements—some technical, others administrative, some national, and others bilateral or multilateral. Many are already in existence, while a few, primarily international verification institutions, have simply been proposed. Current verification techniques may be broadly classed in three categories: unilateral means, bilateral cooperative measures, and international verification systems. Unilateral measures predominate in the present deterrence system, but under any viable disarmament agreement cooperative measures will necessarily become more central.

National Technical Means

The principal method of verification of arms control that has been relied upon since the 1960s is called "national technical means," which comprises essentially every instrumental device or system that each nation can think to devise to find out everything it can about the other's military activities. It is an inclusive term, left deliberately vague by all parties to permit development of the broadest range of capabilities without disclosing sources of information. This secrecy is also thought to exert a deterrent effect on a potential violator, who must always labor under the inhibiting knowledge that someone may be watching.

Satellite and Aerial Reconnaissance

The sophistication and sensitivity of these various imaging systems constitute the single most important means of treaty verification, and their capabilities have improved dramatically over the past quarter century. Satellite and aerial surveillance have reached so fine a degree of resolution that so-called close-look satellites are capable of distinguishing objects a foot or less across from a distance of a few hundred miles. "You can see the tanks, you see the artillery, but you may not quite see the insignia on the fellow's uniform," said William Colby, former director of the CIA.[1] The U.S. Air Force's SR-71, nicknamed "Blackbird," can survey 100,000 square miles from 15 miles above the earth in just one hour and includes a pair of cameras that automatically produce 1,800 overlapping photographs of up to 1,600 miles of terrain with a ground resolution of as little as 12 inches.[2] In addition to these optical means of surveillance, which operate in the visible light spectrum, there is a range of infrared imaging systems (including photographic and thermal), which register the heat radiating from objects and activities not otherwise visible or hidden underground. Though incapable of the degree of resolution achieved by visible-light photography, thermal imaging can detect large clandestine industrial operations and would be useful in verifying a shutdown of plutonium production facilities under a system of comprehensive disarmament.

Radar

Capable of penetrating darkness and cloud cover, radar constitutes a second major category of national technical means, "an all-time, all-weather sensor . . . not limited by any environmental factor."[3] The most sophisticated among these installations are capable of tracking as many as 100 vehicles at once from a distance of 2,000 km, precisely calculating their speed and trajectories. This capability is vital for tracing a potentially massive attack by thousands of missile warheads equipped with MIRVs (multiple independently targeted reentry vehicles). For the purposes of verification, three types of radar are most relevant: large ground- or ship-based phased-array radars (PARs), used for early warning of attack, missile test monitoring, and space object tracking; over-the-horizon (OTH) radars, used to observe distant objects hidden from line-of-sight radars by the curvature of the earth; and synthetic aperture radars (SARs), used to produce high-resolution images of objects on the ground from aircraft or satellites.[4] Synthetic aperture radars now generate detailed computer-enhanced images with high resolution.

Seismic Instruments

Seismic technologies have been under development for more than thirty years and a vast body of literature on the subject now exists in the public domain. Designed in part to detect clandestine underground nuclear tests, seismic monitors measure the vibrations triggered by terrestrial disturbances thousands of miles away. Seismic instruments are now sufficiently sensitive to distinguish between nuclear explosions and natural earthquakes down to 1 kiloton, a level below which little useful information could likely be gleaned from a test. Even so-called decoupled explosions, detonated in dry alluvium or large underground cavities to reduce the apparent yield of a nuclear test, can now be effectively detected. Extensive feasibility studies have also explored the possibility of placing a network of unmanned, tamperproof seismic "black boxes" throughout the territory of each party to a test ban agreement to monitor possible violations and assure compliance.

Electronic Signal Collection

In addition to these relatively well-documented verification technologies, intelligence devices to intercept the signals and communications of friends and foes alike constitute a vast additional set of lesser-known capabilities. These techniques range from the tapping of telephones to the interception of missile telemetry during flight tests to the monitoring by satellites of microwave transmissions from earth-based transmitters. Termed SIGINT (signals intelligence) and COMINT (communications intelligence) by the U.S. intelligence community, this information is gleaned from a wide variety of electronic systems, including radar, radio transmitters, beacons, transponders, and ferrets (electronic satellites to listen in on military radio communications and signals from missile tests).

The National Security Agency (NSA), one of two U.S. agencies assigned to gather electronic intelligence, reportedly seeks to collect and preserve "*all* Soviet radio transmissions, including the full daily broadcast of every conventional radio station in all the Soviet republics, every transmission to every embassy abroad, every broadcast to a ship at sea, every transmission by military units on maneuvers in Eastern Europe, the radio traffic of every control tower at Soviet airports."[5] In addition to these relatively open sources, the great powers also monitor many of one another's most tightly secured personal communications.

In sum, wrote verification specialist Allan Krass,

> this capability to monitor virtually all of the communications of another state must act as a powerful inhibiting factor on any attempts by that state to carry out clandestine activities, especially activities which require the cooperation of several separate facilities and substantial numbers of people. Almost any significant violation of an arms control agreement would fit this definition and would therefore face serious risks of discovery unless highly elaborate and expensive precautions were taken, precautions which would not only reduce the efficiency of the clandestine activity, but which might in themselves arouse suspicion and increased attention.[6]

National Nontechnical Means: Human Intelligence

In addition to the technically based capabilities described above, both superpowers and many other nations as well utilize a wide variety of nontechnical means to gather information about one another. Termed HUMINT by the U.S. intelligence community, the data is gathered by two chief means: gleaning the open sources (newspapers, periodicals, published research journals, and the like), and espionage. Almost nothing is admitted by governments or written about the activities of spies by the reputable research community. The enormous body of literature on the subject in popular fiction and the mass media is not likely a reliable source of information. But that spying exists and is extensive can be assumed. Though not officially considered a legitimate means of verification, espionage is in practice factored into the composite image each nation maintains of the activities and capabilities of its adversaries and allies.

Existing Cooperative Measures

National technical and nontechnical means alone will not suffice to detect the increasingly invisible weapons now being developed. So-called cooperative measures, involving a modest degree of collaboration between the superpowers to facilitate their independent procedures of verification, have already played a significant role in verifying the SALT agreements and can be expected to grow in importance in any future accords.

The Standing Consultative Commission

The Standing Consultative Commission (SCC) is a U.S.-Soviet joint forum where questions and complaints regarding alleged infractions of treaties can be discussed and resolved. Established by the ABM Treaty, it has been called "probably the single most creative and significant product of the SALT process."[7] By most accounts, prior to the Reagan administration, the commission operated with admirable efficiency. Nearly all the issues that were brought before the body were resolved. Many were found upon investigation to have been misinterpretations of data. In other cases, the very act of making the complaint caused the violator to cease the proscribed activity. During the 1980s the SCC has been increasingly bypassed as the superpowers have traded public charges of noncompliance, a strategy that has strained U.S.-Soviet relations without resolving the issues themselves. Still, the SCC has proven itself to be a useful and effective forum for certain specific purposes and provides an embryonic model for future disarmament agreements. Though it presently includes just the United States and the Soviet Union, it could readily be extended from a bilateral to a multilateral arrangement.

Data Exchanges, Counting Rules, and Dismantling Procedures

Other cooperative measures include the development of various arms control protocols designed to make the task of independent verification easier. These protocols include counting rules, data exchanges, agreed data bases, and functionally related observable differences (FRODs). Counting rules include, for example, requirements that any missile tested with MIRV capabilities be counted as a MIRVed missile. Agreed data bases, established during SALT II negotiations, provide for the exchange of information between the United States and USSR about their respective weapons systems, enhancing verification for both by allowing each side to measure its monitoring capabilities through cross-checking with the other's data. FRODs, established by SALT II, provide for readily observable differences to be designed into certain weapons systems to make them distinguishable by an adversary's national technical means from other similar-seeming systems with different capabilities. So, for example, FRODs are used to distinguish launchers of MIRVed from non-MIRVed ICBMs. Existing cooperative measures also include agreed dismantling and destruction procedures, designed to make the process totally visible to reconnaissance satellites and to take the disassembling process sufficiently far that reassembling the weapons would be as time consuming as building them anew.

Proposed International Means of Verification

All of the aforementioned technologies and techniques are now in existence; most are controlled exclusively by one or the other of the two superpowers. Multilateral institutions of verification, none of which yet exist, will likely become increasingly necessary, especially in the event of comprehensive disarmament. The problem, in brief, is that as long as only the two primary contestants in the arms race control the data base, only they are in a position to keep score. Given the antipathy that characterizes all aspects of the U.S.-Soviet relationship, their accountings of one another's arsenals are all too likely to exaggerate the threat while diminishing the visible profile of their own menacing activities. There is no referee in the contest, no independent source of information to verify the truth of each power's allegations against the other.

To provide an impartial source of information to verify arms control agreements (as well as to monitor developing crises and unusual troop movements), various proposals have been made to establish an international verification capability. Introducing the McCloy-Zorin Agreements to the UN General Assembly, President Kennedy proposed to put "the final responsibility for verification and control where it belongs—not with the big powers alone, not with one's adversary or one's self, but in an international organization within the framework of the United Nations."[8]

International Satellite Monitoring Agency

In 1978 the French government introduced at the United Nations a proposal to establish an international satellite monitoring agency (ISMA) under UN auspices. A three-year UN study[9] resulted in a technical report concluding that such an agency would be both feasible and desirable, at a cost of not more than 1 percent of what the major nations now spend on weapons. The UN plan calls for a three-stage process of development. Phase 1 establishes a data processing and interpretation center while still utilizing information from existing (national) sources. Phase 2 establishes the agency's own ground receiving stations, and Phase 3 establishes the agency's own space satellite system. The proposal was brought before the General Assembly in 1983 and endorsed by more than one hundred nations. Due to the uncharacteristically united opposition of both the United States and Soviet Union, however, the proposal was not enacted, and as of 1988 remained a promising but unfulfilled idea.

International Seismic Data Exchange

A similar proposal has been made more recently by Jerome Wiesner, former presidential science adviser and ex-president of MIT. His "international arms verification and study center"[10] would collect and process photographic, seismic, and other pertinent information made available by its own and other accessible sources. It would maintain a cadre of technical and legal analysts to interpret data and treaty provisions, as well as a staff of inspectors to monitor compliance with arms control agreements. The Swedish government has also conducted an extensive research program to consider the feasibility of establishing an international seismic network and data exchange system that would permit all states equal access to seismic data related to nuclear tests.

A number of commentators have suggested that these and other functions would most effectively be clustered into one comprehensive organization. Alva Myrdal, the Swedish disarmament advocate, has proposed the establishment of an International Disarmament Control Organization to act as a clearinghouse to provide information about the implementation of disarmament agreements. She stipulates that the IDCO "should never itself pronounce verdicts. It should only assemble, collate, coordinate and transmit data."[11] Whatever international systems of verification are considered, nations other than the superpowers will need to take the initiative. For whereas the superpowers control the vast majority of militarily useful monitoring technologies, they are no more inclined to share them or the information gleaned from them with a global authority than they are to share the weapons these systems are designed to verify.

Seismic Monitors: A Private Sector Initiative

In a most unusual agreement completed in spring 1986, a private U.S. environmental group, the Natural Resources Defense Council, arranged with the Soviet Academy of Sciences to place seismic monitors (popularly known as "black boxes") near a Soviet test site in Semipalatinsk and another set of monitors at the Nevada test site, each to be accompanied by three seismologists from the other nation. "We see this agreement as the most important private sector arms control initiative ever undertaken," said Adrian DeWind, NRDC chairman.[12]

Though it is a purely private demonstration-scale arrangement, the agreement is intended to spur both governments to initiate a much more extensive network of unmanned, tamper-proof seismic monitors in both nations, as has often been proposed in the past as a means to verify a comprehensive test ban. Seismologists still disagree about how many "black boxes" would be necessary. A research team from Lawrence Livermore Laboratory believes that detection of a one-ton "decoupled" detonation (exploded in soft alluvium to cushion the impact) would require a set of thirty arrays of about twenty-five monitors each scattered throughout the Soviet Union. A second team of seismologists from the

U.S. Geological Survey and elsewhere maintains that twenty-five single monitoring devices would suffice.[13]

The Future of Verification Technologies

Impressive as they are, current technical means of verification are rapidly being outdistanced by contrary trends in nuclear weapons developments—towards more mobile missiles, more clandestine "stealth" technologies, more widespread deployment, and more dual-capable vehicles (able to carry both nuclear and conventional warheads). Cruise missiles and antisatellite weapons, for example, are both so easily concealed that verification would be effectively impossible.

Chemical and biological weapons present a special challenge to verification techniques, one that is likely to grow more significant with time as the United States and the Soviet Union resume production of chemical weapons after a hiatus of seventeen years. Such weapons have not played a large role in military thinking or combat in recent times but could become more attractive to strategists if, for one reason or another, nuclear weapons became politically unacceptable. Always an Achilles' heel of verification, chemical and biological weapons require none of the heavy hardware of nuclear delivery systems; minute quantities can kill millions of persons. Attempts to monitor the production and stockpiling of such weapons will inevitably demand more intrusive and politically sensitive measures than are required to verify nuclear arsenals, and purely technical systems alone are unlikely ever to suffice.

Some observers believe verification is being made obsolete by these developments, or at the very least much more difficult. This contest between secrecy and detection has been called "a race between hiders and finders." Verification technologies can be expected to continue to improve steadily, achieving better resolution in photo reconnaissance, deploying sophisticated radar on satellites, and performing more sensitive electronic monitoring. But since technologies of stealth and secrecy will also proliferate, no dramatic breakthroughs are predicted.

Verification Under Comprehensive Disarmament

All of these capabilities and institutions—technical and political, national and international—would be useful, indeed essential, to an effective verification process under any of the alternative security systems proposed here. There are, however, a few factors that distinguish the tasks of verification in existing arms control agreements from those that would result from a comprehensive disarmament process. The first point to keep in mind is that outright bans and freezes on the production of weapons are easier to verify than limits, since in the case of a ban even a single detection of a violation is sufficient to determine that an agreement is being breached. In addition, verification would probably become increasingly important as the numbers of weapons decrease. With the superfluous killing capacity of present arsenals, small errors in the calculation of an adversary's stockpile do not translate into militarily significant advantages. But as those numbers dwindle, the margin of safety appears to narrow, so that when the arsenals reach relatively low numbers (several hundred or less), a small number of hidden missiles could be perceived as posing a genuine threat.

Nothing can be done to alter this basic trend in the disarmament process. But other aspects of the process help compensate for the greater stringency required by a diminishing margin for error. In a gradual disarmament regime extending over decades, there is ample time for nations to develop the cooperative machinery and political confidence to make mutual verification possible. Furthermore, their stake in the process rises as the weapons diminish; that is, they have ever more incentive to respect a process that is successfully assuring their security and ever less incentive to violate it for limited short-term advantages. However, as the number of weapons diminishes, fear of enemy "breakout" could become more acute, fostering one's own impulse to exceed established limits.

Cheating "on the margins" will continue to occur, as it now occurs. Nations can be expected to utilize the loopholes they have carefully sewn into the fabric of their treaties. But just as most citizens in any nation obey the spirit if not the letter of the laws of the land most of the time, trusting their legitimacy and accepting that they exist largely for the common good, so nations engaged in an extended disarmament process can be expected to become habituated to its mutual restraints over time and to become increasingly reluctant to break out of the system.

Growing Trust in the Process

It is important to distinguish here between trust in one's adversary and trust in a process that binds both to a system of mutual restraints. Suspicion is so deeply embedded in the relationship between the superpowers that to stipulate the establishment of trust between them as a precondition to agreement is to doom all such negotiations to certain failure. Such trust in one another is neither likely nor necessary, at least in the near term. Trust in the process, on the other hand, requires only that nations heed their own self-interest which, when rightly understood, leads them to cooperate with one another to the minimal extent necessary to assure their own survival. It is possible to distrust one another while trusting the process to provide each with a measure of security that can be attained by no other means.

Over time a second and deeper level of trust in one another may evolve from the experience of a successful disarmament process, but it will not likely precede it. Henry Stimson, secretary of war in the Roosevelt and Truman administrations, wrote in his resignation letter to President Truman, "The chief lesson I have learned in a long life is that the only way you can make a man trustworthy is to trust him; and the surest way to make him untrustworthy is to distrust him and show your distrust."[14]

On-Site Inspections

To reinforce national technical means and cooperative measures, an increasingly rigorous system of on-site inspections may well become necessary. Proposals have been tabled over the years to open certain weapons installations to inspection. For three decades the Soviet Union resisted all such arrangements, but with the 1988 INF agreement, dramatic changes have taken place. The INF Treaty, which eliminates intermediate- and (certain) short-range missiles from Europe, represents an unprecedented advance in verification, stipulating more rigorous and comprehensive measures than any previous arms control agreement. In fact, its verification procedures may well become its most enduring contribution to future disarmament treaties.

The terms of the agreement include, for the first time, extensive on-site inspections of Soviet and U.S. missile manufacturing and storage facilities. Within a thirteen-year verification regime, each nation is to be permitted twenty short-notice inspections per year (at sites approved in a memorandum of understanding included in the treaty) during the first three years, fifteen per year during the next five, and ten per year during the final five years. In addition, each nation is permitted to maintain a continuous, 24-hour-a-day presence of inspectors at specified missile production sites still in use by the other nation. Thus, twenty U.S. inspectors will be deployed at a Soviet SS-20 missile assembly site in Vatkinsk where SS-25s are still in production, while thirty Soviet inspectors will monitor activities at a Magna, Utah, Pershing missile production facility.[15]

In addition to these bilateral arrangements, Soviet General Secretary Gorbachev has suggested a "third-party verification process," in which an international agency including neutral nations would undertake to inspect national arsenals and verify compliance with disarmament agreements. This proposal bears a strong resemblance to the principle enunciated by President Kennedy a quarter century ago. In addition, in spring 1987, the Soviet Union proposed that Soviet and U.S. scientists conduct nuclear tests on one another's territory and then take measurements of the size of the blast. "Since each side would know the size of its own device, the tests would permit each side to determine the accuracy of its measurements."[16]

In the current political climate it is difficult to imagine the great powers acceding to third-party inspection. But if they were once to summon the requisite mutual will to disarm, they would likely insist upon such stringent inspection measures as a precondition for agreement and as their best defense against "breakout." Furthermore, the long duration of the process would provide ample time for nations to phase out their secrecy and phase in a system of shared information to strengthen their mutual security.

A freeze on the production and deployment of nuclear weapons and a comprehensive test ban have both already been determined to be verifiable in all their most important aspects, even in the absence of measures like on-site inspection. As nations become accustomed to the success of this first step, they will be that much more willing to take the next, larger step. By the time the weapons have dwindled to relatively few, a substantial history of information exchange will have accumulated and the greater rigor of the process will seem both logical and necessary.

A Political More than a Technical Challenge

The verification process has often been likened to a jigsaw puzzle in which some of the pieces are always missing and always a changing set. Only two nations, the United States and Soviet Union, now possess the full range of verification capabilities. Their data, considerable but inevitably incomplete, are subject to a great many conflicting influences and contrary interpretations. The data are also refracted through a prism of politics before they emerge into public view. Despite the technical emphasis of the verification debate, the underlying dynamic is more political than technological and no amount of instrumental hardware will rescue nations from the uncomfortable necessity of accepting some degree of uncertainty and ambiguity in any disarmament accord. The function of the verification technologies is to make certain that this margin of uncertainty remains always within the boundaries of tolerable risk. Next to the hazards that confront the world in the absence of disarmament, current and projected verification capabilities—national, cooperative, and international—offer a far more acceptable risk.

Notes

1. William Colby, in *Military Implications of the Treaty on the Limitation of Strategic Offensive Arms and Protocol Thereto (SALT II Treaty),* U.S. Senate, 96th Congress, First Session (USGPO, Washington, DC, 1979), Part 3, October 9, 10, 11, and 16, p. 1015.

2. Charlie Cole, "Our Spy on High: The Air Force's SR-71 Shows an Eye for Detail," *New York Times Magazine,* May 10, 1987, pp. 32, 34.

3. C. Elachi, "Spaceborne Imaging Radar: Geologic and Oceanographic Applications," *Science,* vol. 209, no. 4461, September 5, 1980, p. 1073.

4. See Allan S. Krass, *Verification: How Much Is Enough?* (Lexington, MA: Lexington Books, 1985), p. 38.

5. Thomas Powers, "The Ears of America," *New York Review of Books,* February 3, 1983, p. 12.

6. Krass, *Verification,* p. 82.

7. Ibid., p. 212.

8. Quoted in Marcus Raskin, "Arms Control Versus General Security and Disarmament." Unpublished paper (Washington, DC: Institute for Policy Studies, 1983), p. 2.

9. *The Implications of Establishing an International Satellite Monitoring Agency* (New York: United Nations Study Series 9, 1983).

10. Jerome Wiesner, "An International Arms Verification and Study Center." Unpublished paper (Cambridge, MA: December 1985).

11. Alva Myrdal, "The International Control of Disarmament," *Scientific American,* vol. 231, no. 4 (October 1974), p. 31.

12. "Private Detection," *Nuclear Times,* July-August 1986, p. 5.

13. Richard Scribner, Theodore J. Ralston, and William D. Metz, *The Verification Challenge: Problems and Promise of Strategic Nuclear Arms Control Verification* (Boston: Birkhauser, 1985), p. 84.

14. Henry Stimson and McGeorge Bundy, *On Active Service in Peace and War* (New York: Harper Brothers, 1948), p. 644.

15. See Betty G. Lall and Eugene Chollick, *The INF Treaty: Verification Breakthrough* (New York: Council on Economic Priorities, 1988).

16. Michael R. Gordon, "Soviet Offering U.S. an Exchange: Nuclear Tests on Each Other's Soil," *New York Times,* April 18, 1987, pp. 1, 4.

CHAPTER ELEVEN

Bringing Law to Bear on Governments

Roger Fisher

The viability of any alternative security system depends on the willingness of nations to comply with its terms and arrangements. The issues of compliance—and the closely related problems of enforcement in the event that voluntary compliance is not forthcoming—are essential to the acceptance by nations of any regime of cooperative security. Recognizing the importance of the compliance issue, the authors decided that it must be addressed in this volume. Because none of us has formal training in international law, we have chosen to turn here to an acknowledged authority on the subject for his observations. Although it was written two decades ago, Roger Fisher's essay is a classic statement on the subject. It has been slightly revised and updated here to reflect recent events.[1]

—The Authors

It has long been suggested that nations could adjust their conflicts of interest amicably and live in peace forever if they would only conform their conduct to international law. Most lawyers hold in common a view of international law that runs somewhat as follows: There is a great difference between positive law—law with a policeman behind it—and so-called international law. International law is a body of vague rules for the attention of the political scientist and the amusement of the law student not much interested in law. It should not be confused with real law, which is the command of a sovereign backed by force. However much it is hoped that nations will abide by acknowledged rules some day, they do not now; nor can they ever be compelled to do so, at least in the absence of world government. Only woolly thinking would confuse positive law enforced by our courts—our Constitution, our civil and criminal laws—with the moral directives that go by the name of international law. So runs the party line of the profession.[2]

Within such a theory, international law is clearly no more than positive morality. But much of the modern law school curriculum besides international law would have to be similarly characterized. Courses in constitutional law, administrative law, and tax law, to name only a few, deal in large part with limitations on governmental action or involve the government as a party to a dispute in courts deriving jurisdiction from itself. More than 75 percent of the cases in which the Supreme Court handed down opinions during its 1984 term adjudicated rights and duties of the federal government.[3] We can suspect that a definition of law that excludes so much may not be useful today.

But we are not concerned here with a mere matter of definition. In denying the status of international law because there is no apparent sovereign issuing the commands, we show a limited understanding of how a court system operates in its relations with a government. In blandly assuming that all law rests on superior force, we have ignored the cases in which the government loses a judgment and honors it.

Is organized force essential to compliance? Clearly it is not. When a judgment is entered against the United States in the Court of Claims, no superior sovereign compels Congress to vote an appropriation. The judgment is paid because that is the law; but the law is not the articulate voice of a superior sovereign. When, in the *Youngstown* case,[4] the Supreme Court ordered the secretary of commerce to return the steel mills that the president had ordered him to seize, the Court had no regiments at its command. But despite the fact that the Supreme Court sitting in Washington had no greater force at its command vis-à-vis the government than does the International Court of Justice sitting at the Hague, the steel mills were returned.

The more closely one examines law within this country and within others, the less significant seems the element of force. Even such hard, positive laws as the criminal and tax laws depend ultimately on compliance with them by the government, and the general pattern is one of compliance. To be sure, Congress, on perhaps a dozen occasions, has failed to honor a judgment of the Court of Claims.[5] But the government, which is never without funds or absent from the jurisdiction, has a far better record than the private judgment debtor. This record, even if less than perfect, demonstrates that a pattern of governmental compliance can be secured without a supragovernmental police force.

Moreover, even where the organized force of a superior sovereign is available it may be difficult to make a government comply. If a government is not persuaded to obey by other reasons, superior force alone may not be enough. In *Virginia v. West Virginia*,[6] the Supreme Court had before it the continuing failure of the West Virginia legislature to raise and appropriate the funds needed to pay Virginia that share of its public debt that West Virginia had undertaken upon becoming a separate state. If we assume that the U.S. Army was at the Court's disposal, what should the army do to enforce the judgment? Should it seize the state capitol and sell it at auction? Should it raise funds at the point of a gun? If so, from whom? However effective force or the threat of force may be when applied to an individual, it is difficult to bring force to bear on a political enterprise that offers no obvious point of application.[7] So long as a rule runs only to a political entity rather than to individuals, a superior power must face the problem of trying to apply force to an abstraction.

If it is not the threat of force that induces governmental compliance with domestic law, it is not the absence of force that explains why our government feels less strongly bound by international law than, for example, by the Constitution. Nor does an explanation lie in the fact that international rules are generically more vague than constitutional rules. They are not. Nor can we look for an answer in our government's denying the binding nature of international law. It does not. Nor is an answer to be found in the assumption that the government will comply more readily with rules benefiting citizens than with those benefiting foreigners. The due process clause protects citizen and alien alike.

What is the difference, then, between a judgment of the Court of Claims and a judgment of the International Court? Is it merely that the United States accepted the jurisdiction of the former one hundred years ago and has not yet really accepted the jurisdiction of the latter? The question is worth exploring. An understanding of the factors inducing governmental obedience to domestic law may shed light on the problem of securing obedience to international law. We would not expect to find factors that guarantee obedience. Governments do not always obey rules. In a given case, what are considered vital interests may lead a government to break the law just as they may persuade an individual to steal. The question, rather, is: What are the forces that tend to induce obedience, the elements that impart strength to the law? Knowing that these elements are in fact strong enough to bring about general governmental compliance with domestic law, we will want to appraise their ability to bring about governmental compliance with international law.

In considering whether to respect a rule, one factor that a government takes into account is the danger of external consequences should it not respect the rule. Even where there is no organized superior sovereign power to compel obedience, a government is not free to ignore the conduct and attitudes of those with whom it must deal. The U.S. government, considered as an entity, respects the Constitution partly because it fears the retaliatory action that might be taken by the citizens if it did not. A focal point for such retaliation might be the polls. And the government respects the right to vote, influenced in part, perhaps, by fear of more violent action if it were denied.

Internationally, the most significant forces external to a government are not its own citizens but other nations. Before a government decides to break a rule of international law, it must consider the possible reaction of other states. It is not only the immediate reaction of the states most affected by the breach that is relevant; the effect on what may be called world public opinion must also be considered. Thus, should the United States consider abrogating a treaty it has signed with the Soviet Union, an intelligent decision could not ignore three factors external to the government: (1) political criticism within the United States; (2) the possibility of direct retaliation by the Soviet Union; and (3) the likelihood of an adverse reaction among our allies and the uncommitted nations. These considerations are analogous to those that an individual must weigh before deciding to disregard domestic law. Although they do not result from the organized will of a superior sovereign, they are not wholly unpredictable and arbitrary. There are rules about punishing rule breakers; an injured state cannot engage in excessive retaliation without itself weighing the consequences.

Some rules of international law have long been maintained largely by the pressure of these external forces. If the Soviet Union catches a foreign diplomat photographing military installations in violation of Soviet law, he is not punished, but rather is declared persona non grata and politely asked to leave the country. Presumably, a major factor inducing this respect for the international rule of diplomatic immunity is the desire of the Soviet government for similar treatment of its diplomats by other countries. Similarly, in the arms-control field, one force—in many cases, the most important force—causing a country to respect a treaty or other form of restraint is apprehension of the various external consequences of not respecting it. Such apprehension keeps limited wars limited and was at least partially responsible for keeping the Reagan administration from exceeding, until late 1986, the numerical limits established in the SALT II agreement. It is a force that can be used to cause respect for rules limiting preparation for war.

In addition to these pressures from outside, there are international forces influencing government action. One of these is comparable to that which supports individual respect for law. Man is by and large a moral creature who is usually anxious to believe that what he does is not only practical but right. Individual moral standards may differ, but it is nonetheless true that each of us is influenced by his idea of what he ought to do. An individual will frequently respect a rule simply by believing that the rule ought to be respected, without appraising the chances of being caught and without a Machiavellian weighing of the pros and cons.

A government is made up of such individuals, and this fact tends to cause governmental respect for law. The strength of this moral force depends on matters of both procedure and substance. It depends on how the rule was established, including such things as the solemnity with which the obligation to respect it was assumed. It depends also on the degree to which the rule coincides with the moral views of the individual officials in the government affected. A rule against assassination of foreign officials might be respected for reasons going beyond a cold calculation of the consequences. On the other hand, rules requiring the officials of one country to inform on their colleagues might be broken because of moral scruples despite a recognized theoretical advantage in compliance.

These pressures from possible external consequences and from internal morality that induce governmental conformity to rules are comparable to those affecting individual behavior. But there are special internal factors that operate on a government that are either not present or are insignificant in the case of an individual. These are at the heart of our problem.

First, a government is an institution that is dedicated to promoting respect for law. In the domestic sphere a government recognizes that rules are necessary for the avoidance of collisions of interest and that it has an affirmative stake in the creation and maintenance of law. But this law-creating and law-maintaining function is less well recognized in the international field. In the United States, the chief legal officer concerned with domestic law, the attorney general, conceives of his job as the promotion of law and justice. In contrast, the comparable official concerned with international law, the legal adviser to the State Department, has rarely considered his job in that light. He has seen himself not as an assistant secretary for international law, whose job is to promote law in the international arena, but rather as a kind of house counsel, whose function is to keep the department out of trouble.

But whatever views particular officials may have of their offices, it is clear that all governments undertake to create and maintain a legal order. One way to promote such an order is for the government itself to respect laws applicable to it. To the extent (but only to the extent) that a government recognizes that its long-run interests require it to promote a legal order in the international arena, such recognition will tend to create respect for international rules as a means of fulfilling that objective.

A second consideration that is peculiarly applicable to governments is that they have a greater interest in the fair and wise settlement of disputes than in advancing their immediate financial or institutional position. Until 1863, when Congress empowered the Court of Claims to enter judgments against the United States,[8] the government could "win" every case simply by congressional failure to vote a private bill. But it was perceived, however dimly,[9] that to win any particular case was less important for the government than to resolve all cases by a demonstrably fair means. Decisions based on executive or legislative discretion must always be justified on the merits; a claim that has been three times rejected may have to be reconsidered. And the possibility of discrimination is great. But if a private claim is determined according to judicial procedure—if it has had its day in court—the government is protected from political criticism, whether the criticism is that the claim should or should not have been paid. In some respects a judicial decision is like an administrative decision. The government has referred a question of policy to persons qualified to decide it. And having obtained a decision, the government follows it simply because the decision has been made, for reasons not unlike those that cause it to follow a decision of, say, the secretary of agriculture.

The political interests of a government may in some cases be particularly well served when the decision is against the government. The judicial process may enable the government to lose an argument gracefully and according to principle. Responsibility for an unpopular but necessary action can often be passed to the courts and immunized from partisan attack. A judicial decision may provide the executive with a good excuse for doing what it would have to do anyway.

These considerations might well apply to decisions of an international court. The international interests of a government may be advanced more by having a matter decided fairly than by refusing to concede the point involved. For example, by having the World Court adjudicate the division of the disputed Gulf of Maine continental shelf and fisheries zones, the United States achieved a sensible solution with far less disadvantage than would be involved in abandoning a tenaciously held position under political pressure, forcing an ally to accept what it considered to be an untenable situation, or indefinitely prolonging an unsatisfactory situation with Canada. Similarly, although the U.S. naval bases in Cuba and the Philippines may be secure for the present, in the future the United States may not be able to insist on maintaining these military bases against the wishes of local governments. Eventually this country might be better served by abandoning Guantanamo, Cubi Point, and Subic Bay pursuant to an order of an international tribunal, which might provide for the removal of property and payments by the

Cuban and Filipino governments, than by lingering on until these bases are pushed out or acquired by other means. Thus, internationally as well as domestically, situations may arise in which compliance with law is not coerced but proceeds directly from self-interest.

There is a final and significant way in which a government's reasons for complying with rules of law differ from those of an individual. A government is a complex structure comprising a great many individuals, a structure that depends for its very existence on respect for rules. Every individual in the government has many rules directly applicable to him. Some of these rules demand obedience to superiors. But others, which in the United States include the Constitution and statutes, lay down substantive law. The latter do not speak out merely to the government as a whole; they speak also to individual officials and are regarded by them as being binding directly upon them. Thus, it is a risky business for a superior to direct his subordinates to disregard a particular rule. Each subordinate will be subjected to conflicting pressures and there is no guarantee of the result. A high official cannot command the breaking of rules without undermining respect for rules generally. And it is upon obedience to rules that his authority to command depends.

This analysis applies to any government. The oustings of François Duvalier of Haiti and Ferdinand Marcos of the Philippines and the increasing civil strife under South Africa's Pieter Botha and Chile's Augusto Pinochet Ugarte attest to the weakness of governments whose officials do not respect law. In sharp contrast, the government of the Soviet Union is highly organized and tends to be rule respecting. It is a mistake to think of that government as lawless and commanding obedience from its officials only at the point of a pistol. No one is holding a pistol to the head of the man who holds the pistol; that man is complying with rules.

Once a rule has become intertwined in the governmental fabric, the government is no longer free to ignore it. Once subordinate officials recognize a particular legal rule as being just as binding upon them as is the concept of obedience to the orders of their superior, it will be difficult for the government to ignore the rule. In the United States, rules created by treaty or executive agreement are thought to be binding on officials only through the presidential chain of command. If the president directs disregard of a treaty obligation, subordinate officials tend to think of that as a matter for his decision alone and, therefore, tend to respect the decision he has reached. If the treaty obligation were incorporated into a statute or constitutional amendment, the president and the government as a whole would find the treaty far more difficult to ignore. Such action would require a collective decision to break one rule while respecting another.

One can see how such a procedure might operate even in the arms-control field. Should a treaty provide for the abolition of nuclear stockpiles, the most complete inspection system that could be devised would be inadequate to guarantee that no weapons remained hidden. But it might be possible to create a structure of rules within each country that would satisfy other countries that there was no evasion of the agreement. The treaty obligation might be incorporated into the national constitutions. The citizens of each country might constantly be reminded by public notices and official speeches that it was their individual duty to notify United Nations officers of any hidden weapons. Rewards might be offered to those who discovered weapons and punishment threatened to those who concealed them. With such a massive effort to develop rules recognized as personally binding by a great number of people, each government would have created significant forces supporting compliance with the international obligation. In addition to the risks of retaliation and adverse world reaction due to the likelihood of detection under such circumstances, it might be difficult to bring about a governmental decision to act against officially declared government policy.

No absolute guarantee can be given that a government will always respect a rule. We have no guarantee that our government will always respect the Constitution or the decisions of the Supreme Court. But by seeking to understand why governments so generally obey domestic law, we shall be better able to undertake the task of securing respect for international law. Current efforts to deal with pressing international issues, such as the jurisdiction of the international court and the arms race, are being hamstrung by antiquated dogma about what law is and by an insufficient realization of why governments comply with law. No more in the international than in the domestic sphere should the argument be heard that governments must be lawless because they cannot be coerced.

Notes

1. This chapter is a revised version of a speech delivered at Boston University Law School on November 17, 1960.

2. See, for example, Briggs, *"The Cloudy Prospects for 'Peace Through Law,'"* 46 *A.B.A.J.* 490(1960).

3. See *"The Supreme Court," 1984 Term*, 99 *Harvard Law Review* 329, Table III(1985).

4. *Youngstown Sheet and Tube Co. v. Sawyer,* 343 U.S. 579(1952).

5. See Note, 46 *Harvard Law Review* 677, 685–686, n.63(1933).

6. 246 U.S. 565(1918).

7. The West Virginia controversy was settled by the party states. See W. Va. Acts Ext. Sess. 1919, ch. 10, at 19.

8. Act of March 3, 1863, ch. 92, 12 Stat. 765 [now 28 U.S.C. 1491–1505(1958)].

9. A tie vote in the Senate was broken by the vice-president. Views uttered by opponents of the Court of Claims are strangely similar to those uttered today by opponents of the International Court of Justice. Senator Hale of New Hampshire prefaced his remarks by declaring: "I think, sir, when some future Gibbon shall write the history of the decline and fall of the great Republic, and shall give the indications which marked its progress to decay, one of them will be that about the year of grace 1863 the Thirty-Seventh Congress took it into their head that they were wiser than everybody that went before them, and departed from all the precedents established by their fathers, and started out on new, untried, and extravagant theories and notions." He went on to object, "But, sir, we are going to give this new Court of Claims power that we have denied and that our fathers have denied always to any and every Court. . . . "(*Cong. Globe*, 37th Congress, 3d Session 310 [1863]).

CHAPTER TWELVE

Economic Conversion: Making Peace More Profitable than War

Adopting any system of alternative security considered in this book will require profound transformations in the economies of all those nations now heavily invested in military spending. Converting the workforce and industrial base of military economies to the production of goods and services in the civilian sector will entail a very substantial shift in the distribution of resources. Without careful planning, sufficient time, and the proper offsetting measures, the transition could be a wrenching experience, throwing large numbers of people out of work, idling vital industries, and driving the U.S. and global economies into stagnation or even depression. Conversion has long been viewed as a deeply problematic proposition. Some economists, and a substantial portion of the public as well, believe that it may not in fact be possible to maintain prosperity without permanently high military spending.

Any such massive transformation would inevitably encounter its share of difficulties in the short term. The ease with which the transition is made will depend in part on the state of the national and global economies at the time the shift is undertaken. In a thriving economy, many jobs are routinely created while others are lost; in an ailing economy, job creation may be more problematic, requiring stimulus from governmental sources. More importantly, proper planning by and coordination among the affected communities, corporations, and local, state, and national government agencies could do much to minimize the negative impacts and inevitable dislocations. In the process, conversion would release from unproductive activities a vast array of resources for the reconstruction and regeneration of the global economy. If the savings from disarmament were wisely invested, there is sound reason to believe that conversion can be accomplished without unacceptable difficulties and that all nations partaking in the process would come out on the far side much better off than they are today.

Although the entire global economy would be affected by the conversion process, we have chosen for the sake of simplicity to focus here specifically on the transition within the United States. Being the world's largest economy and one of its two largest military enterprises, the U.S. military economy presents a most complex and formidable challenge to conversion planning. Upon the success of the U.S. conversion process the prosperity of much of the rest of the global economy will depend. But it is important to realize that conversion could yield equal or even greater benefits for those developing nations that now devote a still larger proportion of their national wealth and productive resources to military spending.

Precedents for Conversion

There is no direct historical parallel for the conversion process that would take place under a comprehensive disarmament system, but there have been other instances of demobilization and phasedown in the aftermath of military conflicts. In the U.S. experience, the demobilization following World War II entailed by far the largest adjustment. In 1945, the U.S. military budget amounted to $75.9 billion; a year later, it had dropped to $18.8 billion, and a year later to $11.7 billion. The U.S. armed forces shrank from 11 million in 1945 to 2 million in 1947, yet unemployment never rose above 4 percent. The defense production work force shrank equally precipitously; employment in the military aircraft industry, for example, dropped from 1,350,000 in 1943 to 240,000 in 1946. The gross national product dipped briefly in 1946 from its wartime high of $224 billion to $198 billion, but regained its former peak again in early 1947. Similarly dramatic shifts of employment and resources occurred in the Soviet and European economies without catastrophic results.

The postwar experience is both instructive and heartening, but it differs in several essential respects from the circumstances in which disarmament would now occur. In the United States, the postwar process of conversion was actually a reconversion because most of the factories manufacturing military goods during the war had previously produced goods for the civilian sector and had only to pull their blueprints from the drawer to resume where they had left off. By contrast, the military production divisions of many of the largest firms supplying goods to the Department of Defense today have never produced for the civilian marketplace. Nurtured in the protected environment of government sponsorship, military industries have developed what Seymour Melman, a leading proponent of conversion, calls "a trained incapacity" for cost-effective production.[1] In several instances where military aerospace firms have sought to diversify into commercial markets, the results have been disappointing and sometimes disastrous. Instructed to emphasize exacting performance characteristics while disregarding cost, they have shown themselves unable to adapt to civilian standards stressing affordability and marketing appeal.

The postwar demobilization also sent millions of women who had joined the labor force for the duration of the war effort back to their homes; there they no longer competed in the job market. Such a massive voluntary retirement would not recur today. Furthermore, the demands of war production laid claim to the major share of available resources and thus denied them to the civilian economy. This temporary scarcity generated a large pent-up demand for housing, plant equipment, and consumer goods and a robust market for them in the early postwar years, which in turn helped absorb a workforce swelled by the return of 9 million veterans. With few consumer goods available during the war, a large reservoir of personal savings accumulated, whereas today's savings rate in the United States is among the lowest in the industrialized West and personal, corporate, and governmental debts have all swelled to unprecedented levels. Finally, the United States emerged from the war in a position of unparalleled advantage, with an economy not simply unscathed but invigorated, without any serious rival in the marketplace. Today, global markets are fiercely competitive and the U.S. share of most essential goods has been steadily shrinking during the 1970s and 1980s.

These and other differences between the early postwar years and the late 1980s indicate that conversion today would present a fresh set of challenges under a somewhat changed set of circumstances. Nevertheless, the successful demobilization of wartime armed forces and the return to a peacetime economy demonstrate that disarmament would not likely be a catastrophic event for national economies. With sufficient planning, concerted effort, and a far more ample time frame in which to accomplish the task than the two-year demobilization process following World War II, the conversion process today stands a reasonable chance of preventing undue distortions of the economy while providing the opportunity to rebuild the foundations of economic and social health that have been steadily eroding in recent years.

The Structure of the Military Economy

In order to comprehend the dimensions of the conversion challenge, it is first necessary to gain a sense of the size and structure of the current

U.S. military economy. Six and a half million Americans (about 6 percent of the total workforce) are directly employed in the three principal categories in the military sector of the U.S. economy—approximately 2.2 million members in the armed forces, 1 million civilians in the Department of Defense (DOD), and 3.3 million workers in industries producing goods and services for the military.[2] In addition to these visible components of the military economy, there are large numbers of employees engaged in military projects in NASA (where they operate an increasingly militarized space program), in the Department of Energy (where the entire nuclear weapons research, development, production, and testing program is housed), and in such vast but largely invisible enterprises as the National Security Agency, a communications intelligence organization at least five times the size of the CIA with a budget reputedly more than $10 billion a year.[3]

Private firms serving the military are the largest and most diverse category within the military economy. While about 100 major corporations do the majority of their work for the Pentagon, some 30,000 companies receive prime contracts and over 100,000 perform subcontracting work.[4] These contracts are very widely distributed across the nation: only 9 of 3,041 counties in the United States received less than $1,000 in DOD funds in 1984.[5] But they are also disproportionately concentrated in a few regions: California, for example, garnered $29.1 billion in prime weapon contracts in 1985, more than the three next largest states combined (New York, Texas, and Massachusetts).[6]

In addition to being geographically concentrated, military production is heavily concentrated in particular industries. More than one-third of the aircraft industry (39.6 percent) and more than one-half of radio and communications equipment (51.8 percent) and shipbuilding (50.4 percent) industries are devoted to military production.[7] And military industry is disproportionately concentrated in particular occupations, employing far more engineers, scientists, and managers than the average among all manufacturing industries.

These data indicate that although military-serving firms employ only 3 percent of the U.S. workforce, their intense concentration within particular regions, industries, and occupations greatly magnifies the potential effects of conversion on those firms, communities, and professions most dependent on military contracts. In addition, the indirect and induced employment generated among local businesses by the presence of military industries and military bases, generally calculated to be double the direct employment figure, further intensifies the potential impact of the conversion process on military-dependent communities. This highly concentrated yet widely distributed structure of the military economy presents a special set of challenges to conversion planners, but also a special set of possibilities. The highly skilled workforce in much of military industry could, with appropriate retraining, provide an invaluable resource for the reconstruction and development of neglected sectors of the civilian economy.

The Supply Side: Resources Released by Disarmament

We are now ready to look at the nature and scale of the resources—financial, material, and human—that the disarmament process would release from the existing military economy. This is what might be called the "supply side" of the military economy. An immense variety of physical assets, industrial equipment, technical skills, and unskilled labor would gradually become available for alternative uses as disarmament proceeds.

The disarmament process can and should be consciously designed to minimize disruptions and dislocations in the economy. Stability is best assured by building gradualness into the process, insofar as the exigencies of verification and other factors allow. Unfortunately, the verification process is best aided by very visible and abrupt cessations of production, which can be more easily detected than gradually increasing restrictions (bans are more easily enforced than limits). Hence some compromise may well be necessary to accommodate the varying requirements of conversion and verification. Finally, it might be wise to begin with small reductions and enlarge them gradually as successful experience reinforces the economic stability and political acceptability of the conversion process.

Financial Resources

The financial savings resulting from not building the enormous array of weapons now scheduled to be manufactured over the next few decades represent the most tangible and incontestable reward for engaging in the disarmament process. Although it is not possible to estimate with any precision the size of this "disarmament dividend," it is clear that for the United States alone, the return during the two decades or so of the disarmament process would likely reach into the trillions of dollars.

It is important to pause for a moment to consider the dimensions of this figure. During its first hundred years, the U.S. government accumulated a debt of one trillion dollars. In the six years between 1981 and 1987, under the Reagan military buildup, the United States accumulated its second trillion dollars of debt. The disarmament process would likely generate savings equal to double the debt that took more than two hundred years to accumulate. This is a truly staggering sum and represents an unprecedented opportunity to reduce the deficit and to repair and rebuild those sectors of the U.S. economy and society that have fallen into decay in recent years as resources have been shifted increasingly into military production.

Human Resources

With the onset of the disarmament process, large numbers of workers will be released from military industries as contracts for new weapons systems are terminated. Parallel reductions in the civilian staffs of the departments of Defense and Energy would further swell the numbers of persons losing employment. In the absence of arrangements for alternative employment, these cuts could raise the national unemployment level by a percentage point or more (given a total workforce of 106 million [1986]). When taken together with the collateral effects of such cuts on jobs in the communities that supply the military-serving installations, that figure could double.

This temporary rise in unemployment is an inevitable and undesirable byproduct of the transition from a war to a peace economy, but it need not be catastrophic. By way of comparison, in the five years between 1979 and the end of 1983, nearly 11.5 million workers lost their jobs as a result of plant closings, layoffs, or automation, twice the number that would likely be displaced in the course of two decades of disarmament.[8] But no sensibly conceived conversion process would simply terminate employment in one sector and do nothing to create alternative employment. Indeed, the entire conversion process would be specifically designed to ease the transition and generate new job and market opportunities in fields and locations close to the original source of employment. In this endeavor it would be greatly aided by the fact that investments in the civilian economy generate significantly more jobs per dollar spent than investments in the military economy, largely because military industry is so capital-intensive and maintains a wage scale higher than most comparable civilian industries. For each $1 billion spent in guided missile production, some 14,000 direct jobs are created; for each $1 billion spent on local transit, 21,500; and for educational services, 63,000.[9]

It is very difficult to determine the distribution of occupations in military industry; remarkably few aggregate data exist. It is well known that managers, scientists, and engineers proliferate in military industry to a degree unparalleled in civilian industries. Whereas in most manufacturing concerns, one manager supervises four or more production workers, in certain military industries (like aerospace) there is closer to a 1:1 relationship. Production workers make up only 30 percent of the workforce in guided missile production, but 76.5 percent in shipbuilding.[10] In the absence of hard data, it is impossible to guess with any great assurance at the relative proportions among occupations in military industry, but an informed estimate might distribute the numbers somewhat equally between production workers, technical workers (scientists and engineers), and managers.

The scientists and engineers employed in military industry represent this country's most expensive human investment in the military economy. Here again the data are not separated from general industry figures, but it is widely accepted that between one-third and one-half of all U.S. scientists and engineers are directly engaged in military research. Attracted by wages and working conditions seldom encountered outside military industry, they are by all accounts among the most talented of the graduates emerging from the nation's engineering schools. Their research absorbs three-quarters of the total federal research and development budget. The resource contained in this national reserve of inventive and trained skill may be the single most precious asset to be released by the conversion process.

Material Resources

Along with the funds and personnel released by disarmament, a very considerable variety of material assets will become available for alternative uses. The United States maintains some 333 military bases in 21 countries, most or all of which would be closed down or redesigned for new activities in the course of a comprehensive disarmament process. In addition, the U.S. government owns wholly or in part a considerable variety of military industrial plants and equipment, as well as several world-class research laboratories (including Lawrence Livermore in California, Los Alamos in New Mexico, and Lincoln Labs in Massachusetts).

The total value of the stock of physical capital owned by the Department of Defense as of September 30, 1983 (the most recent date for which statistics are available), was conservatively estimated at $474.9 billion, nearly half of the $1,011.9 billion value of the combined stock of physical capital owned by all manufacturing establishments in the United States.[11] But the largest single category of assets is weaponry, more than half the total (56 percent), most of which cannot practically be converted to alternative uses. More convertible assets, like real property (land, buildings, and other structures), amounted to $57.4 billion, 12 percent of the total, and plant and equipment directly owned by the military an additional $20.2 billion. These figures do not, however, give a complete sense of the wealth and variety of material resources that would become available for alternative uses in the event of disarmament. The U.S.

Army alone, for example, owns 12.2 million acres of land (officially valued at $25 per acre), including some in environments extraordinary enough to merit their designation as national parklands.

Local and state governments, communities, and private industry together have proven to be remarkably adept at creating alternative uses for former military installations. In its summary of the past quarter century of "civilian reuse," the Pentagon's Office of Economic Adjustment notes that since 1961, communities nationwide have converted 100 military bases and have created 138,000 new jobs to replace the 93,424 DOD-civilian jobs lost through closure. Twelve four-year colleges, 32 community colleges, and 14 high school vocational technical programs have been established on 57 former bases, while industrial and office parks have been located at 75. According to a report by the Pentagon's Office of Economic Adjustment,

> Wherever possible, former military bases are converted for productive civilian uses, i.e., airports, schools, hospitals, recreational areas, industrial parks, etc. Available federal, state and local government resources are utilized to spur private sector investments and jobs. . . . The transition period (often 2–3 years) in securing new civilian uses can be difficult for many communities. Yet the experience of communities affected by earlier base realignments clearly indicates the communities can successfully adjust to dislocations and base closures.[12]

Quoting an editorial in *The Chicago Tribune*, the study also noted, "If cities are not [to] resist . . . the loss of the local military payroll, they need to hear the message that more diversified, stable, and economically valuable civilian payrolls not only may but do follow the departure of the military payroll."

Private corporations doing business with the military still constitute the great majority in military industry. In this instance, the resources are not usually publicly held assets and planning for their redirection in the event of disarmament would be primarily a private initiative. However, in the unique case of military production, a substantial number of firms are owned by the federal government and operated by a private contractor, an arrangement that would give the government a more central role in redirecting their functions. In all cases, the facilities and equipment now devoted to military projects represent, as in federally owned laboratories, the state of the art. Some would not be convertible to civilian production. Many military technologies have become so specialized that they can no longer be adapted to commercial production. Other technologies, like those that produce aircraft, spacecraft, radio communications, and computers, are highly adaptable to alternative uses.

The Defense Department currently absorbs an enormous quantity and variety of resources as both raw materials and finished products. Indeed, it is the largest single consumer in the U.S. economy and its purchases are scheduled to continue to grow, in some cases doubling in just five years. Purchases of organic and inorganic chemicals, for example, are due to rise from $8.3 billion in 1985 to $12.5 billion in 1991; copper from $674 million to $1.05 billion; aluminum from $1.2 billion to $1.6 billion.[13] Many of the raw materials now absorbed by military uses would become available for alternative uses in the event of disarmament. Finished products—computers, communications equipment, and a host of other goods—would continue to be manufactured for other purposes if and as commercial markets are found for them.

The Conversion Process

Having looked at the structure of the current military economy and the variety of resources within it that would be released by disarmament, we are now in a position to examine the conversion process itself. It is important at the outset to realize that though the military economy has been examined in its "macro," aggregate dimensions, the actual conversion process would need to be highly diverse and decentralized to accommodate the great variety of circumstances in which it would occur. Centralized government planning is foreign to the largely free market nature of the U.S. civilian economy (though not to the military economy) and is anathema to its ideology. But it is simply impractical when the detailed information vital to effective planning decisions exists only at the local level, as is most often the case with military industries.

Decentralized Planning

On this point (though on little else) private conversion researchers and economists in the Pentagon Office of Economic Adjustment agree: Planning for conversion must be done primarily within the plants and communities where the transition is to take place by those directly involved in the operations and management of the facilities. State and federal agencies should serve as information clearinghouses and coordinators of special government-funded programs for retraining and reemployment designed to facilitate the conversion process.

Existing Resources for Economic Adjustment

A considerable variety of governmental agencies already exists at all levels to deal with the difficulties of economic adjustment resulting from the cutbacks that regularly occur in the boom-and-bust cycle of the military economy. The Department of Defense maintains a small Office of Economic Adjustment (OEA) that collects data on such dislocations and the programs devised to deal with them. In 1985, at the request of the House Armed Services Committee, the OEA produced a voluminous report on the feasibility of establishing a federal office of conversion within the Department of Defense. While maintaining a steadfastly hostile stance toward the idea of conversion in general, the report provided ample evidence that an effective, if embryonic, infrastructure does exist to handle what it prefers to call "economic adjustment." Surveying past experiences and current resources devoted to the adjustment process, the OEA report made the following recommendations:

1. Provide early warning, up to six months, of the closing of a facility. Based on multi-year planning, the defense budget process is well equipped to predict and plan for phasedowns in production.
2. Encourage employer and labor participation and cooperation.
3. Engage a wide variety of local development organizations.
4. Coordinate public-private cooperation "in which each sector takes responsibility for marshalling resources and carrying out the actions that it can do best."
5. Establish full-service assistance to workers—job search, placement, retraining, relocation, etc.
6. Assess possibilities for reusing the plant and marketing the facility if feasible.
7. Assess ripple effects of the dislocation and actions to limit them.
8. Take many regular steps, even small ones, "to maintain momentum."[14]

Proposed Conversion Planning

Conversion researchers, with disarmament rather than arms control on their minds, believe that more advance planning is needed prior to disarmament to provide assurance that the process can go forward without cataclysmic results. Since the 1960s many drafts of legislation have been presented to Congress that propose to establish a modest conversion planning process within the U.S. government. The most recent of these, H.R. 425, the Defense Economic Adjustment Act, has been introduced by Congressman Ted Weiss (D–NY). The Weiss bill establishes "alternative use committees" at every military facility employing more than 100 persons. These committees are asked to develop detailed plans for converting the plant and reemploying the workforce within two years of losing a military contract. The legislation also provides for two-year adjustment benefits for those thrown out of work by the loss of a job in military industry and establishes a national council to facilitate, coordinate, and advise local conversion committees.

The Demand Side: Identifying Specific Conversion Possibilities

We have dwelt thus far on the supply side of the conversion equation, examining the resources that would become available in the event of disarmament. Now we cross over onto the demand side to consider the uses to which the resources of military-serving industries could best be applied. This in itself is a two-part question. We will first consider what else they are best suited to do instead and where they would find ready markets for profitable alternative production. Then, setting aside for the moment the criterion of profitability, we will consider some of the most pressing needs in the U.S. economy and society that these resources might effectively address. The variety of resources released from military-serving industries and research facilities by disarmament is clearly too numerous to consider specific uses for each, but a few illustrative examples will suffice for our purposes. Here it may be useful to consider both the conversion of whole facilities and industries and the conversion of individual workers seeking new employment.

Conversion of Industries

Four categories of industry would be most directly impacted by disarmament—aerospace, electronics, ordnance, and shipbuilding. Of these, the ordnance industry (ammunition) might find particular difficulty creating alternative uses, although chemicals processing has been suggested as one possibility.

Aerospace. As the lead military industry, aerospace has received the greatest degree of attention from conversion theorists and, at least in a few cases, from within the facilities themselves. In the early 1960s, the Lockheed Corporation was asked by a congressional committee to speculate on what products it could practically and profitably manufacture in place of weapons if disarmament or deep reductions were ever to occur. Though skeptical of the enterprise, the company nevertheless generated a remarkably imaginative set of promising ideas. Among its suggestions were:

- space exploration
- large-scale construction projects
- mining the ocean floor
- sea farming

- urban development
- integrated transportation systems
- revitalizing the merchant marine
- improving weather forecasting
- strengthening air traffic control
- air and water pollution control
- technical assistance to the developing world

Facing the possibility of layoffs during a Labour government, shop stewards at Lucas Aerospace in Great Britain, Europe's largest designer and manufacturer of aircraft systems, organized a six-month study of alternative products the firm could produce in place of weapons. Engaging the inventive energies of 13,000 shopfloor engineers, technicians, and production workers at seventeen factory sites, the so-called Lucas Plan presented 150 proposals for alternative products. Their detailed suggestions spanned six major fields:

- medical equipment
- alternative energy development
- transportation systems
- braking systems
- oceanics
- telechiric (remote control) equipment for the handicapped[15]

Establishing a criterion of "socially useful production" as the basis for deciding the best employment for their skills, Lucas workers proposed a broad spectrum of imaginative inventions, ranging from windmills for energy to vision aids for the blind.

Shipbuilding. The U.S. civilian shipbuilding industry has been in trouble for some years, crippled by a worldwide glut of facilities and intense foreign competition. The military shipbuilding market (which amounts to 65 percent of the industry) would not likely find a niche in the civilian marketplace. Some economists have suggested applying the productive resource to revitalizing the merchant fishing fleet. The Pentagon's 1985 Economic Adjustment study suggested several other "potential niches":

- heavy machinery, off-road vehicles
- bridge building and repair
- turbines and pumps for dams
- railroad cars
- offshore oil rigs and equipment[16]

A Swedish experiment provides a successful example of adaptation. Facing possible closure of its plant in Landskrona in the 1970s, a private shipbuilding firm converted its operation into fifty smaller enterprises, producing hearing aids, aluminum windows, cutting tools, recycling equipment, oil-spill cleanup rigs, and industrial fishing systems.

Electronics. This is a very diverse collection of industries, including radio and television communications, computers, and electrical measuring instruments. Half the communications industry manufactures products for use in the military but only 10 percent of the computer industry services the Pentagon. The 1985 Pentagon study found considerable promise for alternative production by the electronics industry in the commercial marketplace, identifying potential market niches in space and automotive electronics, oil and mineral exploration, cellular radio and paging systems, residential-industrial security systems, and fiber-optic telecommunications.[17]

Federal Laboratories. The resources contained in federally owned and managed military research facilities include much of the best talent and equipment in the nation and indeed in the world. The potential usefulness and adaptability of this reservoir of tools and skills is almost boundless. But very little attention has actually been given to specific alternatives. In 1979 a private research organization called the U.C. Nuclear Weapons Labs Conversion Project issued a study examining alternative uses for the Lawrence Livermore Laboratory (which is operated by the University of California for the Department of Energy). The study focuses on alternative energy research as the most feasible field of concentration for the two-thirds of the lab's work currently devoted to military projects. These projects included:

- solar research—photovoltaic cells, concentrating collectors, thermal electric systems, and industrial process heat
- wind energy systems
- resource recovery, biomass
- fuel cells
- transportation
- energy storage and transfer
- long-range energy planning

Conversion of Individuals

It is also possible to consider the problem of conversion from an individual perspective, reviewing the skills of those employed in the military economy and evaluating their adaptability to employment in the civilian sector. In rough outline, there are at least five broad occupational categories represented in the military economy: technical workers (scientists and engineers), managers and administrators, production workers, clerical workers, and soldiers (including all services). Production workers, clerical workers, and soldiers, all in semiskilled occupations, are thought to be relatively easily transferred to alternative employment with minimal retraining necessary, provided that sound and significant programs can be devised to absorb them. In many instances on-the-job training might suffice. The conversion of managers and administrators might prove most difficult, in that they have become accustomed to a very different set of priorities in the military economy than those that prevail in the civilian economy. Specifically, they will need to reorient themselves to a more cost-conscious and competitive environment where they must establish a more even balance between performance and price.

It is to the scientists and engineers released by disarmament that conversion economists have given primary attention. Lloyd Dumas, a professor of political economy at the University of Texas in Dallas, has surveyed a number of underresearched fields where scientific and engineering talent could be put to good use: developing energy-efficient and cost-effective mass transit and private transportation, devising better construction techniques and technologies, designing less polluting industrial manufacturing processes, and developing alternative energy sources, among others. He estimates that reeducation to adapt engineers to these alternative fields would require not more than one and one-half to two years of additional study.

Addressing Urgent National Priorities

A second way of looking at the demand side of the conversion equation is to consider what sectors of U.S. society and its economy are most in need of additional resources of the kinds released by the disarmament process. The list is long and in many cases the need is urgent. Despite the outward appearance of prosperity in the United States, key indicators of national economic strength continue to decline, some precipitously. Nonproductive and "distractive" investment in military projects have had a considerable role in this decline and could, if redirected, do much to reverse this menacing course of events. The nature and scale of the opportunity to address these manifold needs under a comprehensive disarmament system are almost beyond reckoning. It is difficult to set one need over another. The following inventory is purely illustrative. A short list of essential national priorities might include the following.

Reduce the Federal Deficit. At $155.1 billion in 1988, the federal deficit has grown enormously in recent years. The danger of continuing deficit financing on the scale of the past several years can best be comprehended by calculating what, in the absence of a policy shift, those deficits will be in less than twenty years. Let us assume, optimistically, that by 1989 the deficit has been cut to $130 billion and that it will remain at that figure except for the increased interest payments to service the debt. Let us also assume (again optimistically) that the interest rate will remain at 7 percent through the years between 1989 and 2009. By the year 2004, the annual deficit would reach at least $360 billion, due solely to the steadily increasing cost of servicing the debt.

Although these figures are only estimated projections based on the current situation, two points are clear. First, deficit reductions need to be made sooner rather than later to inhibit even greater deficits in the decades to come. Second, savings from the demilitarization process could easily balance the budget in ten years or less. The remainder of the savings could then be applied to ensuring the ongoing health and productivity of the nation.

Retool U.S. Industrial Base. U.S. industry now operates with much inefficient and obsolete machinery, while Japanese, European, and Asian manufacturing firms operating with more recently purchased equipment (and in many cases paying lower wages) are able to produce at a more competitive price. Between 1960 and 1980 the U.S. share of world manufacturing dropped from 26 percent to 18 percent while Japan's share rose from 6 percent to nearly 14 percent.[18] Although other factors are also at work, the principal cause of this relative decline seems clear and indisputable. The United States government invests a far higher percentage of the research and development resources essential to industrial innovation in its military economy—nearly 75 percent of all government research and development funds, next to 4 percent in Japan and 20 percent in West Germany. Japanese and Asian manufacturers, diverting relatively few resources into military production, have concentrated on commercial innovations and improved industrial efficiency, displacing U.S. leadership in steel, automobiles, machine tools, electronics, and most recently in computer technologies.

In 1982, *U.S. News and World Report* estimated that the total bill for making U.S. industry competitive again would come to an astounding $1.9 trillion.[19] Several years of additional decay, as scarce resources have been increasingly diverted from basic industries toward military production, have likely added considerably to that figure. With the release of both capital and technical skill from the distractive military economy, substantial sums can be invested in more cost-effective and energy-efficient industrial products and processes. But the enormity of the task assures that the reversal will not be sudden.

Reconstruct the Public Infrastructure. In the most comprehensive study to date, the Council of State Planning Agencies issued a report in 1981 entitled, *America in Ruins,* detailing the advanced decay of public facilities in most U.S. cities—streets and highways, sewers and water systems, railroads and mass transit. The study counted one in five bridges in the national highway system as requiring repair or reconstruction. In addition, the interstate highway network, the central nervous system of the U.S. economy, was found to be deteriorating at a rate of 2,000 miles per year. New York State's repair list for the 1980s includes rebuilding 1,000 bridges, 2 aqueducts, 6,200 miles of paved streets, 6,000 miles of water lines, 6,700 subway cars, 25,000 acres of parks, 17 hospitals, 19 university campuses, 950 schools, and 200 libraries.[20]

Clearly there is room for improvement. There is also room for vast numbers of persons to be reemployed in the labor-intensive construction industries that would do the rebuilding. Among the two million members of the armed forces who would gradually be released by disarmament would be many semiskilled persons who could easily adapt to the requirements of heavy construction. The design of urban mass transit and intercity light rail service requires considerable engineering expertise, and technical workers in the military aerospace industry are especially well qualified to provide it. The total bill for these essential reconstruction tasks, estimated by *U.S. News and World Report* in 1982, came to $2.5 trillion.[21] Applying adequate resources in capital and manpower to the job of rebuilding U.S. cities would go far toward making them once again livable, which in some respects they now are not.

Reclaim the Natural Environment. In the atmosphere, on land, and at sea, toxic wastes are accumulating to levels that threaten the health of all living things. Superfund legislation committed $8.5 billion over a five-year period to the cleanup of toxic waste sites in the United States. At the time of its passage this sum was considered by many to be insufficient to meet the problem, and even these funds have been slashed by budget cuts in the late 1980s. In addition, though there is considerable evidence that acid rain is killing a great many lakes and forests in North America and Europe, little action has been taken to reduce the sulphur emissions that are thought to be the primary source and little has been done to repair the spreading damage. Perhaps most significantly, recent climatological research concerning the so-called greenhouse effect indicates that industrial and commercial activity may be radically altering the earth's climate, portending more erratic and violent weather and the possibility of widespread flooding as seas rise with warming temperatures.

These interdependent ecological crises, brought on by overheated production and transportation systems, will at some point demand a great deal of our attention. A key requirement will be to invent means of production and transportation that do not so heavily pollute the atmosphere. This is a very large challenge in itself and would usefully absorb the talents of many scientists and engineers released by disarmament and perhaps many more less-specialized workers to undertake the reclamation of the nation's and planet's polluted environments.[22]

Soil erosion is also accelerating both nationally and globally. Dramatic examples of desertification and its accompanying famine in the Sahel and elsewhere draw our immediate concern, but even in the United States croplands are being eroded at rates at least 25 percent higher than during the Dust Bowl of the 1930s. Each year some 6.4 billion tons of topsoil are lost, an amount sufficient to cover all croplands in New England, New York, New Jersey, Pennsylvania, Delaware, Maryland, Alabama, Arizona, California, and Florida with an inch of dirt.[23] Intimately connected to the destruction of soil fertility is the decline in the quantity and quality of fresh water supplies throughout the world. Irrigation of farmlands in the western United States has drawn down groundwater levels to dangerously low levels, threatening to exhaust aquifers that have accumulated over centuries. In parts of Arkansas, Texas, and Colorado, aquifers are being drained at four times their rate of replacement. Meanwhile, irrigation water, like the soils it nourishes, is becoming increasingly saline in the southwestern United States, stunting plant growth, while pesticides, sewage, and industrial wastes further pollute fresh water supplies.

Restoring both soil and water supplies will require a wide range of long-term measures, including better regulation of industrial chemical and agricultural pesticide practices and more judicious and regenerative farming techniques. In addition, research and development of more efficient means of waste disposal (sewage, radioactive substances, chemical by-products, and others) will require substantial infusions of capital and scientific talent. Engineers released from weapons work can be retrained for such civil engineering tasks with eighteen months to two years of additional study.

Develop Alternative Energy Sources. Intimately related to the problems of pollution and climatic change is the use and overuse of forms of energy that generate insupportable amounts of toxic by-products. U.S. investment in alternative energy research, which was never more than token even during the energy-scarce 1970s, has been cut to the vanishing point during the 1980s while dependence on foreign sources of oil and the exploitation of environmentally sensitive coastal waters have both intensified. Yet alternatives do exist and may well be closer to commercial viability than we realize. A 1976 study by a joint task force of the Federal Energy Administration and the U.S. Army concluded that a single $440 million purchase of photovoltaic cells (the cost of one B-1 bomber) by the Department of Defense, to replace one-fifth of the Pentagon's remote gas generators, would create the necessary economies of scale to plunge the price of solar electricity within one year from $15 per watt to $2 to 3 per watt, within 3 years to $1 per watt; and in 5 years to $.50/watt, when it would become competitive with all other forms of energy for residential use.[24]

Wind, geothermal, hydroelectric, and ocean thermal technologies also promise to contribute substantially to the national energy supply and thus reduce the need to depend on problematic foreign sources. Increased investment in both research and development and large-scale construction of alternative energy and recycling facilities, as well as tax incentives and other market mechanisms, would all reinforce national security in energy in ways that rapid deployment forces can never accomplish.

Cooperate in Space Exploration and Development. Given the urgency and cost of addressing the various earthbound priorities enumerated above, and the large but limited reservoir of resources released by disarmament, it might initially seem irresponsible to consider including cooperation in space between the great powers as a high priority. But space cooperation is not simply an idle escape from earthly difficulties; indeed, if wisely approached, it can become a key to resolving them. "The same technologies that threaten destruction, because they are too massive for the nation-state system to contain, control, or sanely use for traditional security and political objectives, could—if properly utilized—reduce rather than exacerbate underlying sources of global conflict," wrote Daniel Deudney, a key proponent of space cooperation. "It is a way of rechanneling rather than resisting the technology currently being used for military purposes."[25]

The particular advantages of space cooperation are several. It would provide alternative employment for a substantial number (though by no means all) of those now employed in military projects within the aerospace, electronics, and computer industries (among others), and would thus reduce the adverse employment impacts of curtailing weapons production. Space cooperation would also provide a highly visible, dramatic, and popular arena for cooperative effort (unlike many other equally important but more pedestrian forms of collaboration), likely to gain and sustain widespread political support on both sides of the East-West divide. Furthermore, the extraordinary surveillance capabilities of space technologies could be used to facilitate managing the earth's natural resources and monitoring natural disasters.

But most importantly, space cooperation could become the foundation for a global peace monitoring system, providing the means by which the international community could verify existing national arsenals, assure compliance with disarmament agreements, and communicate to control incipient crises (see chapter 10). Although such peaceful uses of space would not likely cost anywhere near what the superpowers now spend on space-related military technologies, they would more than justify their expense by the security benefits that would accrue from establishing a permanently internationalized space commons.

Financing Conversion

It is easy enough to find appropriate uses for the financial resources released by disarmament. But how would conversion be financed? Who would pay? Who would invest the capital necessary to remodel existing facilities for alternative uses and to carry over converting industries until they could become competitive in new markets? In a mostly free market civilian economy with a strong ideological preference for private investment, much of the initiative will need to come from the private sector. But private industry will not be inclined to take on the risks of investing in alternative products and services without substantial support from governmental sources (as they already receive in excessive amounts in the military economy). The 1985 Pentagon study of economic conversion estimates that in the absence of governmental support, a period of five to ten years of adjustment would be required to take a product from its initial planning phase to commercially profitable production.[26]

The rule of thumb would seem to be that private industry will finance its own conversion with appropriate incentives and technical assistance from governmental agencies. Current conversion legislation includes provision for a small percentage of all military contracts to be set aside to finance advance planning for conversion and to create an employee benefit fund for retraining, relocation, and income support. In addition, special investment tax credits would be offered to prospective candidates for conversion.[27] In providing financial incentives to private industry to aid in the conversion process, state agencies will need to calculate carefully how to provide just enough support to enable converting firms to survive and find a niche in their new civilian markets without simultaneously giving them an unfair advantage over other firms already in the industry.

Certain kinds of projects in the public sector, like rebuilding the urban infrastructure, will require direct federal support, although the work itself would be performed by private contractors. Some of these projects can be financed by user fees so that spending of military savings would be largely unnecessary. It is important to realize, however, that U.S. taxpayers already support an immense direct investment in the military economy, amounting to 44 percent of every tax dollar. The reinvestment of even a portion of that amount in rebuilding essential public services would more than repay the investment. Financier Felix Rohatyn has proposed establishing a reconstruction finance corporation similar to that set up under the New Deal to organize and underwrite such a rebuilding effort. "There is no economic or philosophical difference between the government financing needed for defense and the government financing needed for public investment," wrote Rohatyn.[28]

Obstacles to Conversion

Although it is clear from the foregoing analysis that the skills and resources now employed in the military economy could be recycled into alternative uses without intolerable dislocations and to great potential economic and social benefit, there remain both institutional and attitudinal resistances that are not easily dismissed by rational argument.

1. Military-serving industries provide their employees wages, benefits, and working environments rarely matched in the civilian economy. They also provide their investors with profits more substantial than all but a few civilian industries. In 1984 the ten largest military contractors earned a profit twice that of all manufacturing, realizing an average of 25 percent return on equity next to 12.8 percent for all manufacturing. According to a *New York Times* report,

> The measure of profitability—after-tax profits as a percentage of shareholder equity—is widely used on Wall Street and accepted as fair by the companies. Shareholder equity is the amount by which a company's assets exceed its liabilities. The 25 percent average return on equity actually understates how much the contractors make on their military business. The measure includes commercial sales, where profit rates are generally lower . . . [In addition,] when profits are recalculated on the basis of taxes actually paid, instead of simply provided for, the contractors' average profit rate increases to 35 percent on equity.[29]

Military industries operate on a cost-plus-profit basis, establishing a base price for products and then adding a percentage of profit. No commercial firm can afford such spendthrift habits; the market will not permit them. There is good reason to believe that reasonable profits can be made from the alternative goods and services such firms could produce in the commercial economy, but there is some doubt that such extraordinary rates of profit could be expected.

2. The geographical concentration of military industry and military installations in particular regions, as well as the broad distribution of such facilities in nearly every congressional district in the nation, create a potent constituency in every military-dependent community for maintaining high levels of defense spending. Military contractors often organize their employees to lobby for new weapons projects and against proposed

cutbacks. Political representatives in Washington, including even many who otherwise oppose increased military spending, find themselves obliged to vote in favor of weapons systems involving contracts in their own districts. The B-1B bomber, a weapon that many knowledgeable experts considered to be of dubious utility, was rendered veto proof by distributing work on it across 47 states; and more recently, the U.S. Navy, seeking support for building two additional aircraft carriers (at a cost of $7 billion), spread its contracts over 44 of 50 states and thus "coopted all but 10 of the House's 435 members."[30] Although conversion thinking has been initiated in part to allay the concerns of many who fear losing jobs in the process, it has not yet fully succeeded in eliminating those fears and thus reducing resistance to cutbacks.

3. Military manufacturing has become so specialized in recent years that few of its processes are now adaptable to the production of commercial goods. It is no longer a case of reconverting equipment that has previously produced goods in the civilian sector, as in the demobilization after World War II. It is now a matter of redesigning processes that have been evolving for a generation in a very different direction. Not all of this equipment will be usable in a converted economy.

4. The belief persists among some persons that prosperity can only be assured by continued high military spending. It has even been asserted that prosperity is not possible without conspicuous waste. Most evidence suggests that the very reverse is actually the case, that maintaining high levels of military spending detracts from future prosperity. But the impression still lingers to a degree, especially among the generation that endured the Depression, that because even the New Deal failed to fully revive the economy and only the war mobilization finally succeeded, therefore military spending is inherently good for the economy. This "Great Myth," in economist Kenneth Boulding's words, is beginning to disintegrate now in the face of much contrary evidence, and its dissolution may open the way to a more thoughtful and active consideration of the conversion alternative.

5. In arranging the conversion of the military economy, governmental and industry planners will need to make sure that the civilian economic activity spawned by the redirection of resources does not reproduce the dependent relationship that currently exists between military-serving industries and the Pentagon. While federal aid will be vital to ease the inevitable stresses of the transition, it must not be allowed to develop into a permanently favored relationship. The goal of federal aid must instead be to encourage self-sufficiency at the earliest possible date in the affected industries in order to assure that the resources freed from military spending are not simply diverted toward another form of corporate welfare.

Conclusion: The Long-Term Benefits of Conversion

It has been said that there are two kinds of people in the world, those who see the glass half empty and those who see it half full. Conversion has long been viewed, by both its critics and advocates, primarily as a problem—of unemployment, idled capacity, and reduced demand—for which there may or may not be solutions. The many persons and institutions that would be affected by the conversion process have been viewed almost as liabilities, in that their unemployment would exert a severe drag on the economy. There will, no doubt, be problems; there would be in any transformation of such dimensions. But it is also possible to see the glass half full, to see conversion not primarily as a problem but as an opportunity and to see those persons and institutions affected by it not as liabilities but as resources.

The evidence assembled here indicates that given careful attention to the process, conversion is a thoroughly manageable proposition. The key factors that would ensure its success are enough advance planning to assure a smooth transition to new employment for the persons and facilities displaced by disarmament, enough time to distribute the personnel and weapons cuts so as to minimize the impacts at any given moment, and enough imagination and initiative to reap the abundant opportunities for reconstruction and development opened by disarmament. Conversion is not an end itself, but a means toward a more comprehensive process of economic and social renewal that could ultimately set the foundation for the genuine prosperity of a peace economy.

Notes

1. See Seymour Melman, *The Defense Economy* (New York: Praeger, 1970); *Pentagon Capitalism* (New York: McGraw-Hill, 1970); *Profits Without Production* (New York: Knopf, 1983); and *The Permanent War Economy* (New York: Simon and Schuster, 1985).

2. *Defense Monitor*, vol. 15, no. 3 (1986), p. 4.

3. James Bamford, *The Puzzle Palace* (New York: Penguin Books, 1983), pp. 108–109.

4. *Defense Monitor*, p. 3.

5. Ibid.

6. "The Military-Industrial Complex in California." Mountain View, CA: Center for Economic Conversion, undated, p. 1.

7. *Economic Notes*, vol. 54, no. 2 (February 1986), p. 2 (New York: Labor Research Association). Original source: Robert DeGrasse, *Military Expansion, Economic Decline* (New York: Council on Economic Priorities, 1983).

8. *Economic Adjustment/Conversion* (Washington, DC: Office of Economic Adjustment, Office of the Assistant Secretary of Defense [Manpower, Installations

and Logistics], July 1985), Appendix, p. K-2. It is important to note, however, that 1982 and 1983 were recession years with exceptionally high unemployment.

9. See *BLS 1979 Employment Requirements Table*, Office of Economic Growth and Employment Projections, U.S. Bureau of Labor Statistics, October 23, 1981; also Dave McFadden and Jim Wake, *The Freeze Economy* (St. Louis: National Freeze Clearinghouse, 1983), p. 19; and Carolyn Kay Brancato and Linda LeGrande, "The Impact of Employment of Defense Versus Non-Defense Government Spending" (Washington, DC: Congressional Research Service, 1983). This study reported that 8.4 percent more jobs are lost when nondefense spending is cut than when defense spending is cut. The salaries of teachers and bus drivers would likely be significantly lower than those of the weapons engineers they replace, but since some of the cost of employing the engineer is absorbed in providing him with costly equipment and industrial infrastructure, the wage differential will not be as dramatic as the 4:1 ratio in job creation would seem to indicate.

10. *Economic Notes*, p. 3.

11. Lloyd Jeffry Dumas, *The Overburdened Economy* (Berkeley: University of California Press, 1986), pp. 219–221.

12. Office of Economic Adjustment, "25 Years of Civilian Reuse: Summary of Completed Military Base Economic Adjustment Projects" (Washington, DC: Office of the Assistant Secretary of Defense, Force Management and Personnel, The Pentagon, April–May 1986), pp. i, 2.

13. Department of Defense, "Projected Defense Purchases: Detail by Industry and State, Calendar Years 1986 Through 1991" (Washington, DC: Directorate for Information Operations and Reports, Department of Defense, 1986), pp. 27, 28, 47, 49, and 50.

14. *Economic Adjustment/Conversion*, Appendix pp. K-6, K-7.

15. Dave Elliot and Hilary Wainwright, "The Lucas Plan: The Roots of the Movement," in Suzanne Gordon and Dave McFadden, *Economic Conversion: Revitalizing America's Economy* (Cambridge, MA: Ballinger, 1984), p. 97.

16. *Economic Adjustment/Conversion*, Appendix N-10.

17. Ibid., Appendix N-19.

18. Bruce Scott and George C. Lodge, "U.S. Competitiveness in the World Economy: A Problem of Premises" (Cambridge, MA: Harvard Business School Working Paper, September 1984), p. 1.

19. "The Rebuilding of America: A $2.5 Trillion Job," *U.S. News and World Report*, September 27, 1982, p. 57.

20. Pat Choate and Susan Walter, *America in Ruins* (Durham, NC: Duke University Press, 1981), p. 2.

21. "The Rebuilding of America," p. 57.

22. The Cornucopia Project, *Empty Breadbasket?* (Emmaus, PA: Rodale Press, 1981), pp. 31, 32.

23. See Julianne Malveaux and Alden Bryant, "A Plan for Social Action in Reduction of Atmospheric Carbon Dioxide and Climate Stabilization" (Berkeley, CA: Earth Regeneration Society, 1986). Bryant has devised an employment plan involving 20 million persons in tasks including "remineralizing" the soil (6 million jobs), reforestation (2.9 million), reconstruction of damaged environments (1 million), and alternative energy research and development (4.8 million).

24. See Barry Commoner, *The Politics of Energy* (New York: Alfred Knopf, 1979), pp. 34–35.

25. Daniel Deudney, "Forging Missiles into Spaceships," *World Policy Journal*, vol. 2, no. 2, Spring 1985, pp. 274, 277.

26. "Economic Adjustment/Conversion," Appendix M-30.

27. Dumas, *The Overburdened Economy*, pp. 267–268.

28. See Felix Rohatyn, *The Twenty Year Century* (New York: Random House, 1983), p. 26.

29. Jeff Gerth, "U.S. Weapons Makers Ring Up Healthy Profits," *New York Times*, April 9, 1985, p. 40.

30. "Making Carriers Unsinkable," *New York Times*, April 2, 1987, p. 30.

PART THREE

Prospects for Transformation

CHAPTER THIRTEEN

Toward a Common Security System: A Proposal

In part one we examined the United Nations system and six alternative approaches to security, each of which, if implemented, would fundamentally alter the balance of power system by which nations now relate to one another. Each has both strengths and weaknesses, virtues and defects, if not in concept, then in practice. Those strategies requiring the fewest changes in global political and military arrangements (like strategic defense) command the greatest immediate appeal because they are easily comprehended. But they lack the complex range of structures and features necessary to deal with the manifold threats to peace they will inevitably encounter. On the other hand, those that have been scrupulously designed to deal with every eventuality (like the Clark-Sohn Plan) are so comprehensive and demanding that although they might work very well indeed once put into effect, they stand little chance of actually being enacted.

But a closer look at the strengths and weaknesses of each strategy suggests possible syntheses that compensate for one another's individual defects. The whole is once again greater than the sum of its parts. Taken together, these varied approaches provide a rudimentary outline for what might be called a "common security system," based on the commonsense principle of assuring security equally to all nations and peoples.

Before we explore the design of a common security system, it may be useful to summarize the relative strengths and weaknesses of each approach taken alone. We have chosen not to include strategic defense here because in our view it is an intensification of the arms race rather than an alternative to it.

Strengths and Weaknesses of Each Approach

Several approaches share certain characteristics. With the exception of the Clark-Sohn Plan, which makes detailed provisions for a world security system in the broadest sense—global armed forces, conflict resolution procedures and institutions, enforcement, and so forth—the other proposals are far more limited. They are concerned with making certain fundamental changes in the availability or nonavailability of armed forces and armaments and their control. In all cases, the assumption is that the existing UN institutions or a strengthened version of them would remain in place.

In several important respects, the majority of proposals share both their strengths and their weaknesses. Each of them, with the exception of the Clark-Sohn Plan, lacks any reliable means of enforcement other than that provided by the United Nations as it now exists. The entirely voluntary nature of UN participation and action assures that this capacity for enforcement will remain limited. Neither nonprovocative defense, civilian-based defense, nor qualitative disarmament designates a means to assure that other nations comply with the arrangement. But since civilian-based defense and nonprovocative defense have usually been conceived as strategies for individual nations rather than as universal negotiated agreements (or, in the case of CBD, as a complement to other systems), they do not require enforcement mechanisms.

Minimum deterrence could induce compliance with its provisions, though not physical enforcement, by means of a rigorous system of national and international verification techniques. In this respect, it most resembles qualitative disarmament. Nations would be deterred from wholesale cheating by the knowledge that any significant clandestine rearmament would likely be detected by either the national technical means of their adversaries or an international verification agency. In the case of qualitative disarmament, while compliance is voluntary, the incentives to the rational policymaker are considerable. The long-term economic and financial benefits would be greater than under any other system. In addition, rigorous verification and inspection procedures could exercise a powerfully inhibiting effect on the temptation to break out of the agreement. Finally, if national arsenals were stripped to their barest essentials, it would take time and considerable effort to rebuild a war-fighting capability, time during which the other parties to the agreement could themselves take compensatory measures.

The one system considered here that grapples fully with the politically sensitive question of enforcement is the Clark-Sohn Plan, which unequivocally inserts enforcement provisions into its grand scheme. Asserting that the plan would never work without such "teeth," Clark and Sohn established compulsory jurisdiction by a global court system over the limited field of war prevention and a potent peace force to carry out its decisions. It was likely on this critical issue of enforcement that the Clark-Sohn Plan foundered, as no nation was yet ready to cede that degree of national sovereignty. The other systems considered here were developed with the implicit recognition that enforcement would remain perhaps the most troublesome issue of all. It is still an open question whether the absence of enforcement would be the ultimate undoing of these systems or whether requiring enforcement mechanisms would make them unsellable in the first instance.

In addition, none of the systems considered here, again with the exception of the Clark-Sohn Plan, makes provision for strengthening global conflict resolution machinery. Under every other security system, nations would need to make use of the existing facilities of the UN which, though routinely neglected, are considerable. However, in a world in which military competition is minimized or eliminated, some conflicts relating to the maintenance of global power would be diminished in intensity and therefore become more amenable to being mediated by existing conflict resolution procedures and institutions.

Finally, it should be noted that the implementation of a Clark-Sohn Plan, qualitative disarmament, nonprovocative defense, or civilian-based defense would oblige nations to give up their capability of intervening militarily in the affairs of other nations. (This would not apply to a minimum deterrent system, in which conventional forces and some nuclear forces would be retained.) While this characteristic would be an adverse factor in gaining the support of the larger powers, for most of the smaller nations (especially in the Third World), it would represent a substantial gain.

The United Nations

The UN system's greatest strength is that it already exists; it is not a mere theory. Its institutions function, some well and some badly, and it will probably survive the neglect it routinely endures. It is a foundation on which other, more substantial structures may yet be built. But its weaknesses are equally evident. Its security structures are its weakest links. The Security Council, conceived by the Charter's framers to be the executive authority in all matters of international security, has been perpetually stalemated and has become largely irrelevant in recent years. The General Assembly, which has inherited many of the Security Council's functions and responsibilities, issues many strongly worded resolutions but lacks any capacity to enforce them.

Collective security failed to materialize early on in the UN's history. Peacekeeping, the organization's most significant achievement in the field of security, has dwindled in recent years to a few longstanding commitments, its facilities routinely bypassed in the arenas of conflict for which its services would likely be most useful. Some of the weaknesses in the UN system are structural; others are external to the system, the result of misuse and abuse.

A Clark-Sohn Peacekeeping Federation

The Clark-Sohn peacekeeping federation seeks to remedy the structural defects of the UN system in a number of ways, including strengthening the powers of the General Assembly, accompanied by direct election of its members on a modified proportional basis; disarming all nations down to domestic forces required for maintaining internal order; establishing a sizeable world peace force to police the global system; compulsory jurisdiction of the World Court in security matters; and a limited power of taxation. The product of two brilliant legal minds, the Clark-Sohn Plan is hard to fault on formal grounds.

The plan's principal difficulty is that it demands a substantial transfer of sovereignty in the peacekeeping field from the national to the global level. Given the worldwide resurgence of nationalist politics and sentiment in recent years and the continuing resistance of many nations (especially the great powers) to sharing power in matters of security with a global authority, the Clark-Sohn Plan seems likely to remain, for the foreseeable future, outside the realm of possibility. Nevertheless, its architecture is so fundamentally sound that modest adaptations of the plan, or of certain of its component parts, might prove politically practical.

Minimum Deterrence

Minimum deterrence, the first of three defensively oriented "advanced arms control" proposals, has the virtue of being easily implemented. Involving as it does only nuclear arsenals and thus just the nuclear powers, minimum deterrence leaves intact virtually every other feature of the balance of power system. It thus exacts no reductions in conventional weapons. In fact, under some minimum deterrence scenarios, conventional arsenals are even strengthened, especially in their most offensive elements. Indeed, mainstream thinking in the NATO alliance in the mid-1980s tends to support the view that any reductions in nuclear arsenals at the tactical, theater, or strategic level will inevitably require bolstering the alliance's capacity for "forward defense," carrying the battle back to the enemy.

Thus the strength of minimum deterrence, its minimal requirements for structural change and the ease with which it could be implemented, is also its greatest weakness. In the absence of restraints on offensive conventional arsenals, minimum deterrence could easily end up substituting one threat for another. Since it has long been accepted by strategic analysts that conventional forces are more readily "usable" than nuclear forces, this solitary shift, reducing the nuclear offense while increasing the conventional offense, could unintentionally end up destabilizing the balance between nations. By combining nuclear reductions with a freeze or corresponding reduction in offensive conventional arsenals, nations can be certain of a genuine gain in mutual security.

Qualitative Disarmament

The supreme virtue of qualitative disarmament is the simplicity of the concept. Acknowledging that threat (or the perception of threat) is the primary fuel of the arms race and fuse for war, qualitative disarmament seeks to remove the immediate cause of the threat—all weapons capable of attack, nuclear *and* conventional—while simultaneously strengthening border defenses. By this process, qualitative disarmament seeks to render war far less likely, if not physically impossible. At the very least, overt military action would necessarily be delayed for a considerable period while the nations involved rebuilt their war-making capabilities. This period of time could be used by the UN and by other nations to initiate a settlement of the differences by nonviolent means. But qualitative disarmament also requires universal agreement at the outset on a comprehensive disarmament regime and voluntary compliance thereafter, and this degree of consensus could be very difficult to achieve.

Nonprovocative Defense

Nonprovocative defense has the singular virtue of being entirely self-starting. Unlike minimal deterrence and qualitative disarmament, which both necessitate agreement, nations choosing nonprovocative defense decide of their own accord to blunt their swords and gird their shields, transforming their arsenals from offense to defense. No agreement is required between nations and no higher authority is created. Some nations may retain offensive arsenals without penalty while others adopt a nonprovocative defense posture; the two are expected to coexist. Nonprovocative defense as a global system does not enforce uniformity on all nations. Instead of universal arms reductions or disarmament, it highlights the independent initiative of nations and hopes the example will prove infectious. The primary weakness of nonprovocative defense derives precisely from what is also its greatest strength—its unilateral nature. Many nations may choose not to shed the offense and could still pose a threat to those that do.

Civilian-based Defense

The great virtue of civilian-based defense is its thoroughly nonviolent nature. No other system rejects hardware and violence of all kinds. If undertaken as an independent initiative, civilian-based defense requires no changes in the larger global system. However, it does require a very considerable transformation of politics, economy, and culture to cause a nation to relinquish all its weapons and technical devices and to rely instead solely on its bare-handed and unconquerable determination to remain free and independent. But although it is difficult indeed to imagine CBD in the foreseeable future as a global system to which all agree, and still more problematic to conceive a nation transarming alone to CBD while its neighbors and most of the rest of the world remain locked in an offensive arms race, it is much easier to see CBD adopted in conjunction with other systems, to the great benefit of all. Both qualitative disarmament and nonprovocative defense would be greatly strengthened by the addition of citizen training in nonviolent resistance.

Integrating Approaches: A Proposal for a Common Security System

We have now considered these alternative approaches as separate, discrete options. But the more interesting question is how these systems might be combined with one another in order to strengthen those aspects where each is individually weak. Proposals that, taken alone, may seem politically infeasible or strategically unwise might become much more viable when linked with complementary aspects of other systems. In certain important respects, the entire range of alternative strategies surveyed in this volume dovetail with one another, reinforcing strengths and diminishing weaknesses. What none of them can achieve alone, they seem better able to accomplish together.

This proposal for a common security system should be regarded as the first step in an ongoing process as the requirements for managing the world's problems keep changing through the twenty-first century. With the mitigation or elimination of the military threats now permeating so many of the essential relations between nations, however, the recommended changes would create a very different climate from what exists today, a climate far more conducive to making other desirable changes.

Like many of the alternatives reviewed in this volume, this integrated proposal is based on the commonsense principle of common security, the understanding that in the nuclear age there is no ethical or practical rationale for nations to maintain a conventional or nuclear war-fighting capability provided that the defense of those nations can be more effectively managed by other means. It thus implies a fundamental shift of emphasis from unilateral military defense (and offense) to shared security, rooted in the understanding that the safety of nations depends not only on their own independent security arrangements but equally on the security of their adversaries.

Military Security Provisions

Qualitative Disarmament. The principle of qualitative disarmament, first developed by the British military strategist B. H. Liddell Hart in 1932 and subsequently endorsed by President Hoover, President Roosevelt, and the great majority of nations at the Geneva Disarmament Conference of that same year, would form the basis for a new set of negotiations and treaties. Under such a treaty, nations would agree to eliminate their war-fighting capabilities—that is, all conventional weapons other than those useful only for defense, and all nuclear weapons except those required temporarily for minimum deterrence. The process could be scheduled within a limited time period or could be left more open-ended to "rest" for a time at certain plateaus in the disarming process while continuing in the direction of a wholly disarmed world, as in the Forsberg proposal (see chapter 6).

Minimum Deterrence. The sole exception to the retention of only defensive weapons would be the temporary retention by the nuclear powers of a small fraction of their current nuclear arsenals adequate to impede the use of such weapons against them by other nuclear powers. As part of the agreement, development of several other weapon systems would also need to be curtailed (as it would be in any case in the course of the disarming process). Bans on antisatellite and antisubmarine technologies, strategic defenses, and new nuclear delivery systems would be particularly important in assuring that a minimum deterrent regime remained stable and effective. In a minimum deterrent system of 50 to 200 nuclear missiles for each of the two superpowers and a proportionately smaller number for the lesser nuclear powers, there would be little or nothing left to threaten a submarine-based missile force. The stability of this situation would be without precedent.

The retention of a minimum deterrent must be seen as a necessary accommodation to political reality. Time will be required to build confidence in the new system to the point where the deterrent no longer seems necessary or some other accommodation is found, perhaps by turning the remaining nuclear weapons over to a global authority, as was first suggested by the Baruch-Lilienthal proposals of 1946 and subsequently by Clark and Sohn. The exact process by which this minimum deterrent would be finally relinquished is a matter worthy of intensive study by strategic analysts, for while there have been a number of careful studies of reducing nuclear arsenals to minimal levels, there have been almost none as yet of taking the stockpiles from those few down to absolute zero in a manner that will remain safe, stable, and politically practical. However the problem is resolved, the retention of nuclear weapons by any authority, national or global, should be regarded as a purely temporary expedient.

Civilian-based Defense. Nations should be encouraged to adopt civilian-based defense individually as a supplement to the few remaining defenses left to them under a qualitative disarmament agreement. In a world in which all weapons capable of significant offensive action have been eliminated from national arsenals, the remaining protective defenses could be greatly strengthened by a civilian population trained in the tactics of civilian-based defense. Linking qualitative disarmament with civilian-based defense would provide disarmament with the alternative defense policy that it has never yet possessed. Proponents of disarmament have given surprisingly little thought to what can replace the weapons that are eliminated, to what else can protect nations from their adversaries. But while disarmament advocates have neglected the question, disarmament opponents have been preoccupied with it, believing that in the absence of a viable replacement defense, disarmament would be suicide. For their part, some proponents of disarmament believe that nothing needs to replace the existing defense policy because there is no threat. Others, not so sure there is no threat, have begun to look for alternative forms of defense. CBD might provide a long-missing link in making qualitative disarmament at last a viable option.

Common Defense. As development of offensive weapons of all kinds is being eliminated by the process of qualitative disarmament, some portion of the vast resources liberated by the process should be shifted over to the development of mutually protective techniques and technologies—that is, to developing means to protect all sides equally from harm rather than just one against all others. Unlike defensive weapons, many of which remain convertible to offensive uses, mutually protective technologies would not be weapons at all but tools and instruments designed specifically to prevent conflict whenever possible and to minimize injury to all sides if it does occur.

Because they threaten no one and benefit all equally, research ventures into mutually protective techniques and devices would be ideal candidates for transnational joint ventures, especially between archrivals, who often have the greatest investment in one another's security. These technologies would be in effect the military equivalent of fire-fighting equipment, in that instead of fighting fire with fire, which merely feeds the flames, they would fight it with water, which douses the flames. Both verification systems and crisis control technologies are examples of such war-prevention equipment already in place and under development. Other possibilities, both strategic and technical, can readily be imagined. The research possibilities are almost inexhaustible.[1]

The common security system outlined here would offer nations numerous advantages even if no other actions were taken. But it would not in itself resolve the many remaining social, economic, and political problems that give rise to suspicion and disputes between nations. Means must be strengthened for the management and resolution of conflict by nonviolent means. A common security system would be greatly reinforced by the addition of several other elements.

Conflict Resolution Provisions

There seems little question that the provisions for conflict resolution contained in Articles 33–38 of the UN Charter would operate more effectively in a world in which the superpowers and other nations were no longer engaged in an arms race. Many disputes that in today's world are associated with foreign bases or military support for one side or another in internal disturbances would no longer exist. With this military threat largely removed, nations should be more willing to submit many or most other kinds of disputes to the existing conflict resolution machinery of the United Nations. Under these radically changed conditions, nations might well be willing to strengthen the UN's conflict resolution procedures by giving the International Court of Justice compulsory jurisdiction over all disputes that arise over interpretation of or compliance with the qualitative disarmament treaty.

Both the Soviet Union and the United States objected to this delegation of authority when it was first proposed in 1945, and it would still meet with resistance today. At that time, however, the conditions were radically different from those outlined in this proposal. If nations did indeed agree to a process of qualitative disarmament, they would certainly want to assure that no other nation would be able to defy or evade the agreement with impunity. Under these circumstances, the judgment of the World Court on an alleged infraction of the disarming process would probably carry considerably more weight both with governments and world opinion than it now does.

In order to deal with the disputes between nations that are directly related to the treaty, it is suggested that a World Equity Tribunal be established along the lines proposed in the Clark-Sohn Plan. This tribunal could not make binding decisions but only recommendations. Its principal function would be to provide a forum for the expression of world public opinion, adding positive incentives for compliance by virtue of its authoritative and nonpartisan perspective.

Under the umbrella of a reformed and revived United Nations system, other vital components in a common security system could take shelter.

A global arms verification network, along the lines of the French proposal for an international satellite monitoring agency (ISMA), could produce impartial data on weapons stockpiles and provide the essential monitoring of the qualitative disarmament process. A well-funded and well-equipped verification system under the control of the United Nations could go far in inhibiting nations from engaging in clandestine rearmament. Fearing exposure of their transgressions and consequent censure and possible sanctions, nations might largely comply with the agreement even in the absence of physical enforcement.

Peacekeeping Provisions of the Integrated Security System

The elimination of the war-making capabilities of nations will not in itself significantly reduce the number of disputes that will continue to arise between them. In fact, as the world becomes increasingly interdependent, the number of nonmilitary disputes will probably increase. It is essential, therefore, not only to improve the UN's conflict resolution procedures but to strengthen its peacekeeping machinery.

A Permanent UN Peacekeeping Force. To become an institution on which nations can reliably depend, the UN needs a permanent peacekeeping force of at least 10,000 persons, with another 20,000 held in reserve. This force would be essentially nonmilitary in nature and tactics, being thoroughly trained in nonviolent techniques and armed to the greatest extent practical with nonlethal hardware. In addition, its members should be individually recruited from the smaller nations, rather than sent on loan by national armed forces. The primary function of these forces would be to prevent border clashes from escalating into larger conflicts and to inhibit third parties from supplying military equipment to the belligerents in civil wars.[2]

A Force of Trained Observers. In addition to the peacekeeping force, the UN could maintain a small force of trained observers to be dispatched, with permission from the affected nations, to regions of incipient conflict. These observers would report their findings back to the Secretary-General. The UN's mediation services could also be expanded so that each peacekeeping force dispatched to the field would include a team of mediators to deal with unresolved differences between the warring parties.

Nonintervention Regimes. In a common security system, the problem of one nation using its armed forces to intervene in the internal affairs of another would be greatly diminished, for nations would no longer be permitted to maintain an interventionary capability. It is highly probable, however, that the larger nations would still occasionally bring unwarranted pressure to bear on the internal affairs of smaller nations and, in cases where an internal revolution is taking place, even attempt to supply one side or the other with small arms. In order to prevent these and other forms of intervention, regional nonintervention regimes could be established. There is a growing literature of proposals that considers the forms such agreements might take.[3]

Verification

An impartial and effective system of verification and inspection would exercise a powerfully inhibiting effect on plans to evade the agreement. As nations under the present system invest most of their military budgets in weaponry, under a comprehensive disarmament regime they could be expected to invest the major portion in verification and information systems to assure themselves that no significant cheating is taking place. As suggested by Jerome Wiesner, former science adviser to presidents Eisenhower and Kennedy, nations would "substitute information for weapons,"[4] so that the capacity to detect replaces the capacity to destroy. The superpowers already employ extensive and sophisticated arrays of national technical means (NTM) to glean information about one another's activities, ranging from highly technical devices such as satellite reconnaissance and radar to a variety of nontechnical means, including espionage. Cooperative measures, while less extensive, already play a significant role.

Joint verification measures would likely be given a much more significant role under a comprehensive disarmament plan. International verification agencies, maintaining equipment, staff, and databases independent of any individual government and perhaps sponsored by all of them, could provide an impartial and authoritative source of information. Its nonpartisan nature would help counteract the inevitable tendency of national intelligence organizations to issue self-serving estimates of their own and their enemy's strength. Three specific recommendations make a good start: an International Satellite Monitoring Agency (ISMA), established under UN auspices; an International Seismic Data Exchange, as recommended by Jerome Wiesner; and a network of seismic monitors installed in nuclear nations to detect possible test explosions. Ultimately, as Swedish disarmament expert Alva Myrdal suggests, it would be useful to create an international disarmament control organization, likely under the auspices of the UN, to act as a clearinghouse for verification information. This agency would not itself pronounce judgments but would only "assemble, collate, coordinate and transmit data."[5] It would then become the responsibility of the parties to the agreement, collectively or independently, to decide the proper response to the information given.

A Reliable Source of Funds

A reliable source of funds to cover all the provisions directly related to the common security system would need to be provided, on an equitable basis, as part of the treaty. This could be accomplished in any number of ways, including an entirely new system of taxation. Clark and Sohn suggested "a grant to the United Nations of adequate powers to raise . . . sufficient and reliable revenues to assure the effective fulfillment of its enlarged responsibilities."[6] This grant of the powers of taxation to the UN would require strict safeguards if agreed upon and would need to be carried out through existing tax-collecting machinery of the various member states to avoid creating yet another huge, bureaucratic tax-gathering organization of its own. Alternatively, the UN's existing revenue system could be expanded, but it would need to be far more effective in collecting pledges than it has been in recent years. Whether or not taxation is part of the revenue-raising process, a means of assuring that it is equitably administered is essential.

Compliance with a Common Security System

A key question affecting both the political appeal and long-term viability of any global security system, including the common security system proposed here, is to what degree nations would comply with the obligations they undertake in signing the agreement. This question has two aspects, enforcement and incentives. Nations can (at least theoretically) be forced by one means or another to obey the terms of a treaty or induced to comply by means of a variety of positive and negative incentives. Enforcement provisions are consciously not built into this design for a common security system because they would of necessity require substantial transfers of sovereignty that seem infeasible in the near or middle term.

But systems without enforcement provisions raise an important question about whether an agreement could be made to stick if there is no penalty for abandoning it. It is true that there are very few enforcement mechanisms built into the arms control agreements already in effect. In the cases of SALT I, SALT II, the Non-Proliferation Treaty and the Partial Test Ban Treaty, for example, there have been no formal provisions to exact a penalty for violations, either in the form of economic or military sanctions. In most of these cases, the self-interest of the contracting parties has combined with national means of verification to inhibit breakout from the agreement.

But it is also widely accepted that cheating has gone on at the margins and perhaps closer to the center as well. Despite the ABM Treaty, for example, both the United States and the Soviet Union quietly continued to research the possibilities of ballistic missile defense throughout the 1970s. And in the mid-1980s, the voluntary restraints in SALT II accepted by both sides in the absence of ratification by the U.S. Senate were eventually abandoned by the United States (which accused the USSR of exceeding the treaty's limits), while the Soviet Union vowed to remain bound by its terms. Whether such cheating as would inevitably occur under any thoroughly voluntary agreement could become militarily significant would be a critical factor in determining whether nations accept the agreement in the first instance and whether they keep to its terms once enacted.

As Roger Fisher pointed out in chapter 11, if a large nation chooses to defy the terms of an international treaty, there is no way to force it to comply short of an all-powerful world government. But there are numerous incentives, both positive and negative, inducing governments to abide by their treaty obligations even in the absence of formal enforcement mechanisms. The threat of retaliation by one's adversaries, the threat of disapproval and discord among one's allies, the weight of adverse world public opinion, domestic opposition, and the possibility of joint economic or political sanctions against the offender, all influence the decision of a government to abide by or abandon the terms of a treaty. In addition, Fisher suggested that treaty obligations could be incorporated into national constitutions and made personally binding on individuals. And, as suggested earlier in this chapter, under the dramatically altered conditions of a disarmament agreement, nations might be willing to give the World Court compulsory jurisdiction over the limited range of disputes arising over interpretation of or compliance with the treaty.

Both governments and their citizens would have a strong vested interest in making certain that all nations abide by the terms of the treaty, since cheating would be seen as a direct and immediate threat to their security. In a world economy of increasing interdependence, economic boycotts could become potent weapons to enforce compliance and penalize violators. Nations continuing to abide by the agreement could be expected to be exceedingly vigilant about verifying that others are not cheating and very severe in their responses if cheating were detected. Despite all these forms of political and economic deterrence and sanction, some nations might still choose to defy the agreement and the full weight of world public opinion—as, indeed, nations like South Africa, Libya, and the two superpowers (among others) now do. These nations might carry with them others that decide that they cannot afford to hold to an agreement that their rivals are violating. Such epidemics of defections are not uncommon. Often one nation will accuse its adversary (rightly or wrongly) of cheating and then respond by exceeding the limits of the agreement itself. Indeed, this is how treaties most often die.

What would prevent such a mass defection from occurring under a system lacking enforcement mechanisms? And what would happen if the defections did occur? Would the world simply revert to its former armed state, with nothing gained but nothing lost? If national arsenals were already stripped back to the purely defensive components specified in the agreement, it would no doubt take years to reassemble a significant arsenal and the project would not likely remain invisible to a rigorous verification and inspection system. Other nations would have plenty of time to exercise their options, either to institute nonmilitary sanctions against the violator or to rearm themselves. Since they would already have invested years in the disarming process, they could be expected to retain a strong attachment to its fruits and a determination to make it work.

The common security system outlined here would provide a wide range of benefits to all participants, rewards that could serve as powerful inducements to its adoption and its maintenance once enacted. It would minimize the possibility of a fatal nuclear exchange by mechanical malfunctioning or human miscalculation; it would reduce the possibility of nuclear war resulting from escalation from a conventional war; it would greatly reduce the problem of nuclear proliferation; it would liberate hundreds of billions of dollars each year from counterproductive military projects to finance the revitalization of ailing industries, the reconstruction of blighted cities, and the restoration of threatened natural environments; and overall, it would permit a redirection of vast human and technical resources from destructive to constructive purposes.

This common security system is not intended to homogenize the nations and peoples of the world or to transform the planet into a unitary system or culture. Quite the contrary. The goal is to make the world safe for its differences—differences in values, histories, cultures, religions, and economic and political institutions. These differences are potentially a blessing rather than a curse, for diversity is what gives interest and meaning to life.

Nor does this outline for a common security system make any pretense of dealing directly with rapidly proliferating social, economic, and environmental problems. We have chosen here to concentrate on the military dimensions of security not because they are more important than other forms but because a collective preoccupation with them distracts nations from addressing other, equally essential dimensions of security. The aim of this proposal is to change the scenery, to set the stage for an effective and sustained effort to meet these challenges by freeing substantial resources, including human intelligence, from concentrating on perfecting ever more efficient killing machines to designing techniques and technologies to assure the health and well-being of all life on this planet.

Notes

1. See, for example, Mark Sommer, *Beating Our Swords Into Shields* (Miranda, CA: Center for a Preservative Defense, 1983).

2. For a specific proposal concerning a transnational peacekeeping force, see Robert C. Johansen and Saul H. Mendlovitz, "The Role of Enforcement of Law in the Establishment of a New International Order: A Proposal for a Transnational Police Force," *Alternatives: A Journal of World Policy,* vol. 6, no. 2 (1980), pp. 307–337.

3. See, for example, Randall Forsberg, "The Case for a Third World Nonintervention Regime," *Alternative Defense Working Paper* #6 (Brookline, MA: Institute for Defense and Disarmament Studies, December 1987); Alexander George, *Managing US-Soviet Rivalry* (Boulder, CO: Westview Press, 1980); Robert Keohane, *After Hegemony* (Princeton, NJ: Princeton University Press, 1984); S. Krasner, ed., *International Regimes* (Ithaca, NY: Cornell University Press, 1983); and Sherle Schwenninger and Jerry Sanders, "The Democrats and a New Grand Strategy: A Third World Policy for the Post-Reagan Era," *World Policy Journal,* vol. 4 (Winter 1986–1987), pp. 1–54.

4. Jerome Wiesner, "An International Arms Verification and Study Center." Unpublished paper (Cambridge, MA: December 1985).

5. Alva Myrdal, "The International Control of Disarmament," *Scientific American,* vol. 231, no. 4 (October 1974), p. 31.

6. Grenville Clark and Louis Sohn, *World Peace Through World Law: Two Alternative Plans* (3rd ed., enlarged) (Cambridge, MA: Harvard University Press, 1966), p. 349.

CHAPTER FOURTEEN

The Peril and the Promise

So let us not be blind to our differences—but let us also direct attention to our common interests and the means by which those differences can be resolved. And if we cannot end now our differences, at least we can help make the world safe for diversity. For, in the final analysis our most basic common link is that we all inhabit this small planet. We all breathe the same air. We all cherish our children's future. And we are all mortal.

—President John F. Kennedy[1]

This moment is rife with peril, but it is also ripe with promise. The means now exist to split the planet asunder. But the possibilities also now exist to link it together as never before in human history. The barriers that remain are not primarily technical but political. Nations need not agree on how best to live or govern themselves. They need only agree to accept that they will often differ and to let those differences stand. So long viewed as a curse, the differences between us are in fact a secret blessing, for their variety imbues existence with interest and meaning. Diversity is a sign of life, an indicator of social and political health. Understood as diversity rather than division, our differences can become a source of creative stimulus rather than destructive struggle.

It is not difficult to construct, at least in theoretical terms, a system for assuring global security that would better serve the interests of the human race than that under which we now live. The challenge before us is to construct a global security system that will not only serve the interests of all nations and peoples but will also stand a reasonable chance of being accepted.

A Broader Definition of Self-Interest

We do not underestimate the political obstacles to constructing a fundamentally new global security system. Make no mistake. Despite the fact that the kind of shift suggested here would serve the most vital interests of all humankind—the avoidance of nuclear war, the elimination of the capacity of any nation to launch large-scale armed aggression against other nations, and the transfer of immense quantities of resources from destructive to productive purposes—despite these and other self-evident rewards, the shift to a nonviolent global security system will meet sustained and determined opposition from a wide variety of interests. These interests range from those who tend to oppose change on principle to all those persons and institutions with financial interests in continuing the present system of arms competition. In the United States, there is scarcely a single congressional district that does not reap rewards from the manufacture and maintenance of military apparatus, even though the society as a whole (and many particular regions) incurs net losses from the displacement of precious resources from other, more urgent priorities. The challenge is not to deny self-interest in nations or people, but to redefine that interest to include a longer time horizon and a broader definition of self. What is in the long-term interest of all nations and peoples, as opposed to the short-term interest of a select few?

Toward a Movement to Dismantle the War System

A movement of the kind required to replace the war system must be something far more bold and decisive than arms control has ever been or could ever become. Arms control negotiations have never aimed at actually reversing the arms race, still less at eliminating the capacity of nations to make war on one another. Believing these larger goals to be laudable in the abstract but wholly unattainable in the real world, arms control advocates have settled for the far more modest goal of stabilizing the arms race, seeking to mitigate its most dangerous and destructive aspects while leaving its essential dynamic intact.

But this cautious, incremental approach has often proven to be too little and too late, lending the impression of progress while masking an inexorable trend toward further acceleration of the arms race. Arms control as it has been practiced does not reach to the root of the problem but only to its symptoms. The unfortunate fact is that despite the completion of numerous arms control agreements, each year since the advent of arms control the arms race has continued to escalate. The stated objectives of arms control are worthy and should be pursued, but only as interim steps in the larger agenda of dismantling the entire war system.

Unlike arms control negotiations to limit or reduce a particular weapon system, negotiations to deny all nations the means to maintain a war-making capability are based on a clear moral imperative rooted in an age-old ethical foundation—thou shalt not kill. Surely if this commandment means anything at all, it means that thou shalt not possess the right or capacity to kill hundreds of thousands or tens of millions of people. Virtually all the successful reform movements of recent history, from the abolition of slavery to civil rights, women's rights, and environmental movements, have been based on sound ethical and moral underpinnings as well as on practical benefits. The issues and principles involved in these movements are easily comprehended. All recognize that life is a precious gift not to be capriciously threatened or denied. All assert that everyone possesses an equal right to life's blessings. All are deeply rooted in universally recognized ethical norms.

Voices for the Abolition

Combining great material rewards with an ethical and moral foundation is the stuff of which great movements are made. Eliminating the war-making capability of nations and replacing it with a system of shared security links principles with pragmatism, yielding dramatic financial incentives and a salient clarity of moral purpose. Ordinary people can understand and say yes. It is for this reason that a big-step approach may ultimately prove a more practical route to peace than the cautious and ineffectual strategies that have been pursued for the past generation. With the mobilization of a broad-based movement linking principles and pragmatism, the transition to a world beyond the threat of cataclysmic war could be underway by the turn of the century.

Statements like these are routinely dismissed as utopian and not given serious consideration by most policymakers or political leaders. But there are significant exceptions, and they are a growing number. Persons of vast practical experience and highly respected judgment have concluded that nothing less than the abolition of war will suffice to assure a human future. General Douglas MacArthur, most widely recognized for his military victories in the Pacific during World War II, reached this conclusion in a remarkable but little-known speech delivered to the American Legion on January 26, 1955:

> Many will say, with mockery and ridicule, that the abolition of war can be only a dream—that it is but the vague imagining of a visionary. But we must go on or we will go under. And the great criticism that can be made is that the world lacks a plan that will enable us to go on. . . . The next great advance in the evolution of civilization cannot take place until war is abolished. It may take another cataclysm of destruction to prove to [leaders] this simple truth. But, strange as it may seem, it is known now by all common men. It is the one issue upon which both sides can agree, for it is the one issue

> upon which both sides will profit equally. It is the one issue—and the only decisive one—in which the interests of both are completely parallel.[2]

MacArthur's statement is noteworthy not only because it was spoken by an impeccable warrior but because he grasped the singular power of this idea, its capacity to transcend the many lesser differences that plague the human family: "It is the one issue upon which both sides can agree, for it is the one issue upon which both sides will profit equally."

A generation later, George Kennan, former ambassador to the Soviet Union, author of the containment doctrine that (when misunderstood and misapplied) dominated U.S. foreign policy during the Cold War years, and widely recognized as the dean of U.S. diplomats, declared that

> I am now bound to say that while the earliest possible elimination of nuclear weaponry is of no less vital importance in my eyes than it ever was, this would not be enough, in itself, to give Western civilization even an adequate chance of survival. War itself, as a means of settling differences at least among the great industrial powers, will have to be in some way ruled out; and with it there will have to be dismantled (for without this the whole outlawing of war would be futile) the greater part of the vast military establishments now maintained with a view to the possibility that war might take place. . . .[3]

Our Choice

The nations of the world face a fundamental choice that they cannot long defer without seeing the decision made for them by events, most likely on terms unfavorable to their survival. They may continue to govern their relations with one another by the system of competitive national armaments under which their peoples have long lived (and died), or they may choose an alternative system based on the relinquishment of their individual war-making capacities and the development of essential institutions and structures of shared security. If they choose the present system, they will continue to arm themselves without effective restraint, but they will also face adversaries with an equal freedom to arm and threaten. There is ample historical evidence to suggest that unrestrained competition in offensive armaments will almost inevitably produce one of two tragic outcomes—economic exhaustion or war. The current contest between the superpowers threatens both.

The alternative is for nations to break out of the syndrome of suicidal threats inherent in the balance of power system by joining with one another in renouncing the capacity to make war or intervene militarily in the sovereign territory of other nations in return for a vastly diminished threat to their own national security and a greatly reduced burden of expense. This is the ultimate trade-off. Either nations continue to deploy arsenals that threaten their adversaries and confront in them an equally menacing freedom to arm, or they relinquish those arms and forces capable of attack and gain both security and savings. The freedom to arm for war is in fact a meaningless freedom, given that it does not actually enhance national security, while relinquishing that freedom is an illusory sacrifice, given that nations gain security by jointly shedding the threatening elements in their arsenals. The choice is clear.

If, as President Eisenhower predicted a generation ago, the era of armaments is drawing to a close, it is time—and past time—to begin preparing for the era of shared security that will succeed it. The ideas and designs surveyed in this volume seek to become a modest contribution to that essential endeavor.

Notes

1. From "A Strategy of Peace," a speech delivered at the American University, Washington, D.C., June 10, 1963, and reprinted in Don Carlson and Craig Comstock, eds., *Securing Our Planet* (Los Angeles: Jeremy Tarcher/St. Martin's Press, 1986), p. 35.

2. Quoted in Norman Cousins, *The Pathology of Power* (New York: W. W. Norton, 1987), p. 68.

3. George Kennan, *The Nuclear Delusion: Soviet-American Relations in the Atomic Age* (New York: Pantheon, 1982), p. 71.

Appendix: Current Proposals for Arms Reduction

The perspective of this book has been large scale and long range, exploring system changes some of which may take many years to enact. But it is also necessary to ask at some point how these ambitious changes relate to the many arms control proposals under consideration in the late 1980s. In a political environment in which the short term and the piecemeal dominate the negotiating agenda, it is important to ask which of the many proposals now on the table would advance the planet in the direction of a stable global security system.

Arms Control vs. Arms Reduction

Arms control as it has been traditionally practiced by the great powers has tended to legitimate rather than lessen arms competition between nations, often setting limits well above existing levels and including spacious escape clauses for circumventing the spirit of the agreements. The proposals listed below, however, are of a different order. Every one of them involves a larger step than existing treaties and stipulates a more comprehensive restriction on the production or deployment of weapons. They are not arms control in the sense that we have known it, but arms reduction, requiring the actual dismantling of existing stockpiles, the disbanding of standing forces, or comprehensive bans on future testing or production. Although the measures listed here would not themselves eliminate the war-making capabilities of nations, taken cumulatively they would appreciably slow the arms race. It would be foolish not to take such achievable steps while preparing for more comprehensive changes. At the same time, their enactment should not be allowed to distract nations from undertaking the larger system transformations explored in this volume.

These proposals do not arrange themselves in any fixed order of priority, but they do congregate around several broad categories. They have been selected on the basis of four primary criteria: verifiability, political practicality, strategic stability, and potential for contributing to a system transformation.

Nuclear Systems

A Comprehensive Nuclear Test Ban (CTB). Gaining substantial support in the early 1960s, a CTB was ultimately shelved in favor of the Limited Test Ban Treaty of 1963, which banned tests in the atmosphere but continued to permit them underground. Now interest in banning all testing is once again accumulating, especially in the wake of the Soviet Union's nineteen-month unilateral moratorium on nuclear testing between August 1985 and February 1987. With sufficient monitoring facilities, adequate verification of compliance is now technically possible.

A Nuclear Freeze. A ban on testing, development, and deployment of nuclear weapons and delivery systems. The object of a spontaneous national movement in the United States in the early 1980s, the freeze has since been endorsed by the United Nations General Assembly, the Soviet Union, the Five Continents Peace Initiative, and thousands of citizens' organizations. Though it has been overshadowed in recent years by the debate over strategic defense, the nuclear freeze remains a priority on the agendas of peace movements worldwide.

Deep Cuts in Superpower Nuclear Warhead Stockpiles. The notion of making radical reductions in current nuclear arsenals has been under consideration for more than two decades. In 1982 George Kennan proposed an immediate, across-the-board 50 percent cut in superpower nuclear arsenals, to be verified by existing national technical means.[1] More recently, former Defense Secretary Robert McNamara has proposed cutting present superpower arsenals from 50,000 to several hundred.[2] Verification capabilities exist to monitor the process.

A Ban on the Production of Weapons-grade Fissile Materials and Placement of Materials Recovered From Disarmed Weapons Under International Safeguards. Any agreement to freeze or reduce warhead stockpiles would be greatly strengthened by ensuring that no nation continued to produce weapons-grade materials. Current International Atomic Energy Agency (IAEA) standards are capable of detecting "within days or months the diversion of enough material to make a single nuclear weapon . . . (and) should be able to detect diversions of less than 1 percent of the fissile material flowing through a nation's nuclear-reactor fuel system. . . . The IAEA safeguards are hundreds of times more stringent than those that would be required to verify a superpower cutoff agreement."[3]

A Ban on Further Development of Destabilizing Strategic Delivery Systems (Multiple Warheads, MX, SS-20, Trident, et al.). The accuracy, speed, and vulnerability of many new delivery systems, most especially those with multiple warheads, render them more useful for preemptive attack than for retaliation. The elimination of these most destabilizing weapons would curb the current drift in superpower arsenals toward a launch-on-warning posture.

Establishment of Nuclear-free Zones. There are currently more than 3,500 nuclear-free zones in 24 nations, including 132 in the United States (of which the largest is the city of Chicago).[4] While the declarations of local governments have sometimes been overridden by national authorities, several national governments have now made similar pledges. In 1986, 13 Pacific island nations, including Australia and New Zealand,[5] signed an accord to establish a nuclear-free zone in the South Pacific, the first such international agreement. A nuclear-free zone in central Europe has been widely proposed to reduce the danger of war by human miscalculation or the technical malfunction of one or more of the thousands of tactical nuclear weapons already integrated into the conventional force structures of both sides.

Adoption of a Policy of No-First-Use of Nuclear Weapons and the Reconfiguration of Arsenals and Force Postures to Conform to that Change of Policy. The Soviet Union has pledged not to be the first nation to use nuclear weapons but the United States currently refuses, expressing concern that without reserving the option to use their nuclear weapons first, NATO forces would be quickly overwhelmed by superior Soviet conventional forces. But no-first-use has received widespread support from established political figures in the United States; an influential proposal by former National Security Adviser McGeorge Bundy, former Ambassador George Kennan, former Secretary of Defense Robert McNamara, and Gerard Smith, chief negotiator of SALT I, was first published in *Foreign Affairs* in 1982.[6] To become more than a mere rhetorical promise, adoption of a no-first-use policy would require changes in nuclear deployments and conventional force structures to render them less threatening.

Other Weapons Prohibitions

A Ban on All Space Weapons, Including Antimissile and Antisatellite Technologies. Strategic defense is likely to be an expensive and futile endeavor and the attempt will entrench weapons in space, perhaps irreversibly. Satellites are vital for effective defense and verification of arms control and disarmament agreements, as well as for communication and commerce. All antisatellite weapons threaten to blind defenses and sever essential communications in time of war, thus preventing effective command of forces as well as contact between the warring parties to negotiate terminating the conflict. A ban on the deployment of space-based weapons is currently verifiable.

A Ban on Antisubmarine Warfare Technologies. Submarines are at present the only invulnerable leg of the strategic triads on which superpower nuclear arsenals depend and would form the foundation for any minimum deterrence regime. Antisubmarine warfare systems would threaten this invulnerability and thus upset the delicate deterrent balance. Nuclear weapons would be far less likely to be used if left invulnerable than if, through their vulnerability, they tempted preemptive attack and thus forced their own first use. Such a ban would presently be difficult to verify, although technical capabilities are likely to improve.

A Ban on All Chemical Weapons and a Strengthening of Current Prohibitions on Biological Weapons Development. After nineteen years of negotiation, the 40-nation Geneva Disarmament Conference in 1988 appeared close to agreement on a treaty to abolish all chemical weapons stocks worldwide. Providing for elimination of all existing weapons and manufacturing sites over a ten-year period, the treaty would establish a chemical verification agency (modeled on the International Atomic Energy Agency), which would monitor the destruction of weapons facilities and the operation of civilian plants to ensure that they do not produce specific toxic chemicals.[7] The current agreement banning biological weapons also needs to be strengthened. The 1972 treaty lacks enforcement mechanisms and has been overtaken by scientific advances and the invention of new kinds of biological weapons.

Conventional Force Reductions

Adoption of a Nonprovocative Defense Posture. This policy would involve an independently initiated restructuring of nonnuclear armed forces to eliminate their most offensive elements. Such a strategy would involve phasing out tanks, long-range attack aircraft, medium-range conventional and nuclear missiles, and other components of "forward defense" and phasing in weapons and tactics more useful for the defense than the offense. Alone among the proposals on this list, nonprovocative defense could be independently initiated—and, indeed, has been adopted in modified form in Switzerland, Sweden, and Yugoslavia, among other nations. It could also be adopted bilaterally or multilaterally, most importantly between the NATO and Warsaw Pact alliances, perhaps as a series of de-escalating steps taken over a number of years. The superpowers would be most likely to undertake a program along these lines within the framework of a bilateral agreement.

Troop Reductions. Troop reductions would also be essential, especially along the European Central Front, perhaps in conjunction with establishing nuclear-free zones. Mutual and Balanced Force Reduction (MBFR) talks have been underway in Vienna between 19 NATO and Warsaw Pact nations since 1973 to discuss the mutual reduction of forces and armaments in central Europe, but no significant progress has yet been made. Interest has recently been rekindled in the so-called Rapacki Plan, first proposed in 1967 by then Polish foreign minister Adam Rapacki. The plan sought to demilitarize the central front in Europe by removing all nuclear weapons from both Germanies, Czechoslovakia, and Poland, and most conventional forces in a 300-mile-wide band along the inter-German border. A new Polish plan introduced in May 1987 calls for the "gradual and mutually agreed withdrawal" of both nuclear and conventional weapons from Poland, Czechoslovakia, East Germany, and Hungary within the Warsaw Pact, and from West Germany, Belgium, the Netherlands, Luxembourg, and Denmark within NATO. In addition, the Polish plan calls for "reshaping European military strategies into clearly defensive arrangements."[8] Troop reductions would be readily verifiable with existing capabilities.

Nonmilitary Measures to Enhance Common Security

Creation of International Arms Verification Facilities to Provide Impartial Data on Current Weapons Stockpiles and to Facilitate Compliance with Existing and Proposed Arms Control and Disarmament Agreements. In 1982, after a three-year study by a special United Nations commission, 123 nations approved the idea of establishing an international satellite monitoring agency (ISMA), under the auspices of the UN, to monitor arms control agreements and perform a variety of other useful tasks. Although the plan was ultimately blocked by the superpowers, support for the idea has continued to grow. Jerome Wiesner, former science adviser to Presidents Eisenhower and Kennedy, has proposed that an international arms verification and study center be established to provide an independent source of information on the arsenals of nations.

Establishment of Crisis Control Machinery to Prevent Accidental War. In mid-1987, U.S. and Soviet negotiators agreed to establish a pair of "risk reduction centers" in Washington and Moscow to facilitate communication between one another's armed forces in times of crisis. This upgrading of the original hot-line concept is just the first step in establishing a comprehensive accident-prevention system to avert the possibility of war through miscalculation or miscommunication. William Ury, director of the Nuclear Negotiation Project at Harvard Law School, sketches a broader agenda for crisis control, including an international mediation service composed of recognized international political figures with experience in negotiation, and a "rapid-deployment peacekeeping force" composed of soldiers from nations other than the superpowers and their allies and armed solely with weapons of self-defense, to be injected as buffers into arenas of conflict.[9]

Although none of these proposals, nor all of them together, presage a global security system of the scope considered in this book, the enactment of any one of them would mark a significant advance beyond any of the arms control agreements in place in the late 1980s. Adopted together or separately, these proposals would substantially reduce the danger of armed confrontation between the great powers and could set the stage for a larger system transformation.

Notes

1. From George Kennan, *The Nuclear Delusion: Soviet-American Relations in the Nuclear Age* (New York: Pantheon, 1982). Reprinted in Don Carlson and Craig Comstock, eds., *Securing Our Planet* (Los Angeles: J. P. Tarcher/St. Martin's, 1986), p. 290.

2. Robert S. McNamara, *Blundering into Disaster* (New York: Pantheon, 1986), p. 123.

3. McGeorge Bundy, George F. Kennan, Robert S. McNamara, and Gerard Smith, "Nuclear Weapons and the Atlantic Alliance," *Foreign Affairs*, vol. 60, no. 4 (Spring 1982).

4. Statistics from Nuclear Free America, 325 East 25th Street, Baltimore, MD 21218.

5. The other 11 nations in the group, called the South Pacific Forum, are Western Samoa, Tuvalu, Niue, Fiji, the Cook Islands, Kiribati, Tonga, Papua New Guinea, Vanuatu, Nauru, and the Solomon Islands.

6. Frank von Hippel, David H. Albright, and Barbara G. Levi, "Stopping the Production of Fissile Materials for Weapons," *Scientific American*, vol. 253, no. 3 (September 1985), pp. 40–47.

7. Paul Lewis, "40 Nations Closer to a Pact Banning Chemical Weapons," *New York Times*, April 30, 1987, p. 1.

8. Michael T. Kaufman, "Polish Chief Offers Plan for Arms Disengagement," *New York Times*, May 9, 1987, p. 3.

9. See William Ury, *Beyond the Hotline* (Boston: Houghton Mifflin, 1984), pp. 86–89.

Selected Bibliography

Chapter 3: The United Nations

Bennett, LeRoy. *International Organizations: Principles and Issues.* 2d ed. Englewood Cliffs, NJ: Prentice-Hall, 1980.

Bloomfield, Lincoln P. *International Military Forces.* New York: Little, Brown, 1964.

______. *The Power to Keep Peace: Today and in a World Without War.* Berkeley, CA: World Without War Council, 1971.

Claude, Inis, Jr. *Swords into Plowshares: The Problems and Progress of International Organizations.* 4th ed. New York: Random House, 1971.

Eichelberger, Clark. *Organizing for Peace.* New York: Harper and Row, 1977.

Elements of United Nations Reform. Wayne, NJ: Center for United Nations Reform Education, 1980.

Fabian, Larry. *Soldiers Without Enemies.* Washington, DC: Brookings Institution, 1971.

Falk, Richard, Friedrich Kratochwil, and Saul H. Mendlovitz, eds. *Studies on a Just World Order Series, Volume II: International Law: A Contemporary Perspective..* Boulder, CO: Westview Press, 1985.

Falk, Richard, and Saul H. Mendlovitz. *The Strategy of World Order,* vol. 3. New York: Institute for World Order, 1966.

Florini, Ann, and Nina Tannenwald. *On the Front Lines: The United Nations' Role in Preventing and Containing Conflict.* New York: United Nations Association of the United States, 1984.

Franck, Thomas. *Nation Against Nation: What Happened to the UN Dream and What the U.S. Can Do About It.* New York: Oxford, 1985.

Hudson, Richard. "The Case for the Binding Triad" (28-minute videotape). New York: Center for War/Peace Studies, 1986.

Johansen, Robert C. "The Reagan Administration and the UN," *World Policy Journal,* vol. 3 (Fall 1986), pp. 604–641.

Johansen, Robert C., and Saul H. Mendlovitz. "The Role of Law in the Establishment of a New International Order: A Proposal for a Transnational Police Force," *Alternatives: A Journal of World Policy,* vol. 6, no. 2 (1980).

Mische, Gerald, and Patricia Mische. *Toward a Human World Order.* New York/ Ramsey, NJ: Paulist Press, 1977.

Rikhye, Indar Jit, Michael Harbottle, and Bjorn Egge. *The Thin Blue Line: International Peacekeeping and Its Future*. New Haven, CT: Yale University Press, 1974.

———. *The Theory and Practice of Peacekeeping*. London: C. Hurst and Co., 1984.

Stoessinger, John G. *The United Nations and the Superpowers*. 4th Ed. New York: Random House, 1977.

Tinbergen, Jan. "Revitalizing the United Nations System," *Waging Peace Series Booklet 13*. Santa Barbara, CA: Nuclear Age Peace Foundation, 1987.

Tinbergen, Jan, and Dietrich Fischer. *Warfare and Welfare: Integrating Security Policy into Socio-Economic Policy*. New York: St. Martin's, 1987.

Weston, Burns H., Richard A. Falk, and Anthony D'Amato, eds. *International Law and World Order*. St. Paul, MN: West Publishing Co., 1980.

Wiseman, Henry, ed. *Peacekeeping: Appraisals and Proposals*. New York: Pergamon Press, 1983.

———. "Peacekeeping and the Management of International Conflict," Background Paper #15. Ottawa: Canadian Institute for International Peace and Security, September 1987.

Woito, Robert. *To End War: A New Approach to International Conflict*. New York: Pilgrim Press, 1982.

Chapter 4: A World Peacekeeping Federation

Clark, Grenville, and Louis Sohn. *World Peace Through World Law: Two Alternative Plans* (3d ed., enlarged). Cambridge, MA: Harvard University Press, 1966.

Dunne, Gerald. *Grenville Clark: Public Citizen*. New York: Farrar, Straus, and Giroux, 1986.

"Joint Statement of Agreed Principles for Disarmament Negotiations of the Soviet Union and the United States," September 20, 1961.

McVitty, Marion. *Preface to Disarmament: An Appraisal of Recent Proposals*. Washington, DC: Public Affairs Press and World Law Fund, 1970.

Raskin, Marcus. *Program Treaty for General Security and Disarmament*. Washington, DC: Institute for Policy Studies, 1984.

Chapter 5: Minimum Deterrence

Bundy, McGeorge. "Existential Deterrence and its Consequences." In *The Security Gamble*, ed. Douglas MacLean, pp. 3–13. Totowa, NJ: Rowman and Allanheld, 1984.

Carver, Michael. *A Policy for Peace*. London: Faber and Faber, 1982.

Feiveson, Harold, Richard Ullman, and Frank von Hippel. "Reducing the U.S. and Soviet Nuclear Arsenals," *Bulletin of the Atomic Scientists*, vol. 41 (August 1985), pp. 144–150.

Ferraro, Vincent, and Kathleen FitzGerald. "The End of a Strategic Era: A Proposal for Minimal Deterrence," *World Policy Journal*, vol. 2 (Winter 1984), pp. 339–360.

Gayler, Noel. "How to Break the Momentum of the Nuclear Arms Race," *East/West Outlook* (June-July 1982), pp. 2–5.

______. "If Each Side Had Only 100 Weapons," *Washington Post*, February 1, 1986, p. A17.

Halperin, Morton. *Nuclear Fallacy*. Cambridge, MA: Ballinger, 1987.

Hippel, Frank von. "Tenfold Reductions in the U.S. and Soviet Nuclear Arsenals: Why and How." Opening talk of the International Forum of Scientists on Drastic Reductions and Final Elimination of Nuclear Weapons, Moscow, February 14, 1987.

Johansen, Robert C. "How to Start Ending the Arms Race," *World Policy Journal*, vol. 1 (Fall 1983), pp. 71–100.

McNamara, Robert S. *Blundering into Disaster*. New York: Pantheon, 1986.

Chapter 6: Qualitative Disarmament

Forsberg, Randall. "The Freeze and Beyond: Confining the Military to Defense as a Route to Disarmament," *World Policy Journal*, vol. 2, no. 2 (Winter 1984).

Hollins, Harry B. "A Defensive Weapons System," *Bulletin of the Atomic Scientists*, vol. 38 (June-July 1982), pp. 63–65.

Jervis, Robert. "Cooperation Under the Security Dilemma," *World Politics*, vol. 30, no. 2 (January 1978), pp. 167–214.

Kruegler, Christopher. *Liddell Hart and the Concept of Civilian-Based Defense*. Ph.D. diss., Syracuse University, 1984.

Liddell Hart, B. H. *Deterrent or Defence?* New York: Praeger, 1960.

Noel-Baker, Philip. *The First World Disarmament Conference 1932–33, and Why It Failed*. New York: Pergamon Press, 1979.

______. *The Arms Race: A Program for World Disarmament*. Dobbs Ferry, NY: Oceana Press, 1960.

Sommer, Mark. *Beating our Swords into Shields*. Miranda, CA: Center for a Preservative Defense, 1983.

______. "Forging a Preservative Defense," *Bulletin of the Atomic Scientists*, vol. 39 (August-September 1983), pp. 5–7.

______. "An Emerging Consensus: Common Security through Qualitative Disarmament," *Alternative Defense Project Pamphlet #1*. New York: Alternative Defense Project, 1988.

Chapter 7: Nonprovocative Defense

Agrell, Wilhelm. "Offensive Versus Defensive: Military Strategy and Alternative Defense," *Journal of Peace Research*, vol. 24 (March 1987), pp. 75–86.

Alternative Defence Commission. *Defence Without the Bomb*. London: Taylor and Francis, 1984.

______. *The Politics of Alternative Defence: A Role for a Non-Nuclear Britain*. London: Paladin, 1987.

"Alternative Defense and Security" (Special Issue), *Bulletin of Peace Proposals*, 1978, no. 4.

Alternative Defense Reading Packets and Working Papers. Alternative Defense Network, Institute for Defense and Disarmament Studies, 2001 Beacon Street, Brookline, MA 02146.

Barnaby, Frank, and Egbert Boeker. *Defense Without Offence: Non-Nuclear Defense for Europe*. Bradford, West Yorkshire, U.K.: University of Bradford Peace Studies Paper #8. Also published in London by Housmans, 1983.

Blackaby, Frank. "Arms Control and Nonprovocative Defence in Europe." Speech prepared for the Consultation on Non-Nuclear Alternatives in Europe, University of Bradford, July 15–18, 1986.

Boserup, Anders. "Nuclear Disarmament: Non-Nuclear Defence." In Mary Kaldor and Dan Smith, eds., *Disarming Europe*. London: Merlin, 1982.

Boston Study Group, *Winding Down: The Price of Defense*. San Francisco: W. H. Freeman, 1982.

Clarke, Michael. "The Alternative Defence Debate: Non-Nuclear Defence Policies for Europe." *ADIU Occasional Paper*, no. 3. Brighton, U.K.: Armament and Disarmament Information Unit, Science Policy Research Unit, University of Sussex, August 1985.

Consultation on Non-Nuclear Alternatives in Europe, University of Bradford (U.K.), July 15–18, 1986.

Dankbaar, Ben. "Alternative Defence Policies and Modern Weapons Technology," in Mary Kaldor and Dan Smith, eds. *Disarming Europe*. London: Merlin, 1982.

Evangelista, Matthew. "Offense or Defense: A Tale of Two Commissions." *World Policy Journal*, no. 1 (Fall 1983), pp. 45–69.

Fischer, Dietrich. *Preventing War in the Nuclear Age*. Totowa, NJ: Rowman and Allanheld, 1984.

———. "Invulnerability Without Threat," in Burns H. Weston, ed., *Toward Nuclear Disarmament and Global Security: A Search for Alternatives*. Boulder, CO: Westview Press, 1984, pp. 504–532.

Forsberg, Randall, and Rob Leavitt. *Alternative Defense: A New Approach to Building a Stable Peace*. Brookline, MA: Institute for Defense and Disarmament Studies, 1988.

Galtung, Johan. *There Are Alternatives: Four Roads to Peace and Security*. Nottingham: Spokesman, 1984.

———. "Transarmament from Offensive to Defensive Defense." *Journal of Peace Research*, no. 21 (1984), pp. 127–139.

Non-Offensive Defense (newsletter), ed. Bjorn Moller. Copenhagen: University of Copenhagen Centre for Peace and Conflict Research, Vandkunsten 5, 1467 Copenhagen K, Denmark.

Oberg, Jan, Wilhelm Nolte, and Dietrich Fischer. *Frieden Gewinnen*. Freiburg, Federal Republic of Germany: Dreisam-Verlag, 1987. *Winning Peace* (English translation). London: Taylor and Francis, forthcoming.

Roberts, Adam. *Nations in Arms: The Theory and Practice of Territorial Defence*. 2d ed. New York: St. Martin's, 1986.

Sommer, Mark. *Beyond the Bomb: Living Without Nuclear Weapons. Alternative Strategies for Building a Stable Peace*. Boston: ExPro Press, 1986.

Tromp, Hylke, ed. *Non-Nuclear War in Europe: Alternatives for Nuclear Defense*. Groningen, Netherlands: Groningen University Press, 1984.

Unterseher, Lutz. "Defending Europe: Towards a Stable Conventional Deterrent." University of Maryland: Working Group on Nuclear Policy and Morality, August 1986.

Chapter 8: Civilian-based Defense

American Friends Service Committee. *Instead of War: An Inquiry into Nonviolent National Defense*. New York: Grossman, 1967.

Atkeson, Brigadier General Edward B. "The Relevance of Civilian-Based Defense to U.S. Security Interests," *Military Review* (Fort Leavenworth, KS), vol. 56, no. 5 (May 1976), pp. 24–32; no. 6 (June 1976), pp. 45–55.

Bondurant, Joan. *The Conquest of Violence*. Berkeley: University of California Press, 1971.

Boserup, Anders, and Andrew Mack. *War Without Weapons*. New York: Schocken Books, 1975.

Bruyn, Severyn, and Paula Raymon, eds. *Creative Conflict in Society: Nonviolent Theory and Action*. New York: Wiley, 1978.

Civilian-Based Defense Bibliography. Omaha, NB: Civilian-Based Defense Association, P.O. Box 31616, Omaha NB 68131, 1987.

Civilian-Based Defense: News and Opinion (newsletter). Omaha, NB: Civilian-Based Defense Association, P.O. Box 31616, Omaha, NB 68131.

Fogg, Richard. *Nonmilitary Defense Against Nuclear Threateners and Attackers*. Stevenson, MD: Center for the Study of Conflict, 1983.

Geeraerts, Gustaaf. *Possibilities of Civilian Defense in Western Europe*. New Brunswick, NJ: Transaction Books, 1977.

Glick, Edward Bernard. *Peaceful Conflict: The Nonmilitary Use of the Military*. London: Stackpole, 1967.

Irwin, Robert, and Beverly Woodward. *U.S. Defense Policy: Mainstream Views and Nonviolent Alternatives*. Waltham, MA: ISTNA, 1982.

Keyes, Gene. "Force Without Firepower: A Doctrine of Unarmed Military Service," *Co-Evolution Quarterly*, no. 34 (Summer 1982), pp. 4–25.

King-Hall, Stephen. *Defence in the Nuclear Age*. Nyack, NY: Fellowship Publications, 1957.

Lakey, George. *Strategy for a Living Revolution*. New York: Grossman, 1973.

Mahadevan, T. K., Adam Roberts, and Gene Sharp. *Civilian Defense: An Introduction*. New Delhi: Gandhi Peace Foundation, 1967.

Roberts, Adam. *Civilian Resistance as a National Defense*. Harrisburg, PA: Stackpole, 1968.

Sharp, Gene. *The Politics of Nonviolent Action*. 3 vols. Part I, *Power and Struggle*; Part II, *The Methods of Nonviolent Action*; Part III, *The Dynamics of Nonviolent Action*. Boston: Porter Sargent, 1974.

______. *Social Power and Political Freedom*. Boston: Porter Sargent, 1980.

______. "Making the Abolition of War a Realistic Goal." New York: Institute for World Order, 1981.

______. *Making Europe Unconquerable: The Potential of Civilian-Based Deterrence and Defense*. Cambridge, MA: Ballinger, 1985.

———. *National Security Through Civilian-Based Defense*. Omaha, NB: Civilian-Based Defense Association, 1985.

Waskow, Arthur. *Towards an Unarmed Force of the United States*. Washington, DC: Institute for Policy Studies, 1965.

Chapter 9: Strategic Defense

American Physical Society Study Group. *Science and Technology of Directed Energy Weapons*, April 1987.

Boffey, Philip M., William J. Broad, Leslie H. Gelb, Charles Mohr, and H. B. Noble. *Claiming the Heavens: The New York Times Complete Guide to the Star Wars Debate*. New York: Random House, 1988.

Bowman, Robert M. *Star Wars: Defense or Death Star?* Chesapeake Beach, MD: Institute for Space and Security Studies, 1985.

Mische, Patricia. *Star Wars and the State of Our Souls*. Minneapolis, MN: Winston Press, 1985.

Office of Technology Assessment. *SDI: Technology, Survivability, and Software*, 1988. See Warren E. Leary, "'Star Wars' Runs into New Criticism," *New York Times*, April 25, 1988, p. A8.

Tirman, John, ed. *The Fallacy of Star Wars*. New York: Vintage, 1984.

Waller, Douglas, James Bruce, and Douglas Cook. *SDI: Progress and Challenges*. Staff report submitted to Senator William Proxmire, Senator J. Bennett Johnston, and Senator Lawton Chiles, March 17, 1986.

Zuckerman, Lord Solly. "Reagan's Highest Folly," *New York Review of Books*, April 9, 1987.

Chapter 10: Verification

Buchan, Glenn C. "The Verification Spectrum," *Bulletin of the Atomic Scientists*, vol. 39, no. 9 (November 1983).

Hafemeister, David, Joseph J. Romm, and Kosta Tsipis. "The Verification of Compliance with Arms Control Agreements," *Scientific American*, vol. 252, no. 3 (March 1985), pp. 39–45.

Hippel, Frank von, David H. Albright, and Barbara G. Levi. "Stopping the Production of Fissile Materials for Weapons," *Scientific American*, vol. 253, no. 3 (September 1985), pp. 40–47.

"Implications of Establishing an International Satellite Monitoring Agency." New York: United Nations Study Series 9, 1983.

Krass, Allan. "The Politics of Verification," *World Policy*, vol. 2 (Fall 1985), pp. 731–752.

———. *Verification: How Much Is Enough?* Lexington, MA: Lexington Books, 1985.

Krepon, Michael. *Arms Control: Verification and Compliance*. Headline Series, no. 270. New York: Foreign Policy Association, 1984.

Myrdal, Alva. "The International Control of Disarmament." *Scientific American*, vol. 231, no. 4 (October 1974), p. 31.

The Nuclear Weapons Freeze and Arms Control. Cambridge, MA: Center for Science and International Affairs, John F. Kennedy School of Government, Harvard University, 1983.

Potter, William C., ed. *Verification and SALT.* Boulder, CO: Westview Press, 1980.

Rowell, William F. *Arms Control Verification: A Guide to Policy Issues for the 1980s.* Cambridge, MA: Ballinger, 1986.

Scribner, Richard A., Theodore J. Ralston, and William D. Metz. *The Verification Challenge: Problems and Promise of Strategic Nuclear Arms Control Verification.* Boston: Birkhauser, 1985.

Sykes, Lynn R., and Jack F. Evernden. "The Verification of a Comprehensive Nuclear Test Ban." *Scientific American,* vol. 247, no. 4 (October 1982), pp. 47–55.

Tsipis, Kosta, David Hafemeister, and Penny Janeway. *Arms Control Verification: The Technologies that Make it Possible.* Elmsford, NY: Pergamon-Brassey, 1985.

Wiesner, Jerome. "An International Arms Verification and Study Center." Unpublished paper, December 1985.

Chapter 12: Economic Conversion

Anderson, Marion. *Converting the Workforce: Where the Jobs Would Be.* Lansing, MI: Employment Research Associates, 1979.

Arms Control and Disarmament Agency. "Panel on Economic Impacts of Disarmament," January 1962; "Economic and Social Consequences of Disarmament," 1964.

______. *Economic Impacts of Disarmament.* Economic Series 1, Publication 2, January 1962.

Benoit, Emile, and Kenneth E. Boulding, eds. *Disarmament and the Economy.* (Final Report of the Program of Research on Economic Adjustments to Disarmament [READ], sponsored by the Center for Research on Conflict Resolution, University of Michigan, Ann Arbor). New York: Harper & Row, 1963. Republished in Westport, Conn., by Greenwood Press, 1978.

Bolton, Roger E. *Defense and Disarmament: The Economics of Transition.* Englewood Cliffs, NJ: Prentice-Hall, 1966.

Conversion Planner. Bimonthly newsletter on economic conversion. Washington, DC: SANE/Freeze, 711 G Street, SW, Washington, DC 20003.

DeGrasse, Robert, Jr., *Creating Solar Jobs: Options for Military Workers and Communities.* Mountain View: Mid-Peninsula Conversion Project, 1978.

______. *Military Expansion, Economic Decline.* New York: Council on Economic Priorities, 1983.

Department of Defense. *Economic Adjustment/Conversion.* Washington, DC: Office of Economic Adjustment, Office of the Assistant Secretary of Defense (Force Management and Personnel), July 1985; with revisions and additions, February and April 1986.

Dumas, Lloyd J., *The Political Economy of Arms Reduction: Reversing Economic Decay.* AAAS Selected Symposium no. 80. Boulder, CO: Westview Press, 1982.

———. *The Overburdened Economy: Uncovering the Causes of Chronic Unemployment, Inflation, and National Decline*. Berkeley: University of California Press, 1986.

Economic Impact of Reductions in Defense Spending: Summary of Research Prepared for the U.S. Arms Control and Disarmament Agency. Washington, DC, 1972.

Gordon, Suzanne, and Dave McFadden, eds. *Economic Conversion: Revitalizing the American Economy*. Boston: Ballinger, 1984.

Hartung, William. *The Economic Consequences of a Nuclear Freeze*. New York: Council on Economic Priorities, 1984.

International Economic Conversion Conference. *Proceedings: Transforming the Economy for Jobs, Peace and Justice*. Boston College Conference on Conversion, June 22–24, 1984.

Lall, Betty G. *Prosperity Without Guns: The Economic Impact of Reductions in Defense Spending*. New York: Institute for World Order, 1977.

Leontief, Wassily, and Faye Duchin. *Military Spending: Facts and Figures, Worldwide Implications and Future Outlook*. New York: Oxford University Press, 1983.

McFadden, Dave, and Jim Wake. *The Freeze Economy*. St. Louis: National Freeze Clearinghouse, 1983.

Melman, Seymour, ed. *Conversion of Industry from a Military to a Civilian Economy* (6 vols.). New York: Praeger Special Studies, 1970.

———. *Barriers to Conversion from Military to Civilian Industry—in Market, Planned and Developing Economies*. Prepared for the United Nations Centre for Disarmament, April 1980.

———. *The Permanent War Economy: American Capitalism in Decline*. New York: Simon and Schuster, 1974.

Mosley, Hugh G. *The Arms Race: Economic and Social Consequences*. Lexington, MA: Heath and Co., 1982.

Plowshare Press. Newsletter of the Center for Economic Conversion, 222 C View Street, Mountain View, CA 94041.

Sanger, Clyde. *Safe and Sound: Disarmament and Development in the Eighties*. Ottawa: Deneau, 1982.

Thorsson, Inga. *In Pursuit of Disarmament: Conversion from Military to Civil Production in Sweden* (2 vols.). Stockholm: Liber Allmanna Forlaget, 1984.

Udis, Bernard. *From Guns to Butter: Technology Organization and Reduced Military Spending in Western Europe*. Cambridge, MA: Ballinger, 1978.

United Nations Center for Disarmament. *Report of the Secretary-General on the Relationship Between Disarmament and Development*. New York, 1982.

U.S. Executive Office of the President. "Report to the President from the Cabinet Coordinating Committee on Economic Planning for the End of Vietnam Hostilities," published in *Economic Report of the President*. Washington, DC, 1969.

Wallensteen, Peter, ed. *Experiences in Disarmament: On Conversion of Military Industry and Closing of Military Bases*. Uppsala, Sweden: Uppsala University Department of Peace and Conflict Research, Report No. 19, 1978.

Webre, Phil. *Jobs to People: Planning for Conversion to New Industries*. Exploratory Project for Economic Alternatives, 1983.

Weidenbaum, Murray. *The Economics of Peacetime Defense*. New York: Praeger, 1974.

Wong, Cary. *Economic Consequences of Armament and Disarmament: A Bibliography*. Los Angeles: Center for the Study of Armament and Disarmament, 1981.

Chapter 13: Toward a Common Security System

Carlson, Don, and Craig Comstock, eds. *Securing Our Planet*. Los Angeles: Tarcher/St. Martin's, 1986.

Deudney, Daniel. *Whole Earth Security: Towards a Geopolitics of Peace*. Worldwatch Paper no. 55. Washington, DC: Worldwatch Institute, July 1983.

Falk, Richard, Friedrich V. Kratochwil, and Saul H. Mendlovitz, eds. *International Law and a Just World Order*. Boulder, CO: Westview Press, 1983.

Galtung, Johan. *There Are Alternatives: Four Roads to Peace and Security*. London: Spokesman, 1984.

______. *The True Worlds*. New York: Free Press, 1980.

Independent Commission on Disarmament and Security Issues. *Common Security: A Blueprint for Survival*. New York: Simon and Schuster, 1982.

Johansen, Robert C. "Towards a Dependable Peace: A Proposal for an Appropriate Security System." New York: Institute for World Order, 1978.

______. "Towards an Alternative Security System." *World Policy Paper #24*. New York: World Policy Institute, 1983.

______. "Toward National Security Without Nuclear Deterrence." *ExPro Papers #8*. Boston: Exploratory Project on the Conditions of Peace, 1987.

Kaldor, Mary, "Disarmament: The Armament Process in Reverse," in E. P. Thompson and Dan Smith, eds. *Protest and Survive*. New York: Monthly Review Press, 1981.

Smoke, Richard, and Willis Harman. *Paths to Peace*. Boulder, CO: Westview Press, 1987.

Sommer, Mark. "Constructing Peace as a Whole System," *Whole Earth Review*, no. 51 (Summer 1986), pp. 12-19.

Stephenson, Carolyn, ed. *Alternative Methods for International Security*. Washington, DC: University Press of America, 1982.

Weston, Burns H., ed. *Toward Nuclear Disarmament and World Security: A Search for Alternatives*. Boulder, CO: Westview Press, 1984.

Index

ABM (antiballistic missile) Treaty (1972), 14, 15, 102, 104, 105, 133, 188
Abrahamson, James (General), 114
ACDA. *See* Arms Control and Disarmament Agency
Acid rain, 3, 165
Advisory Committee for the UN Emergency Force (1956), 27
Aerial reconnaissance, 130
Aerospace industry, 160–161, 165, 167
Afghanistan. *See under* Soviet Union
AIDS (acquired immune deficiency syndrome) epidemic, 3
Air Force Systems Command Space Division, 112
Air force technical community, 103, 119
AirLand Battle strategies (NATO), 82
Air-launched cruise missiles, 57, 121
Almonte, Jose T., 98
Alternative Defence Commission (Great Britain), 82
Alternative defense. *See* Civilian-based defense; Nonprovocative defense
Alternative energy, 166–167, 172(n23)
America in Ruins (Council of State Planning Agencies), 165
American Expeditionary Force, 39
American Physical Society (APS), 107–108, 109, 116, 123(n19)
Antiaircraft technology, 60
Antiballistic missile technology, 60, 101–102, 103, 104, 199. *See also* Strategic Defense Initiative
Antisatellite weapons, 136, 183, 199
Antisubmarine warfare technologies, 59, 60, 183, 200
Antitank weapons, 83
APS. *See* American Physical Society
Aquino, Corazon, 98
Argentina, 4
Aristophanes, 89
Arms control, 4–5, 14–15, 19(n3), 51, 58, 193, 197
  "advanced," 17–18, 180
  protocols, 133
  and SDI, 116
  See also Arms reduction proposals; Deterrence, minimum; Verification
Arms Control and Disarmament Agency (ACDA), 51
Arms race, 14, 18, 51, 54, 68, 78, 177, 181, 193
Arms reduction proposals, 197–201
Aspin, Les, 85
Assured destruction, 55–56. *See also* Mutual Assured Destruction
Atlantic Charter (1941), 21
Australia, 40, 199
Austria, 31
Aviation Week and Space Technology (journal), 115

Balance of power, 13, 34, 40, 41, 177, 195

Ballistic missile defense research and development, 15, 101
Barr, Stringfellow, 38, 42
Baruch-Lilienthal proposals (1946), 183
Belgium, 29, 40, 84, 94, 201
Biological weapons, 136, 200
Blackbird. *See* SR-71
Black Monday (1987), 2
Blundering into Disaster (McNamara), 57, 61
Bombers, 118, 121. *See also* Long-range bombers
B-1 bomber, 121, 166
B-1B bomber, 170
Booz Allen and Hamilton, Inc., 111
Botha, Pieter, 147
Boulding, Kenneth, 93, 170
Bowman, Robert M., 112
Brazil, 4
Brewster, Kingman, 38, 41
Brzezinski, Zbigniew, 109
Bulletin of the Atomic Scientists, 56
Bundy, McGeorge, 199

California, 153, 156
Cambodia, 34
Camp Crame (Philippines), 97
Camp David Accords (1979), 32
Canada, 31, 40, 146
Carter, Ashton T., 117–118
CBD. *See* Civilian-based defense
Cecil, Robert, 64–65, 66, 69
Central Intelligence Agency (CIA), 74, 112
Chemical weapons, 74, 136, 200
Chicago (Ill.), 199
Chicago Tribune, 157
Chile, 147
Chiles, Lawton, 106
China, People's Republic of
  nuclear weapons, 3, 58, 69
  and UN, 21, 26
Christian Phalangists, 32
Churchill, Winston, 21
CIA. *See* Central Intelligence Agency
Civil defense shelter program (Sweden), 81
Civilian-based defense (CBD), 18, 83, 86, 89–90, 94–97, 98–99, 178, 179, 181–182
  and common security proposal, 183
  pilot studies, 94, 96
  preparation, 91, 93–94, 96
  resistance techniques, 90, 91–92, 93
Civil rights movement, 98, 194
Clark, Grenville, 38, 39, 40–43, 46, 52, 178, 183, 188
Clark-Sohn Plan, 17, 38, 43–47, 48, 50, 51, 52–53, 75, 94, 177, 178–179, 180, 185
Claude, Inis, Jr., 23, 25
Coalition for the Strategic Defense Initiative, 113
Colby, William, 130
Cold War, 21, 24, 26, 27, 31, 195
COMINT. *See* Communications intelligence
Committee of Imperial Defence (British), 65
Committee of Jurists, 22
Common defense, 184–185. *See also* Security, common; Security, global
Common Security: A Blueprint for Survival (Palme Commission), 72
Communications intelligence (COMINT), 131
Comprehensive nuclear test ban (CTB), 60, 70, 198
Compulsory military training, 39
Computers, 104, 117, 167
"Confining the Military to Defense as a Route to Disarmament" (Forsberg), 69
Conflict resolution, 1, 2, 3, 8, 85, 141, 179
  and common security proposal, 185–186, 201–202
  institutions, 16, 95. *See also* United Nations

See also Arms control; Security
Congo crisis (1960), 22, 29, 30, 31
Containment strategy, 26, 195
Conventional forces, 61, 69, 70, 74, 180
reduction proposal, 200–201
Conventional war, 3, 61, 85
Conventional weapons, 61, 62, 83, 180, 181, 183
Council of State Planning Agencies, 164
Council on Economic Priorities, 113
Counterforce capability, 54, 60, 84
Court of Claims, 142, 143, 146
Cousins, Norman, 38, 41
Cranston, Alan, 38, 41
Crisis control management proposal, 201–202
Cruise missiles, 57, 59, 73, 118, 121, 136
CTB. *See* Comprehensive nuclear test ban
Cuba, 146, 147
Cubi Point, 146
Cyprus, 28–29, 32
Czechoslovakia, 84, 90, 97, 201

David, Edward E., 111
Decolonization, 7, 33
Deep strike (NATO), 82
Defense, Department of (DOD), 107, 111, 121, 151, 153, 155, 156, 157, 158, 159
Office of Economic Adjustment (OEA), 157, 158, 159, 161
Defense Economic Adjustment Act, 159
Defensive defense. *See* Nonprovocative defense
Deforestation, 3
Demisch, Wolfgang H., 111
Denmark, 31, 40, 84, 97, 201
Desertification, 3, 166
Détente, 14
Deterrence, minimum, 17, 54, 55–62, 78, 178, 179, 180–181
and common security proposal, 183–184
defined, 54–55
See also Civilian-based defense
Deudney, Daniel, 167
Developing world, 18
DEW. *See* Directed energy weapons
DeWind, Adrian, 135
Diplomatic immunity, 144
Directed energy weapons (DEW), 108, 114, 116
Disarmament, 17, 47–52, 136, 137, 138
first conference. *See* Geneva Disarmament Conference, 1932
global, 69–71, 76. *See also* Security, common; Security, global
and peacetime economy, 152, 154–158, 159, 163
qualitative, 64–68, 71, 74–76, 178, 179, 181, 182
qualitative, and common security proposal, 183, 184
qualitative, compared to nonprovocative defense, 79
See also Arms control; Cecil, Robert; Hoover, Herbert; Liddell-Hart, B. H.; Roosevelt, Franklin Delano
"Divine right of kings," 7
DOD. *See* Defense, Department of
Dow Jones Industrial Average, 2
Draft Treaty Establishing a World Disarmament and World Development Organization, 43
Dublin One meeting (1940s), 41–42
Dulles, John Foster, 21, 54
Dumas, Lloyd, 163
Dumbarton Oaks proposals, 41
Dust Bowl (1930s), 166
Duvalier, François, 147

Eastern bloc, 2–3, 72
East Germany, 84, 201
East-West relations. *See* Cold War; Détente; Disarmament

Economic and Social Council (ECOSOC), 33
Economic interdependence, 3
Economic warfare, 112
ECOSOC. *See* Economic and Social Council
Egypt, 29, 30, 32
Eighteen-Nation Disarmament Committee (1961), 48, 49
Einstein, Albert, 5, 42, 43
Eisenhower, Dwight D., 49, 196
Electronics industry, conversion possibilities, 162, 167
Energy, Department of, 153, 155, 162
Enrile, Juan Ponce, 97
Environment, 3, 18, 165–167, 172(n23), 194
European Central Front, 200, 201
Executive Council, 44, 46

Fabian, Larry, 27, 28
FAO. *See* Food and Agriculture Organization
Federal Energy Administration, 166
Federation of American Scientists, 107
Federation of Free Peoples, 40, 42
Feiveson, Harold, 56, 57, 60
Finland, 31, 40
Finletter, Thomas K., 41
First Boston Corporation, 111
First strike, 59, 109, 110, 113. *See also* No-first-use
Fisher, Roger, 189
Five Continents Peace Initiative, 198
Fixed-position arms, 74
Fletcher, James, 104
Fletcher Commission, 104
Food and Agriculture Organization (FAO), 33
Foreign Affairs, 199
Forsberg, Randall, 69, 75. *See also* Disarmament, qualitative
Fortress America, 103
Forward defense, 91, 180, 200
France, 40, 67
  and CBD, 94
  MNF, 32
  nuclear weapons, 3, 55, 58
  and UN, 21, 29, 134, 186
Frankfurter, Felix, 42
FRODs. *See* Functionally related observable differences
Functionally related observable differences (FRODs), 133

Gandhi, Mohandas, 97
Garwin, Richard, 57, 119
Geneva Disarmament Conference
  1932, 64, 67, 68, 69, 183
  1988, 200
Genscher, Hans Dietrich, 78
Geothermal energy, 167
Germany, 67, 68, 97. *See also* East Germany; West Germany
GNP. *See* Gross national product
Goddard Institute for Space Studies (NASA), 113
Gorbachev, Mikhail, 19(n3), 31, 70, 73, 78, 101, 138
Graham, Daniel O., 113
Great Britain, 40, 65, 66, 82, 161
  and CBD, 94
  MNF, 32
  nuclear weapons, 3, 58
  and UN, 21, 25, 29
Great Powers, 20
Greece, 28
"Greenhouse effect," 3, 165
GRIT strategy (1962), 84
Gromyko, Andrey, 22
Gross national product (GNP), 151
Guantanamo (Cuba), 146
Guderian, Heinz, 65
Guerrilla warfare, 82
Guidance systems, 104

Hague conferences (1899 and 1907), 13
Haiti, 147
Hamburg Proposals (1986), 70
Hammarskjöld, Dag, 22, 29, 30, 31, 36(n2)

Harvard Law School, 201
Heritage Foundation, 102
High Frontier, 102–103, 113
Hiroshima (Japan), 27
Hitler, Adolf, 68
Hoffman, Stanley, 35
Holliday, William T., 38
Hoover, Herbert, 66, 183. *See also* Disarmament, qualitative; Hoover Plan
Hoover Plan (1932), 66–67, 68
Hot-line upgrading, 201
House Armed Services Committee, 159
How to Make Nuclear Weapons Obsolete (Jastrow), 113
Human intelligence (HUMINT), nontechnical means, 132
HUMINT. *See* Human intelligence, nontechnical means
Hungary, 84, 201
Hutchins, Robert, 38
Hydroelectricity, 167

IAEA. *See* International Atomic Energy Agency
ICBMs. *See* Intercontinental ballistic missiles
IDCO. *See* International Disarmament Control Organization
ILO. *See* International Labour Organisation
IMF. *See* International Monetary Fund
Independent Commission on Disarmament and Security Issues. *See* Palme Commission
India, 3, 31
INF (Intermediate Nuclear Force) Agreement (1988), 73, 85, 138
Infrared imaging, 130
Inspection Service, 45
Intercontinental ballistic missiles (ICBMs), 57, 103, 119, 133
Intermediate-range missiles, 52, 56, 73
International arms verification and study center proposal, 201
International Atomic Energy Agency (IAEA), 33, 198, 200
International Court of Justice, 22–23, 44, 142, 143, 146, 185
International Disarmament Control Organization (IDCO), 135
International economy, 2–3, 4, 18, 195
  conversion costs, 168–169
  conversion from war to peace, 16, 150–152, 154–158, 169–171, 193
  conversion process, 159–168
International institutions, 69. *See also* United Nations
Internationalism, 34, 42
International Labour Organisation (ILO), 33
International law, 142, 143, 146–148
  and moral force, 145
  and positive law, 141–142
  and public opinion, 144, 145, 189
International Monetary Fund (IMF), 33
International Peace Academy, 28
International peacekeeping forces, 70. *See also* United Nations, peacekeeping operations
International relations, 5–7, 13. *See also* Security; United Nations
International satellite monitoring agency (ISMA), 134, 186, 187, 201
International Scientists' Peace Congress (1986), 70
International Seismic Data Exchange, 187
Interventionism, 5, 32, 69, 75, 186–187, 196
Investment capital, 2
Iran, 4
Iran-Iraq cease-fire, 34
Iraq, 4
Ireland, 31, 40
Iroquois nation, 89
ISMA. *See* International satellite monitoring agency

Israel
  and Lebanon, 32
  nuclear weapons, 3, 61
  and UN, 29, 30
Italy, 32, 67

Japan, 69, 164
Jaruzelski, Wojciech, 84
Jastrow, Robert, 113
Johansen, Robert C., 34
Johnston, J. Bennett, 106
Joint Chiefs of Staff, 104
"Joint Statement of Agreed Principles for Disarmament Negotiations" (1961), 48, 49

Kahn, Herman, 52
Kampelman, Max, 109
Kashmir, 28
Keel, Alton, 84
Kellogg-Briand Pact (1929), 66
Kennan, George F., 57, 91, 195, 198, 199
Kennedy, John F., 2, 48, 49, 50, 55, 60, 134, 139
Khrushchev, Nikita, 31, 60
Kissinger, Henry, 109
Kokoshin, A. A., 84
Korean action (1950–1953), 26
Kortunov, A. V., 84
Krass, Allan S., 132
Kruegler, Christopher, 65

Land-based ballistic missiles, 56, 59
Larson, Arvid G., 111
Laser weapons, 104, 116, 119
Lawrence Livermore National Laboratory, 106, 110, 135, 156, 162
League of Nations, 14, 20, 22, 24, 27, 64, 68
Lebanon, 28, 32
Liddell Hart, Basil H., 65, 66, 68, 69, 183. *See also* Disarmament, qualitative
Limited Test Ban Treaty. *See* Partial Test Ban Treaty
Lincoln Labs (Mass.), 156
Lockheed Corporation, 160
Long-range attack aircraft, 200
Long-range bombers, 56, 57, 59
Los Alamos (N.M.), 156
Low-intensity conflict, 1, 8, 9(n2)
Lucas Aerospace (British firm), 161
Lucas Plan, 161
Luxembourg, 84, 201
Lysistrata (Aristophanes), 89

MacArthur, Douglas, 194–195
McCloy, John J., 48, 49
McCloy-Zorin Agreements (1961), 48–49, 51, 134
MacDonald, Bruce W., 102
McFarlane, Robert C., 104
McNamara, Robert S., 55, 56, 57–58, 61, 74, 109, 198, 199
MAD. *See* Mutual Assured Destruction
Magna (Utah), 138
Maine, Gulf of, 146
Marcos, Ferdinand, 97, 147
"Marginal cost deterrence," 81
Marshall, George C., Institute, 113
Massachusetts, 153, 156
Massive retaliation policy, 54
MBFR. *See* Mutual and Balanced Force Reductions
Mediation and reconstruction (UN), 28–29
Medium-range missiles, 200
Melman, Seymour, 151
MFO. *See* Multinational Force and Observers
Middle East, 29, 31, 32, 34
Midgetmen missiles, 57
Military alliances, 70
Military industries, 151–152, 153, 156–158, 169–170, 193
  demand-side transformation, 160–168
  raw materials, 158

supply-side transformation, 154, 155–160
work force, 155–156, 159, 162–163, 167
Military spending, 14, 62, 76, 151. *See also* International economy, conversion from war to peace; *under* Soviet Union; United States
Military Staff Committee (UN), 24, 25–26, 45
Military Training Camps Committee (1915), 39
MIRVs. *See* Multiple independently targeted reentry vehicles
MNF. *See* Multinational Force
Mozley, Robert, 114
Multinational Force (MNF), 32
Multinational Force and Observers (MFO), 32
Multiple independently targeted reentry vehicles (MIRVs), 130, 133
Multiple warheads, 59
Mussolini, Benito, 67
Mutual and Balanced Force Reductions (MBFR), 84, 201
Mutual Assured Destruction (MAD), 103, 119
MX (missile experimental), 121, 198
Myrdal, Alva, 135, 187

Nagasaki (Japan), 27
Namibia, 34
NAS. *See* National Academy of Sciences
NASA. *See* National Aeronautics and Space Administration
Nasser, Gamal Abdel, 29
National Academy of Sciences (NAS), 107
National Aeronautics and Space Administration (NASA), 113, 115, 153
National Security Agency (NSA), 131, 153
National technical means (NTM), 129–132, 138, 187, 198
NATO. *See* North Atlantic Treaty Organization
Natural Resources Defense Council (NRDC), 135
Netherlands, 31, 40, 84, 94, 201
Nevada, 135
New Deal, 170
New Mexico, 156
"New thinking" (Soviet Union). *See* Mikhail Gorbachev
New York State, 153
New York Stock Exchange, 2
New York Times, 169
New Zealand, 40, 199
Nicaragua, and U.S. mining of harbors (1984), 22, 74
Nitze, Paul, 113, 115
Nobel Peace Prize (1988), 34
Noel-Baker, Philip, 66, 67
No-first-use, 199
Nonaligned movement, 32
Nonmilitary defense. *See* Civilian-based defense
Nonoffensive defense. *See* Nonprovocative defense
Non-Proliferation Treaty (1968), 14, 188
Nonprovocative defense, 17, 78–80, 83–87, 178, 179, 181, 182, 200
characteristics of, 82–83
types, 80–82
Nonviolent action, 89, 90, 97–98, 181–182
Nordic standby force, 31
North Atlantic Treaty Organization (NATO), 21, 42, 69, 180
conventional forces, 61, 82, 199, 200
and restructuring toward defense, 78, 83–85
and Warsaw Pact cooperation, 83, 201
North Korea, 22, 26
Norway, 31, 40, 97

NRDC. *See* Natural Resources Defense Council
NSA. *See* National Security Agency
NTM. *See* National technical means
Nuclear blackmail, 92–93
Nuclear freeze proposal, 69, 181, 198
Nuclear-free zones, 199, 201
Nuclear Negotiation Project (Harvard Law School), 201
"Nuclear peace," 1
Nuclear war, 3, 193
  and SDI, 109–110
Nuclear weapons, 1, 3, 13, 27, 46, 55, 58, 61, 70, 82, 86, 181, 183
  miniaturization, 118
  proliferation, 3–4, 15, 92
  reduction proposals, 198–199
  tactical, 59
  testing, 60, 131
  See also Deterrence, minimum; *under* Soviet Union; United States
"Nuclear winter," 3
Nunn, Sam, 121

Ocean thermal energy, 167
OEA. *See* Defense, Department of, Office of Economic Adjustment
Offensive defense, 109
Office of Technology Assessment, 117
On-site inspections, 138–139
ONUC (UN force), 29
Optics, 104
Osgood, Charles, 84
OTH. *See* Over-the-horizon radars
Over-the-horizon (OTH) radars, 131
Ozone layer, 3

Packard Commission, 111
Pakistan, 4
Palestine, 28
Palme, Olof, 72
Palme Commission, 72
Parnas, David L., 106
PARs. *See* Phased-array radars
Partial Test Ban Treaty (1963), 14, 50, 60, 188, 198
Partisan warfare, 82
Peace, 1
Peace Force, 45, 46, 47
Peacekeeping federation. *See* Clark-Sohn Plan
Peace movements, 6
Peace observation (UN), 28
Peace Observation Corps, 50
Perestroika: New Thinking for Our Country and the World (Gorbachev), 73
Perez de Cuellar, Javier, 34
Permanent Court of International Justice, 22
Pershing IIs, 73, 138
Phased-array radars (PARs), 130
Philippines, 146, 147
  revolution (1986), 90, 97–98
Photovoltaic cells, 166
Pinochet Ugarte, Augusto, 147
Plan for Peace, A (Clark), 43
Poland, 84, 90, 97, 98, 201
Polaris missiles, 55
Population growth, 18
Prague Spring (1968), 90
Pravda (Moscow), 31, 70
"Preliminary Draft of a World Constitution" (Hutchins et al.), 38
Princeton Project on Finite Deterrence, 56, 57
"Problem of Land Disarmament, The: A Solution—Simple and Complete" (Liddell Hart), 65
"Program Treaty for Security and General Disarmament." *See* Raskin Plan
"Proposal for a Federation of Free Peoples" (Clark), 40
Proxmire, William, 106

Radar, 130–131, 187
Ramos, Fidel, 97
Rapacki, Adam, 84, 201
Rapacki Plan, 201
Rapid-deployment peacekeeping force proposal, 201

Raskin, Marcus, 51
Raskin Plan, 51–52, 53(n13)
Reagan, Ronald, 19(n3), 34, 35, 52, 57, 71, 101, 103, 105
"Reasonable sufficiency" principle, 70, 78, 84. *See also* Mikhail Gorbachev; Soviet Union
Republic of China (Taiwan), 21
Resistance, civilian. *See* Civilian-based defense
Reykjavik (Iceland) summit (1986), 52, 73, 101
Risk reduction centers, 201
Roberts, Adam, 79, 81
Roberts, Owen, 41, 42
Rohatyn, Felix, 168–169
Rommel, Erwin, 65
Roosevelt, Franklin Delano, 21, 26, 39, 67–68, 183. *See also* Disarmament, qualitative
Rouse, James W., 6

Saar plebiscite (1935), 27
Salinization, 166
SALT. *See* Strategic Arms Limitation Talks
San Francisco conference (1945), 27, 41
SARs. *See* Synthetic aperture radars
Satellites, 116, 118, 130, 133, 134, 136, 187, 199
SCC. *See* Standing Consultative Commission
SDI. *See* Strategic Defense Initiative
SDI: Progress and Challenges (Waller et al.), 106, 114
SDIO. *See* Strategic Defense Initiative Organization
Security
  and attitudes, 16
  collective. *See subentry* global
  common, 71–72, 177
  common, proposals for, 182–191
  global, 2, 3, 8, 14, 15, 16, 70, 75, 86, 192–193, 196. *See also* Disarmament, global; United Nations, and global security
  national, 13, 14, 16
  nonmilitary, 201. *See also* Civilian-based defense
  nuclear-free, 75
  shared, 182, 194, 196
  system, defined, 16
  See also Arms reduction proposals; Disarmament; Strategic defense
Seismic information, 131, 134–136, 187
Selective Service Act (1940), 39–40
Self-interest, 3, 137, 147, 193
Semipalatinsk (Soviet Union), 135
Senate Defense Appropriations Subcommittee, 114
Shared interest, 3
Sharp, Gene, 89, 90, 91, 92, 93
Shipbuilding industry, 161–162
Short-range missiles, 73
Shultz, George, 57
SIGINT. *See* Signals intelligence
Signals intelligence (SIGINT), 131
Simon, John, 66, 67
SIPRI. *See* Stockholm International Peace Research Institute
Slavery, 7–8, 194
Smith, Gerard, 199
Social change, 6, 7–8
Social Democratic party (W. Germany), 78
Social dissent. *See* Civilian-based defense
Social justice, 83
Sohn, Louis, 38–39, 41, 43, 46, 52, 178, 183, 188
Soil erosion, 166
Solar electricity, 167
Solidarity movement (Poland), 90, 98
South Africa, 3, 40, 61, 93, 147
South Korea, 4, 26
South Pacific Forum, 202(n5)
Soviet Academy of Sciences, 135
Soviet Union, 67, 82, 97
  ABM defense, 104–105, 113–114, 119, 120, 188–189
  and Afghanistan, 34
  economy, 2, 4, 112, 151

military spending, 4, 101
and nonprovocative defense, 78
nuclear weapons, 3, 54, 56, 58, 69, 92, 113, 198
and SDI, 120
space station, 115
and UN, 21, 22, 25, 26, 29, 31, 34, 48, 185
and verification, 135, 138–139. *See also* Standing Consultative Commission
See also Arms control; Arms race; Cold War; Disarmament
Space cooperation, 167–168, 187
Space debris, 116
Space weapons ban proposal, 199–200
Special Committee on Peacekeeping Operations (1965), 27
SR-71 (Blackbird), 130
SS-18s, -19s, -20s, and -25s, 73, 138, 198
Standing Consultative Commission (SCC), 132–133
Stanford Linear Acceleration Center, 114
Star Wars. *See* Strategic Defense Initiative
Stimson, Henry, 40, 138
Stockholm International Peace Research Institute (SIPRI), 69
Stock prices plunge. *See* Black Monday
Strategic Arms Limitation Talks (SALT), 132, 133
I (1972), 14, 102, 188
II (1979), 14, 15, 73, 86, 133, 144, 188, 189
Strategic defense, 17, 18, 101, 102–103, 119, 183
defined, 121–122(n1)
See also Strategic Defense Initiative
Strategic Defense Initiative (SDI), 71, 101, 103–104, 105–113, 118–121, 177
and arms control, 117–118
cost, 113–115, 121
defined, 110
effectiveness, 106–108
spin-off technologies, 110–112
vulnerability, 115–116, 119–120
Strategic Defense Initiative Organization (SDIO), 105, 106, 107, 114, 117
Panel on Computing in Support of Battle Management, 106
Strategic launchers, 55, 56
Strategic Modernization Program, 121
Strategic warheads, 56, 57, 58, 59, 73
stockpile reduction, 198
Subic Bay (Philippines), 146
Submarine-launched ballistic missiles, 56, 57, 58–59
Suez Canal Company nationalized (1956), 29
Suez crisis (1956), 22, 29
Supreme Court (U.S.), 142
Sweden, 31, 40, 135, 162
and CBD, 94
defense system, 81–82, 200
Switzerland, 40, 200
armed neutrality, 80–81, 86
Synthetic aperture radars (SARs), 131
Syria, 32
System, defined, 15

Taiwan. *See* Republic of China
Tanks, 65, 80, 200
Technology, 18, 83, 110–112, 157
Telecommunications, 104
Territorial defense, 79–80, 91
Terrorist groups, 4
Texas, 153
Third World, 69, 179
Toxic pollution, 3, 165, 166
Trained observers force, 186
"Transarmament," 93, 99(n7). *See also* Civilian-based defense
Transnational joint ventures, 184
Treaty of Versailles (1919), 67, 68
Trident missile, 198
Truman, Harry, 41, 138

Tugwell, Rexford, 38

U.C. Nuclear Weapons Labs Conversion Project (1979), 162
Ullman, Richard H., 56, 57, 58, 60
UNEF. *See* United Nations, Emergency Force
UNESCO. *See* United Nations Educational, Scientific and Cultural Organization
UNHCR. *See* United Nations High Commissioner on Refugees
UNICEF. *See* United Nations Children's Fund
Union of Concerned Scientists, 107
United Nations, 14, 21, 33–34, 35–36, 38, 41
  agencies, 33
  Charter, 17, 20, 23, 24, 25, 26, 32, 43, 47, 48, 49, 179, 185
  disarmament resolution (1959), 47–48
  Emergency Force (UNEF), 29, 30
  General Assembly, 21, 22, 26, 30, 33, 35, 41, 44, 46, 47, 49, 51, 134, 179, 198
  and global security, 17, 18, 20–23, 24–27, 33, 34–35, 36, 75, 95, 177, 178, 179–180, 185–188, 201
  military force, 24–27, 29–30, 32
  Nobel Prize (1988), 34
  and nonmilitary sanctions, 23, 24
  peacekeeping operations, 27–32, 33, 34, 50, 179, 186–187
  revenues, 188
  Secretariat, 22, 34
  Security Council, 21, 22, 23, 24, 25, 27, 28, 31, 32, 44, 50, 179
  veto in, 21, 24, 25, 26, 27, 41, 44, 49, 50
  See also Clark-Sohn Plan
United Nations Children's Fund (UNICEF), 33
United Nations Educational, Scientific and Cultural Organization (UNESCO), 33
United Nations Fund for Population Activities, 33
United Nations High Commissioner on Refugees (UNHCR), 33
United States
  debt, 154
  deficit, 163–164
  and deterrence, 54, 55–56, 57
  economy, 4, 151, 152, 155, 158
  and Federation of Free Peoples, 40
  industry, 164
  infrastructure, 164–165, 168
  and international law, 143, 146
  isolationism, 20, 39
  Marines compound bombing (Beirut), 32
  military bases abroad, 146, 156
  military spending, 4, 101, 151, 153–154, 169–170
  MNF, 32
  nuclear weapons, 3, 54, 56, 61, 69, 188–189. *See also* Deterrence, minimum
  and UN, 21–22, 24–25, 29, 31, 34–35, 48, 185
  unemployment, 155
  world manufacturing share, 164
  See also Arms control; Arms race; Cold War; Disarmament; International economy, conversion from war to peace
United World Federalists, 38
Uniting for Peace Resolution (1950), 22, 26
Universal conscription system, 86
University of California, 162
University of Chicago, 38
Ury, William, 201
U.S. Army, 157, 166
U.S. Geological Survey, 136
U.S. Navy, 55, 146, 170
U.S. News and World Report, 164, 165

Vance, Cyrus, 72
Vatinsk (Soviet Union), 138
Verification, 49, 58, 60, 87, 136–138, 154, 167, 178, 198

chemical, 200
and common security proposal, 184, 186, 187, 188, 201
functions, 129
methods, 129–136, 138–139
techniques, 129
Virginia v. West Virginia (1918), 142–143
Von Hippel, Frank, 56, 57, 60

Walesa, Lech, 98
War, 1, 2, 3, 194–195. *See also* Conflict resolution
War-making capability, elimination of, 193–194, 196
and CBD, 95
and SDI, 118–120
Warsaw Pact, 69
conventional forces, 61, 199, 200
and NATO cooperation, 83, 201
Political Consultative Committee, 84
and restructuring toward defense, 78, 83–85
Warsaw Treaty Organization (WTO). *See* Warsaw Pact
Washington Post, 84
Water supply, 166
Weapons-grade materials, 198
Weinberger, Caspar W., 103, 120
Weiss, Ted, 159
Western Sahara, 34
West Germany, 78, 84, 164, 201
West Virginia, 142–143
WHO. *See* World Health Organization
Wiesner, Jerome B., 55, 134, 187, 201
Wilson, Woodrow, 20
Wind energy, 167
Women's rights movement, 194
Wood, Lowell, 110
World Conciliation Board, 44, 47
World Court, 180, 185, 189
World Development Authority, 45
World Equity Tribunal, 44, 47, 185
World government, 17, 38, 42, 141
World Health Organization (WHO), 33
World orders, 13, 19(n4)
World peacekeeping federation. *See* Clark-Sohn Plan
World Peace Through World Law: Two Alternative Plans (Clark and Sohn), 38, 43–45, 52–53
World War I (1914–1918), 64, 66
World War II (1939–1945), 65, 68, 82, 97
demobilization, 151, 152
WTO (Warsaw Treaty Organization). *See* Warsaw Pact

Yalta conference (1945), 27
Yom Kippur War (1973), 29
Youngstown Sheet and Tube Co. v. Sawyer (1952), 142
Yugoslavia, 82, 200

Zorin, Valerian, 48, 49